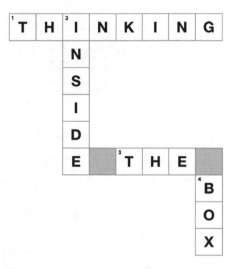

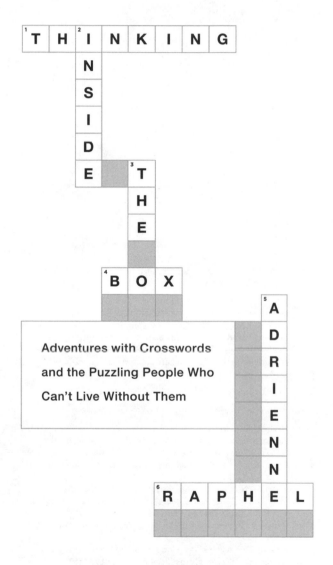

THINKING
INSIDE THE
BOX

ADRIENNE RAPHEL

Adventures with Crosswords
and the Puzzling People Who
Can't Live Without Them

Penguin Press ■ New York ■ 2020

PENGUIN PRESS
An imprint of Penguin Random House LLC
penguinrandomhouse.com

LIBRARY OF CONGRESS CATALOGING-IN-PUBLICATION DATA

Names: Raphel, Adrienne, author.
Title: Thinking inside the box : adventures with crosswords and the
    puzzling people who can't live without them / Adrienne Raphel.
Description: New York : Penguin Press, 2020. | Includes bibliographical
    references and index.
Identifiers: LCCN 2019022874 (print) | LCCN 2019022875 (ebook) |
    ISBN 9780525522089 (hardcover) | ISBN 9780525522096 (ebook)
Subjects: LCSH: Crossword puzzles—History.
Classification: LCC GV1507.C7 R287 2020 (print) | LCC GV1507.C7
    (ebook) | DDC 793.73/2—dc23
LC record available at https://lccn.loc.gov/2019022874
LC ebook record available at https://lccn.loc.gov/2019022875

Printed in the United States of America
10 9 8 7 6 5 4 3 2 1

Book design by Daniel Lagin

To my grandparents

The pattern of the thing precedes the thing. I fill in the gaps of the crossword at any spot I happen to choose.

—Vladimir Nabokov, interview, *The Paris Review*

Crossword fan, presumably

—YOU (10D, Friday, March 13, 1998,
The New York Times)

C O N T E N T S

INTRODUCTION

t's hard to imagine modern life without the crossword. The puzzle originated in 1913, and it soon became part of the fabric of daily existence. (Quite literally, the fabric: over the past century, solvers have sported, among other articles, crossword-patterned stockings, scarves, sweaters, and sneakers.) The crossword flared as a fad in the 1920s, but unlike other trends of the era—flagpole sitting, marathon dancing—the puzzle endured and thrived.

For many, the crossword is a daily ritual. Morning crossword people do the puzzle with coffee, on their commute, to wake up the brain; midday crossworders retreat to the puzzle to escape the day's demands; nighttime solvers use the puzzle as a winding-down routine. Others do crosswords more casually—usually in limbo spaces, like the dentist's office or on a plane. *If you fill in the crossword, please take the magazine with you so it's replaced,* some in-flight magazines instruct readers. Some people solve when they get bored, or when they need to place their minds elsewhere. Some use the crossword to give a sense of accomplishment—*if I've done nothing else all day*, they reason, *at least I've done this.*

Celebrities often solve to carve out a private routine in the clamor of their daily lives. Jon Stewart, Bill Clinton, Yo-Yo Ma, Bill Gates, Martha Stewart, Nancy Pelosi: all crossworders. While waiting out rain delays in matches, the tennis player Lindsay Davenport did crosswords; quarterback Brett Favre is also a solver. Actors and musicians frequently do puzzles between scenes or sets: Kate Hudson, Natalie Portman, Dustin Hoffman, Daniel Craig, Sting, and Nine Inch Nails's Trent Reznor, among many others, have been spotted with crosswords.

Writers use the crossword as cross-training, working on another kind of word problem to let their subconscious minds simmer. Vladimir Nabokov composed butterfly-shaped crosswords in letters to his wife. T. S. Eliot did the crossword like clockwork every day on the omnibus. "I have a completely overactive mind," poet Alice Notley told me, and crosswords are one of the only things that relax it. W. H. Auden loved crosswords. Poet James Merrill, who contacted Auden through his decades-long experiments with the Ouija board, doodled grids and word patterns in the margins of his notebooks. Stephen King does crosswords, though it's difficult to say whether to escape or enter his horror-filled imagination. Composer and lyricist Stephen Sondheim brought British cryptic-style crosswords to America.

Although the crossword seems engineered for solo consumption, it's just as important in its social function. Families, roommates, lovers, soldiers in barracks, anxious hospital waiting room acquaintances— groups of all kinds complete the puzzle together. The crossword draws already close people still closer together, letting their brains sync as they solve. It gives people a way to interact who otherwise might have nothing in common. It helps people pass time that doesn't seem to be going anywhere but desperately needs to be passed.

Solvers build their own personal puzzles inside the crossword. The New York Public Library's Cullman Center, which offers year-long research and writing fellowships, regularly hosts an unofficial crossword coterie; every day over lunch, several fellows solve the day's *New York Times* and *Wall Street Journal* puzzles together. One fellow, a historian of science, told me that when she was growing up, her father had invented a system to make the Monday *Times* crossword, histori-cally the week's easiest, more interesting. He would arbitrarily choose a pattern of squares to leave empty—all the squares touching a black square, say—but wouldn't allow himself to write down which pattern he was choosing or the letters in those squares, according to the clues; he had to hold all the "filled" blanks in his head while filling in only the blank blanks on the page. At Lollapuzzoola, an annual crossword tournament in Manhattan, there's a special "Downs Only" category for solvers who try to fill in the whole grid—down and across—while receiving only the down half of the clues.

Some people do crossword puzzles constantly, like breathing. My favorites are the superfans who bring crossword collections to cross-word tournaments. As soon as they've completed one regulation puz-zle and have a down moment before the next one begins, they'll flip open a volume and start solving.

People solve aspirationally, wanting to be seen as the kind of per-son clever enough to figure out the crossword. Lord Uffenham, a bum-bling aristocrat in the P. G. Wodehouse novel *Something Fishy*, begs crossword answers off his butler sotto voce so that, should a visitor happen to enter at any moment, he could appear to be dashing off the puzzle with ostentatious *sprezzatura*, easy-peasy. I met a graduate student who was looking for a way to add discipline to her life, so she decided to set herself a goal of solving the crossword puzzle every day for a year. She did—but the mission backfired. She ended up becoming compulsive about the crossword, unable to do anything until she'd finished. The week became a barometer of anxiety, as Friday and Saturday's difficult puzzles could keep her trapped at the kitchen table for hours. When her partner tried to help, she snapped at him. After the year ended, neither of them did the puzzle again for some time.

▢▮▢▮▢

I started writing this book when I was three. That's when I discovered what the alphabet could do: using only a combination of these shapes on the page, I could beam down messages from my brain, which other people could put back together, making my message get wormed into their brains. Whenever I rode in the car, I'd play the Alphabet Game with my brother: we each had to find the letters of the alphabet, in order, somewhere in the landscape zooming by, shouting out the letter and its site upon sighting. Whoever got from A to Z fastest was the winner. Dairy Queen, Quiznos, and Jiffy Lube became shrines.

When I was growing up, children's book author Roald Dahl's reader par excellence, Matilda, was my hero. I stared at the towel rack in the bathroom so hard my eyes blurred, willing myself to move something by shooting telekinetic beams from behind my eyeballs, the way Matilda used her mental power to pick up chalk. But I was even more excited about the other things that letters could do: how letters could arrange themselves into any words, and how certain combinations of letters suggested other ones, even when they seemed unrelated.

Monday nights during high school, my family had crossword races. My father would make photocopies of the Monday *New York Times* puzzle, hand them out to us, and send us to separate corners of the house; at his shout, we'd flip them over and begin. I'd scramble to finish before hearing my brother crow "Done!" I'd scrawl the final capital letters and rush into the living room, where my mom would be coolly reading the rest of the day's arts section, having breezed through the grid several minutes earlier. Dad would be pretending not to care anymore, a few scattered blank squares mocking him.

As a senior in high school, I had to do a capstone research project that included a community service component. I did mine about crosswords. The centerpiece was a spiral-bound book of crosswords that I brought into a local eighth-grade classroom, along with blank grids for the students to try their hand at puzzle making. My puzzles back then were objectively terrible. I didn't realize you should make the grids symmetrical, or that all the letters should interlock with each other, so my puzzles looked like jack-o'-lanterns instead of neat quilts, clues slashed snaggletoothed across the page.

Thinking Inside the Box investigates the crossword from all sides. I start with the crossword's origins, tracking how that first crossword in 1913 evolved from novelty to craze to routine. I construct a puzzle from soup to nuts, and I go behind the scenes with crossword editors to discover how a crossword goes from rough draft to publication. I investigate the myths around crosswords. Are crosswords frivolous toys that fritter your brain away? Will crosswords stave off dementia? I go to crossword tournaments to learn from the best solvers and constructors in the business. I even take a crossword-themed ocean crossing aboard the *Queen Mary 2*.

The more the crossword changes, the more it stays the same. The crossword is a reflection of everything happening around it, but it's also an anchor. In the wake of a particularly harrowing presidential election, an editor at the *New Yorker* said he found himself turning to the crossword puzzle as a life raft of stability in a world that had gone topsy-turvy. It's no accident that the crossword grew up during World War I, and that the *New York Times* introduced its crossword during World War II. No matter how chaotic life is, solving a crossword puzzle gives you a sense of control: seeing where the letters lead you sets the mind free.

FUN: ARTHUR WYNNE,
MARGARET PETHERBRIDGE FARRAR,
AND THE ORIGINS OF THE PUZZLE

The story of the crossword begins with the birth of Arthur Wynne on June 22, 1891, in Liverpool, England, where his father was the editor of the local *Liverpool Mercury*. When Wynne was nineteen, he emigrated to Pittsburgh, where he took a job on the *Pittsburgh Press* and played violin in the city's symphony orchestra. Soon, Wynne moved to New York and joined the staff of the *New York World*.

The *World* had launched in New York City in 1860. Each issue cost a penny. In 1864, the paper's editor published forged reports supposedly from President Abraham Lincoln that urged men to join the Union army. Lincoln was furious, the editor was arrested, and the *World* shut down for several days. The paper limped along printing propaganda for its various owners until 1883, when famed publisher Joseph Pulitzer bought the operation. In an aggressive circulation-boosting campaign, Pulitzer pumped the paper full of pulpy news and yellow journalism, transforming the *World* into one of the most popular publications in the country and the first in America to reach over one million subscribers daily. Pulitzer hired blockbuster reporters like Nellie Bly, who performed such gonzo stunts as traveling, for the *World*, around the world in seventy-two days, just to best Phileas Fogg's famous eighty. In 1890, operations moved into a brand-new, eighteen-story, gold-domed skyscraper next to City Hall on Park Row at the bottom tip of Manhattan, making the *World*'s home the world's then-tallest office building. In 1911, the paper launched its weekly color supplement: FUN.

By 1913, Arthur Wynne had been put in charge of FUN. For that year's Christmas edition, set to run on Sunday, December 21, Wynne was in a jam: he had space to fill but nothing to fill it with. He'd been instructed to add more puzzles to FUN, and Wynne, in desperation, turned his writer's block into a grid, a diamond-shaped interlocking set of squares flanked by clues that ran differently across and down. "FUN's Word-Cross Puzzle" instructed readers, "Fill in the small squares with words which agree with the following definitions." The crossword conceit—here are clues, here is a grid, go forth and fill the grid with the answers to these clues—was born.

Wynne's Word-Cross looks like a modern crossword, with obvious differences. It's a diamond, not a square, and rather than black spaces throughout, there's one concentrated blank in the middle, like a doughnut hole. Rather than separating the clues into Across and Down, Wynne listed clues by giving their beginning and ending squares.

Wynne's puzzle doesn't deploy pyrotechnic layers of wordplay. The clues proceed as fairly straightforward definitions; none of them ask the reader to solve a riddle, or decode an acrostic, or undo a pun to arrive at the solution. Ambiguity is on the level of information rather

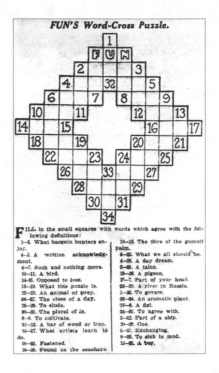

than imagination: "A bird" (DOVE), for example, could have any number of solutions, but this puzzle is looking only for flying animals, not, say, jailbirds or stool pigeons. Most clues are fairly generic. Many of the clues establish a bond between the clue writer and the solver, a wink from Wynne to us: "What we should all be," for example (MORAL), or, "What this puzzle is" (HARD). The puzzle also repeats itself: "A pigeon," like "A bird," is also DOVE. Some require extremely esoteric knowledge—"The fibre of the gomuti palm" (DOH) would likely be impossible for most non-botanists, particularly since the gomuti is far more common in Indonesia than Manhattan—so filling in the puzzle relies not only on the reader's capacity to get the clues via the definitions alone but on the simultaneous ability to deduce the answer from corresponding letters in the grid.

FUN and the origin myth of Wynne's invention notwithstanding, part of the ingenuity of Wynne's Word-Cross is that it isn't original at all. Wynne's genius wasn't to reinvent the wheel, but to move the needle precisely enough so that his new game would excite but not befuddle solvers. Victorian newspapers and magazines frequently featured word squares that challenged readers to fill in blanks with words that read the same horizontally and vertically; a simple example might be the following:

O   F   F
F   O   E
F   E   D

Wynne freely acknowledged that his Word-Cross did not come to him sui generis. He'd based the puzzle on similar word puzzles that had been published in children's newspapers in England. The popular children's magazine *St. Nicholas* had regularly been publishing acrostics and word puzzles since 1873. Its "Riddle Box" featured games such as a "cross-word enigma," a riddle that asks readers to tease out a word from a rhyming poem of cryptic clues. Other magazines had also started to print word-grid games. The September 1904 edition of the *People's Home Journal* featured a blended square, or five word squares that interlocked at the corners. The blank grid wasn't printed, though, meaning that solvers had to draw the squares for themselves to fill it in. And proto-crosswords weren't only in English. In 1890, Italian journalist Giuseppe Airoldi had introduced a four-by-four word game printed with a grid.

But Wynne's crossword was the first that incorporated crossed words directly on the page with blocked-out squares, pushing beyond the natural limitations of the word square and creating a much more flexible, and expandable, game. Wynne took advantage of advances in twentieth-century printing technology that made it easier to print large grids in the newspaper itself. Rather than posing a problem and asking readers to draw their own grids or write the answers elsewhere, Wynne's puzzle provided the empty squares, inviting the reader to engage with the puzzle right in the newspaper. Wynne also introduced black squares into his symmetrical rows and columns, which gave the puzzles clear units of negative space and allowed for more varied grids. If music comes to life in the spaces between the notes, the crossword became the crossword because of the gaps in the puzzle.

Each week, Wynne printed a new puzzle of this word-crossed type in the *World*. A typographical error two weeks after Wynne's original Word-Cross transposed the title's two words, suggesting that readers "Find the Missing Cross Words," and the following week, the paper presented the puzzle under the heading "Fun's Cross-Word Puzzle." Eventually, the hyphen disappeared, as did the capital letters, and the Cross-Word became the crossword. The trend of disappearing hyphens isn't unique to the crossword; the early twentieth century saw many words that were once hyphenated become either two separate words or closed compounds (*to-day, ice-cream, bumble-bee*). Cross-Word, like Xerox or Band-Aid, shifted from becoming descriptive of a certain kind of word game in one particular paper to the generic name for the puzzle itself.

Jokes, riddles, comics, rebuses, advertisements, and other layers of subcutaneous information insulated FUN from the rest of the *World*. (A full-page ad in January 1914 proclaims, *LET US MAKE YOU*

FAT. By March, another advertisement, in exactly the same location, declared that *FAT IS DANGEROUS*.) Readers soon began to submit their own crossword puzzles to the paper. The grids were usually diamonds but erratic in size and shape. No black squares interrupted the white squares, as is typical in crosswords today. Mostly, these puzzles used diamond-shaped grids, but the shapes were not standardized: in January 1915, for example, one week's grid was in the shape of an F; the next week, a U; and the following week, an N. "That spells FUN for every one of FUN's puzzle solvers," wrote Wynne.

Wynne's first Word-Cross already had one answer filled in—FUN—so that even readers who did not go to the trouble of filling out the rest of the grid would be cued that this was a FUN activity. The brand added another ritual dimension to the nature of solving. Crossworders were, from the beginning, social. You filled in the same grid with your remote fellow crew, week after week. Already in 1915, Wynne imagined his readers as a loyal coterie, turning to FUN religiously each Sunday to fill in the same grid with your cohort members far and wide. Once you were a crossworder, you were in the club.

Wynne tried to patent the crossword, but the *World* refused to foot this bill, and the crossword remained open for all to use. In 1920, it cost thirty-five dollars to file and issue a patent, and a typical patent lawyer's fee would have been about seventy dollars.

Wynne's invention of desperation became an institution overnight.

After constructing the paper's first seven crosswords himself, Wynne slyly suggested to *World* readers that it was more difficult to create a crossword than to solve one. Like Tom Sawyer's friends eagerly picking up the pail of whitewash to join the "fun" and paint the fence, Wynne's readers took the bait and started doing his work for him. In February 1914, a Mrs. M. B. Wood became the first constructor to be given a byline. By the following year, Wynne's trick had worked too well. In a headnote to the puzzle of March 7, 1915, Wynne painted a vivid picture of the deluge at his office: "Everywhere your eyes rest on boxes, barrels and crates, each one filled with cross-word puzzles patiently awaiting publication," he wrote. He begged readers to curb their zeal: "The puzzle editor has kindly figured out that the present supply will last until the second week in December, 2100." Current crossword editors face the same problem. Will Shortz at the *New York Times* typically has a backlog of at least three to four months. Though topical puzzles can be pushed through more quickly, for evergreens, or themes that aren't pegged to a particular news cycle, puzzle gestation can take as long as human gestation. (In 2018, one constructor told me that he knew he had a puzzle coming out that year around Halloween. It was March.)

Wynne was getting sick of the crossword. He became a careless editor, regularly publishing puzzles riddled with errors. Angry solvers wrote into the paper in droves, badgering Wynne about clues that didn't match their definitions, misspellings baked into the grid, or answers that led to nowhere. And yet the crossword was more popular than ever. Every Sunday's *World* contained several sidebars scattered throughout the sections instructing readers to look for the crossword in FUN, less a reminder about the puzzle's existence—after all, the puzzle had long been established as a staple of Sunday's FUN—than a promotional teaser for one of the paper's most popular features. Readers grumbled at poorly constructed puzzles, but they exploded on the occasional weeks that FUN didn't publish a crossword at all: "The only thing I give a hang about on your page or in your Sunday magazine is the crossword," wrote one solver.

By 1921, the crossword had outgrown Wynne, and Wynne, desperate to rid himself of the albatross, turned to John O'Hara Cosgrave, the *World*'s executive editor, for help. Cosgrave had no more time or interest than Wynne in devoting his days to placating vociferous cruciverbalists (that is, people skilled in solving or creating crosswords, from Latin *cruci-*, "cross," plus *verbum*, "word"). But he did have one asset Wynne lacked: a secretary.

▢ ▮ ▮ ▢

Margaret Petherbridge was born in 1897 in Brooklyn, New York, where her father owned a licorice factory. She attended the Berkeley Institute in Park Slope, one of the oldest and most highly regarded independent schools in New York, where seniors routinely received automatic entry into the top women's colleges.* Though most of Brooklyn was still farmland, Park Slope had established itself as a genteel residential neighborhood with easy access into Manhattan, and Petherbridge's classmates hailed from the borough's socioeconomic crème de la crème. A Berkeley girl's[†] schedule followed the so-called Vassar model: academics from nine to noon, home for luncheon, then physical education in the afternoon. After attending Berkeley, Petherbridge graduated from

---

*A 2016 *New York* magazine article referred to Berkeley—now, after a merger in the 1970s, the Berkeley-Carroll School—as "the Harvard of Brooklyn's K–12 institutions."
†Berkeley was co-ed until the fourth grade, when boys typically transferred to Poly Prep in Bay Ridge, until 1974, when the institute became fully co-educational.

Smith College in 1919, then returned to New York, where, with the help of a roommate's stepfather, she landed a job in 1921 as secretary to the executive editor of the *New York World*.

An aspiring journalist, Petherbridge hoped that working for Cosgrave would provide her foray into writing for the *World*. So when Cosgrave assigned Petherbridge to help Wynne with the crossword, Petherbridge was less than thrilled. She, like many of the people in her office, saw the crossword as undecorative filler, schlocky drivel to puff out the paper and placate the masses.

With her career stalled in crossword Siberia, Petherbridge devoted as little time as possible to the puzzle. She'd never done a crossword before, and she wasn't about to start now. Rather than bothering to test the puzzles that readers submitted to the paper, she selected grids based solely on aesthetic appeal and waved them untouched to the typesetters, just as a bored high school student might create fill-in-the-blank bubble-grid patterns in her standardized test booklets. Readers continued to complain, but Petherbridge brushed aside their concerns as "the work of cranks."

The stalemate between miffed readers and diffident editor might have persisted for years, if not for a hiring coup and a quirk of intra-office geography. In 1922, the *World* poached legendary columnist Franklin Pierce Adams—"F.P.A.," as he signed his work—from the rival *New-York Tribune*. A feature in F.P.A.'s most famous column, "The Conning Tower," launched the careers of writers such as Dorothy Parker, Moss Hart, George S. Kaufman, and Edna St. Vincent Millay. F.P.A. was also an avid cruciverbalist, and the *World* happened to install him in an office next to Petherbridge's. Until recently, Sunday's FUN insert had reliably brought F.P.A. a weekly dose of immense pleasure. Now, F.P.A. could unleash his irritation at the puzzle's decline to the source. Hardly known for his demure manner, F.P.A. marched into Petherbridge's office every Monday morning and chewed her out, clue by poorly constructed clue. Petherbridge ignored F.P.A. at first, but the "comma-hunter of Park Row" harangued Petherbridge week after week, and finally she consented to at least try solving one of these things.

The cranks were right. Under her supposed watch, the puzzle, she discovered, was a mess: clues left out, wrong numbering, warped definitions, and words, she said, "that had no right to be dragged out of their native obscurity." Petherbridge was mortified, but she also saw an opportunity. If personages as esteemed in the world of letters as Franklin Pierce Adams were poring over the crossword week after week, the puzzle might be her opportunity. Everyone who was anyone, it seemed, was addicted to the thing, and what had seemed like a major nuisance could be her chance to make her mark. Like an architect renovating a house that has great bones but has fallen into disrepair, Petherbridge realized that fixing the crossword puzzle could be her ticket to a career after all—but it was going to take some doing.

Placing her left hand on a dictionary and raising her right, Petherbridge vowed to take up the crossword. Thenceforth, Margaret Petherbridge's crosswords would be, she declared, "the essence of perfection." She insisted that she would test every puzzle herself, establishing as her motto: "If it be not fair to me, what care I how fair it be?"*

---

*Petherbridge adapted her mantra from seventeenth-century poet George Wither's "Shall I wasting in despair": "If she be not so to me, / What care I how fair she be?"

Having discovered that the crossword was such a mess, Pether-bridge whipped the puzzle into respectability. She set the puzzles a week in advance rather than green-lighting them at the eleventh hour, giving her time to fix clues, correct grid errors, and test-solve the page proofs before the puzzle went public. Petherbridge also established industry standards, such as permitting only dictionary words and eschewing unchecked letters (that is, ones that didn't cross other squares).

By the end of 1923, with the assistance of F. Gregory Hartswick and Prosper Buranelli in the editorial department, Petherbridge had transformed the crossword from its unruly state to an efficient machine. The puzzle might not have seemed different to the casual skimmer, but the solving experience had radically improved. Early crosswords pre-sented across and down clues in a single column, cued by the first and last number square of the word (2-3, 4-10, etc.); now, clues appeared with a single number, marked Across and Down. Grids were symmet-rical, and all letters interlocked.

Once Petherbridge had become obsessed, Wynne gladly abdicated all crossword duties to her and left the *World* altogether. He spent most of the rest of his career working for papers owned by print mogul William Randolph Hearst, chief rival of *World* owner Joseph Pulitzer. In 1925, Wynne convinced King Features Syndicate—Hearst's distribution conglomerate for puzzles, comic strips, and other games—to pay for the application fee and achieved a patent on a "step-word puzzle." The game is a word ladder: starting with two words at either end of the ladder, the player has to find a chain of other words that links the two, in which every word in the chain changes by exactly one letter. (To turn *cat* into *dog*: CAT → COT → DOT → DOG.) It was not a new idea.

Lewis Carroll had popularized word ladders in Victorian England, and later, the narrator in Vladimir Nabokov's *Pale Fire* would become enamored of a similar "word golf." Wynne's patent was for a specific iteration of the concept: "a cross word puzzle card embodying a multiple series of stepped enclosures for the reception of letters, there being the same number of enclosures in each horizontal series, each series having thereon a letter to form a basic letter of the word to be placed in said series, each series to receive letters to form progressively from the top to the bottom series, different words." Wynne tried to sneak in the term *cross word*, but though he got his step-word patent, he'd lost the war: the stepchild might be his, but the parent technology was free for the world to use as it pleased.

▭▮▯▮▮

In 1919, a fourteen-year-old named Ernie Bushmiller arrived at the *New York World* as a new copy boy. Born and raised in the Bronx, the son of a German immigrant and an Irish immigrant, Bushmiller attended Theodore Roosevelt High School for six months before his self-described "lucky break": quitting and joining the *World*. (Teen Bushmiller's other career option was becoming a cabin boy for the Cunard steamship line, at which thought he later shuddered: "Thank God! Otherwise I'd probably be a steward on the *Queen Mary*!"*)

Every morning, Bushmiller rode the Lexington Avenue IRT for nearly an hour from the Bronx to Brooklyn Bridge–City Hall, where he exited the subway and entered the palace on 63 Park Row. Bushmiller

---

*More on the *Queen Mary* later.

spent as much time as possible around the art department, raptly hanging over the cartoonists at work. By 1920, he'd been promoted to art department assistant, where he was given menial assignments such as lettering word balloons and laying out the weekly crossword puzzle. Bushmiller showed a flair for this latter task, and by age fifteen, Bushmiller had become the *World*'s expert crossword-puzzle line tracer.*

Bushmiller's grids were extremely accurate, but he never sacrificed panache. Bushmiller got jazzier with his grids the longer he found himself drawing them. One grid had a faux-woodcut finish, as though Albrecht Dürer had been resurrected to print the crossword; another grid looked as though he'd drawn it with a calligraphy pen. The thickness of his lines waxed and waned over the weeks. Sometimes the black squares were solid black, sometimes striped, and sometimes speckled.

The crossword soon started to spread from the *World* to the rest of the country. The *Pittsburgh Press* began publishing a crossword in 1916; the *Boston Globe*, in 1917. In 1922, Clare Briggs, a prominent newspaper comic strip artist with a recurring sequence called "Movie of a Man," drew a "Movie of Man Doing a Crossword Puzzle." The strip features a beleaguered solver, cigar clutched in his mouth, pen clutched in his hand, who grows increasingly bombastic in his frustration: "87

---

*Though one might imagine a certain nostalgia for other tactile aspects of newspaper life—Linotype machines, slugs, those massive scrolls—it's hard to picture anything but a unanimous appreciation for the digitization of the grid. Though the creator still has to figure out where the blank squares occur in any given grid, it's infinitely easier to get a more perfect grid than any human could ever draw simply with a few strokes of a computer program, and there's nothing inherent about a hand-drawn grid that provides the sanctity of the puzzle.

Across 'Northern Sea Bird' !!??!?!!? Northern Sea Bird??? Hmm-m-m-m Starts With an 'M' Second Letter is 'U' . . . " He looks up the answer, crows in triumph, and returns to the grid, his smoke spiral chugging in a tidy line again rather than a frustrated squiggle.

But the crossword didn't get its big break until it made the leap from newspapers to books.

THE *CROSS WORD PUZZLE BOOK* AND THE CROSSWORD CRAZE

n January 1924, Richard ("Dick") Simon, an aspiring publisher on the verge of starting his own company, went to dinner with his aunt Wixie, who asked him where she might find a book of crossword puzzles. A niece had become addicted to the things, she said, and Wixie wanted to buy her a collection. Simon brought up the conversation to his business partner, Lincoln Schuster, and they realized that no such book existed.

Simon and Schuster were still in the process of forming their fledgling house, and the crossword collection would be their first foray into the world as publishers. Afraid that the book would make their new publishing house seem trivial, and afraid it would flop, they decided they'd release the book under the moniker "Plaza Publishing," a dummy imprint named after their telephone exchange. Simon and Schuster hired Petherbridge, Buranelli, and Hartswick to edit the volume, paying them a twenty-five-dollar* advance to assemble a

---

*About $365 in today's dollars.

book-length collection from their backlist, and they also hired Bushmiller to draw the squares and number the grids. They attached a sharpened pencil to every book and priced the volume at $1.35.

In April 1924, Plaza Publishing released *The Cross Word Puzzle Book*. The company took out a one-inch ad in the *New York World* that they hoped would be a self-fulfilling prophecy:

> 1921—Coué
> 1922—Mah Jong
> 1923—Bananas
> **1924—THE CROSS WORD PUZZLE BOOK**

Still nursing his old grudge against the crossword higher-ups, F.P.A. predicted in January that Simon and Schuster would "lose their shirts" in the endeavor. Dick and Lincoln were also worried, not only that they'd go broke but that they'd lose any hope of goodwill and respectability in the industry. But by the time *The Cross Word Puzzle Book* was released, on April 10, 1924, F.P.A. decided to help the project along, giving the venture a loud fanfare in his column: "Hooray! Hooray! Hooray! Hooray! / The Cross-Word Puzzle Book is out today."

F.P.A. also featured gallows-humor crossword doggerel in his column. "The Cross Word Puzzle," by humorist Newman Levy, takes cross words between husband and wife to dramatically rhymed ends. The husband lives with his wife in perfect domestic bliss, save for those few moments when he has to bop her over the head, and she has to hurl a cooking pot at his skull to retaliate. But the crossword wreaks irritation beyond what he'd ever known. The wife pesters the husband with questions, which infuriates him—he's trying to escape into a novel, and she keeps pulling him back into the world with maddeningly simple clues ("My, / What pronoun in three letters starts with Y?"). The husband gets so cross at these interruptions that eventually, to restore peace and quiet, he's obliged to murder her.

The Cross Word Puzzle Book quickly proved to be Simon & Schuster's cornerstone. Simon & Schuster's crossword compendia became the longest continually published book series in existence. Since its inception, the house has never not had a crossword book in print.

In 1926, Petherbridge married publisher and poet John C. Farrar, and she left her post at the *World* to raise a family. Despite her marital allegiance to a rival publisher, Farrar continued to edit Simon & Schuster's puzzle series, bringing out at least two Simon & Schuster crossword collections per year until her death, when she was at work on her 134th compilation. Each night, once she'd put her two children to bed in her apartment on the Upper East Side, Farrar worked late into the night on crosswords, diplomatically insisting that the arrangement was conducive to puzzle inspiration: after the phone stopped ringing, she claimed, was the best time to think up "that magical definition."

As *The Cross Word Puzzle Book*'s sales exploded, the *World*'s puzzle offerings expanded, including not only a daily crossword but more word puzzles, rebuses, and riddles. In November 1924, in addition to drawing the daily crossword, Bushmiller was placed in charge of "Red Magic," the *World*'s bigger and bolder puzzle supplement, ostensibly edited by Harry Houdini. Bushmiller, who still wanted to break into the comic strip world, realized that his livelihood could be his ticket out. If people were so nuts about puzzles, he reasoned, presumably they'd want to read about puzzles in his preferred form. In the spring of 1925, Bushmiller quietly slipped his new strip into "Red Magic": *Cross Word Cal*, the adventures of a mild-mannered cruciverbalist. One strip, for instance, features Cross Word Cal as a frustrated cabbie idling for passengers when a pedestrian tells him to get a "checkered cab." Cal dives into a stack of newspapers, cuts out the crossword from each one, and spackles them to his car; in the final panel, he's zipping along, a fare in the backseat and people frantically running alongside him to hail his cab.

The Cross Word Book, just as Simon and Schuster's advertisement had aggressively prognosticated, was a hit, selling 350,000 copies in its first year. Every morning for weeks, the door to the offices of Simon & Schuster was physically blocked with mailed-in orders for the new book. For *The Cross Word Book*'s second volume, priced at twenty-five cents, one distributor alone ordered 250,000 copies, the largest book order to date ever placed in the United States.

Success bred competition. Crossword-puzzle books were great for the publishing industry. The books were easy to produce, since they all followed essentially the same formula, and unlike prose writers, crossword constructors and editors offered their puzzles for little to no fee.

To mitigate booksellers' losses, Simon & Schuster offered to take back unsold copies, which created an equally powerful though less foreseen effect of the crossword on the publishing world: the practice of returns. Though returns initially protected bookstores, traditionally much smaller entities than the huge houses, by the end of the twentieth century, the tides had shifted, and megachains' very real threat of returning huge orders often loomed over the now-struggling publishing industry. The largess that crosswords had allowed Simon & Schuster to extend to bookstores would one day become publishers' threat.

▭▪▮▪▭

By the end of 1924, readers everywhere had gone crossword crazy. Gelett Burgess, a humor editor and author most famous for his four-line nonsense ditty "The Purple Cow" ("I never saw a purple cow / I never hope to see one / But I can tell you anyhow / I'd rather see than be one"), celebrated the craze by submitting a crossword to the *New York World*. On the occasion of his first puzzle's publication in November 1924, Burgess commemorated the event through self-parody:

> The fans they chew their pencils
> The fans they beat their wives
> They look up words for extinct birds
> They lead such puzzling lives.

When Mildred Jaklon, the *Chicago Tribune*'s society editor, heard about the new crossword craze, she thought that the *Tribune* should join the trend, so she created a puzzle and sold it to the paper for twenty-five dollars. The *Tribune* printed Jaklon's crossword in September 1924, pronouncing that the nation had caught "cross-word-puzzle-itis" and unless "you're a babe in the arms or a doddering idiot you're certain to fall victim." On October 8, 1924, the *Tribune* published a story about Mary Zaba, a woman filing for divorce on the grounds that her husband wasted his time doing crossword puzzles instead of working; in December of that year, the paper ran advertisements for the *Chicago Evening American*'s crossword contest. In 1929, Jaklon spearheaded a crossword-puzzle contest for the *Tribune*, with a $5,000 prize; the contest proved so popular that the paper instituted a regular daily puzzle, with Jaklon as its editor, a role she would hold for the next forty years.

The first issue of the *New Yorker*, published February 21, 1925, featured a "Jottings about Town" column by "Busybody," with bite-sized aphoristic remarks about life in the city. One of Busybody's signature humorous tics was the overstatement of the obvious or banal as a faux-profound observation. "A richly dressed woman left a badly torn umbrella at a Broadway repair shop late Tuesday evening. The umbrella was recovered." "Many people may be interested to know that the real name of Edna Ferber, the writer, is Edna Ferber." Busybody further noted, "Judging from the number of solvers in the subway and 'L' trains, the crossword puzzle bids fair to become a fad with New Yorkers." The joke was not the revelation, but the commonplace: the crossword had become so prevalent that to proclaim its ubiquity was akin to "discovering" that people seemed to enjoy drinking coffee in the morning.

Crossword enthusiasts wore their devotion on their sleeves with grid-pattern dresses, jackets, jewelry, and special wristbands with tiny dictionaries strapped to them, like ür-Fitbits. One solver who was equally zealous with a needle created a quilt featuring forty-eight separate embroidered crossword puzzles, one for each state in the union. The University of Kentucky offered a class on crossword puzzles. Puzzlers danced to "Crossword Puzzle Blues" and "Cross Word Mama You Puzzle Me (But Papa's Gonna Figure You Out)." Solvers could eat their words with Cross-word Cream Biscuits, made by Huntley & Palmers, Ltd. In 1925, Broadway triple threat Elsie Janis wrote, directed, and starred in *Puzzles of 1925*, a revue that featured a crossword sanatorium for puzzlers whose obsession had driven them to insanity.

Commuters loved crosswords. In late 1924, a man on a train from New York to Boston did a survey of his fellow passengers and found that at least 60 percent were doing crosswords. The B&O Railroad placed dictionaries in train cars for the convenience of crossword-crazed commuters. Not to be outdone, the Pennsylvania Railroad printed crosswords on the menus. Train stops frequently served as a stopwatch for solvers: as a reader to the *Times* of London wrote, her father returned home one day and announced, "Ah, it was a tough one today, took me between Barming and Swanley to complete." If you calculate it out, this reader's father had mastered the art of the crossword humblebrag. At only six stops, Barming to Swanley—East Malling, West Malling, Borough Green & Wrotham, Kemsing, Otford, and Swanley—is about half an hour, a perfectly respectable time.

One Sunday, a Reverend George McElween in Pittsburgh set up a large blackboard with a crossword grid in front of his pulpit and told his congregation to solve it before the service began; the solved puzzle contained the text for his sermon. Members of a church in Atlantic City distributed crosswords in pamphlets to promote a missionary campaign.

Contests of all stripes were big in the 1920s, particularly ones that involved some sort of grueling feat of discipline for a useless skill: dance marathons, flagpole sitting, egg-eating races, yo-yo competitions, gum-chewing contests, and even a "Noun and Verb Rodeo"* in the Park Avenue Armory on Christmas Day, 1928, in which the competitor who could keep talking the longest was promised a one-thousand-dollar prize. Puzzle contests, a popular subset of the contest mentality, merged seamlessly with the crossword craze. Newspapers and magazines ran crossword contests for cash, making the crossword not only a game you played against yourself to while away a commute but a way to show off your intellect with your friends and family and, as an added incentive, turn a profit from your prowess.

Crosswords diverted readers from novels to grids, and crossword contests wreaked special havoc on booksellers and libraries. Bookstores blamed crosswords for lagging sales of novels but had trouble keeping reference books such as dictionaries and glossaries in stock. Traditional volumes moldered as readers dove into puzzles. A 1924 Reuters report from Canada claims, "Cross-word puzzles and the radio have been given as the reason for a marked decline during the

---

*Like senators in a filibuster, rodeo participants could say whatever they wanted—sing songs, read the Bible out loud, recite monologues—as long as their mouths kept moving. Contestants had to take three half-hour breaks every twenty-four hours; any more time off would result in penalties. The winner was anyone still left standing with a perfect record after four days and four nights. Ticket sales were sparse, but news outlets adored the Noun and Verb Rodeo (the only daily in New York City that didn't send a reporter was the Communist *Daily Worker*), and copywriters jockeyed to come up with the contest's best sobriquet: "tonsil derby," "carnival of cacophonies," "the hoarse race of the century," and "jawtauqua." The contest's organizer, hard-boiled small-time hustler Milton Crandall, hoped that rubbernecking would bring people to the torture spectacle as the days wore on, but he lost tens of thousands of dollars on the event. When the four days ended in a dead heat, he proposed a tiebreaker jawbreaker marathon. No further Noun and Verb Rodeos were recorded.

recent months in the demand for books at the Ottawa Public Library." But the facilities themselves were far from abandoned. Indeed, as in the case of bookstores, demand for dictionaries and encyclopedias overwhelmed reading rooms, particularly when prizes were attached. As literary critic Elaine Scarry has pointed out to me, the crossword puzzle was seen by libraries and bookstores as the same kind of threat as online booksellers: a new technology changing the way people used texts. The annual report of the New York Public Library for 1924 gives a tart indictment of the craze. Puzzles have their place, notes the report—"as recreation, in the hospital, or on an ocean voyage or a railway journey, or as a cure for insomnia"—but when "the puzzle 'fans' swarm to the dictionaries and encyclopedias so as to drive away readers and students who need these books in their daily work," the report sniffs, "can there be any doubt of the library's duty to protect its legitimate readers?"

In February 1925, Walt Disney released the animated short film *Alice Solves the Puzzle*, the fifteenth of his *Alice Comedies*. ("Alice" is a clear homage to Lewis Carroll, as the first film in this series is called *Alice's Wonderland*.) Alice, a cherubic girl with a dark bob and bangs, and her animated cat, Julius, go on various adventures. Everything in the film is animated except for Alice, portrayed by a live-action actress. When the film opens, Alice frowns over a crossword puzzle. *Little Alice—never had a cross word, not even with a puzzle*, a title slide announces. Crumpled puzzle grids are scattered on the floor around Alice, and two large volumes labeled *SYNONYMS* and *DICTIONARY* are stacked next to her on the desk. *Three Letter Word* pops up in a thought bubble above Alice's head, and for the next few seconds, a phonics lesson unspools: *CAT*, she thinks. *RAT. BAT.* As though *CAT* has summoned him, Julius comes bounding in. *I JUST NEED ONE WORD*, a speech bubble above her head declares. Julius's grin flips: *Let's go swimming instead!* he mutters. Alice needs little persuasion to procrastinate, and she scampers after him.

When Alice returns to her crossword, the plot thickens. Bootleg Pete, a collector of rare crossword puzzles who also happens to be a peg-legged black bear with a leering snout, bursts into Alice's chamber. *GIMME THAT PUZZLE*, he demands. *NO*, says Alice. She quickly folds up the puzzle, tucks it into her prepubescent bosom,* slaps Pete across the face, and dashes away. Bootleg Pete chases her up a lighthouse and starts to tussle with her, and just when all seems lost, Julius launches to her rescue, knocking away Pete and saving both Alice and the puzzle. As Julius preens, Alice squeals: *I GOT IT!* The film zooms in on her grid, which, it turns out, isn't a proper crossword at all but a souped-up title card with a crosswordlike aesthetic. *AN ALICE COMEDY*, reads the grid, though *AN* is actually attached to the *I* in *ALICE*, making the answer technically *ANI*. The answer running parallel to *COMEDY* is *LAFTER*, a misspelling that the viewer will presumably find hilarious. As Alice fills in the solution—*THE END*—the film diegetically ends too.

▯▮▯▮

On June 13, 1922, Mr. and Mrs. James J. Franc of 120 West Seventieth Street, Manhattan, announced in the *New York Times* the engagement

---

*There's some disturbing interspecies sexual innuendo in the film: Julius is fascinated by Alice's figure when she emerges in a bathing suit, whistling in admiration, and when Alice gets dressed again, he peeks inside her bloomers on the pretense of smoothing out her outfit.

of their daughter, Wellesley College sophomore Miss Ruth Lois Franc, to a William von Phul, "of this city and New Orleans," who had served as a lieutenant in World War I and had just graduated from Harvard. Born and raised among progressive intellectuals on the Upper West Side ("my mother even smoked," as she later told the *New Yorker*), Ruth Franc went to Horace Mann School—at the time, girls attended a separate campus at Columbia Teachers College—and then Wellesley, though she'd wanted to stay in New York and go to Barnard.

After marriage, Ruth von Phul dropped out of Wellesley, but she needed something to do with her brain. As legend has it, she discovered crosswords while attending baseball games with her husband; bored with one pastime, she latched onto another. In 1924, at age twenty, von Phul won the *New York Herald Tribune*'s inaugural National All Comers Cross Word Puzzle Tournament, making her officially the fastest cruciverbalist in America. She set the bogey time for several newspapers' crosswords: the paper published her solving time next to the puzzle as the gold standard for solvers to best. Today, most crossword-puzzle apps display the time that you've spent on the puzzle, though without a record-setting speed to beat. (Though many recreational solvers linger over the puzzle, letting the subconscious chew a clue for hours to return to it triumphantly, for other solvers, the time taken to solve is a major aspect of crossword bragging rights and the basis for today's crossword tournaments. British ghost-story writer M. R. James used the crossword as erstwhile egg timer, claiming to solve a puzzle in the time it took to boil his breakfast—and, he boasted, he hated a hard-boiled egg.) In March 1925, *Cross Word Puzzle Magazine* featured von Phul on its cover, with the caption *The champion trains for her next bout.*

On April 4, 1925, the *New Yorker* profiled von Phul in "The Hour Glass," a column of short profiles featuring some of the city's most intriguing figures. Someone who is freakishly good at crosswords will of course be male, be socially awkward, and have a face made for radio, the writer assumes. So it comes as both a surprise and a delight to find that crossword's champion is not only a young woman but an accomplished one who's easy on the eyes as well. This "vivacious young lady" is not the sort of person you'd expect to see accompanied by "Noah Webster in one hand and the wrong Roget in the other." "Imagine the blow to the Hellenic Shipbuilder's Board of Trade if Helen hadn't had that sort of face," the writer claims. "One thousand ship contracts unlet. Then you may consider what manner of hurt the cross word industry would have suffered had its official champion been a lady who didn't photograph well. The disease might have struggled along, but it never could have become epidemic." A thumbnail sketch of von Phul depicts a smooth-skinned, attractive young woman, her face framed in a fashionable hat.

The crossword had found its first ingénue.

A few personality types have dominated the collective crossword cultural imagination since its origins. The crossword geek took for granted the crossword as a marker of both high intelligence and nerdiness to the point of obliviousness: the geek could list every river in Africa but not when he (the geek is always a "he") last ironed a shirt. Another narrative of the successful crossword solver was the expert grandmother, zipping through the puzzle with the same autopilot skills as when crocheting her afghans. Even when crosswords were a brand-new fad, the little old solver was an established concept. After all, it was Dick Simon's elderly aunt who initially asked him to put together a book of the puzzles (albeit for her niece).

The crossword ingénue subverted the anticipated types of geek and granny. You wouldn't expect someone so good at the crossword, so the stereotype goes, to also be young, attractive, and female—hence the allure. The ingénue made the crossword hot, the vehicle for the woman to whip off her glasses and flip from bedraggled bookworm to sexy librarian. The 2009 film *All About Steve* starred Sandra Bullock as a crossword constructor who began the film as an old maid spouting cheesy mottos. Of course, Bullock did eventually get to be her A-list self: the audience waited for when, not if, she'd emerge from her crossword cocoon into a full-blown word-nerd butterfly.

In 2014, when twenty-three-year-old Anna Shechtman became Will Shortz's assistant, the media story about her echoed von Phul's: there's a new, brilliant figure making waves in the crossword world— and not only is she a woman, she's attractive, young, and fashionable to boot! Opening Ceremony, a trendy SoHo clothing store, ran an interview on its blog with Shechtman that focused more on her outfit than her contribution to crosswords. When Shechtman took the stage at the American Crossword Puzzle Tournament, the interviewer writes, she stunned the crossword world: "To pretty much everyone's surprise, out walked a pint-size stunner (or shall we say a dime?) with a refined yet humble vibe." (Shechtman, known among crossworders for pumping clever contemporary swag into the *Times*, had persuaded Shortz that *dime* as a term for an attractive person was culturally enough of a thing to be included in a puzzle.) And just as the *New Yorker* had described von Phul as the epitome of brains and beauty, the

Opening Ceremony article also highlighted Shechtman's academic cred, noting that she would be attending Yale in the fall as a PhD student. It's exactly the same story as a century earlier, and the story still hasn't moved beyond the novelty that a crossword expert might be a smart young woman—and, by implication, that a young woman might be an expert at anything.

Ruth von Phul, like all ingénues, grew up. Husband William's work as a civil engineer kept the family on the move, and in the twenties and thirties, between raising her two daughters and packing and unpacking their house at least a dozen times, von Phul bowed out of the crossword limelight.

By World War II, the family had returned to New York City, and von Phul took a cryptanalysis course at Hunter College. Naturally, she excelled, and she soon landed a job as a censor in a secret Special Security division of the New York Office of Postal Correspondence, where she hunted for codes in mail. After the war, several government agencies offered von Phul positions as a cryptanalyst, but she turned them down—she'd had enough of that kind of thing, she said. She was still restless. Crosswords were too juvenile; cryptanalysis, too one-dimensional. She solved puzzles almost automatically, but she also grew easily bored. Then she found James Joyce.

Ruth von Phul took to Joyce the way evangelists take to Jesus, reading *Ulysses* "the way some people read the Bible—cover to cover, every year or eighteen months." She initially rejected *Finnegans Wake* but slowly became obsessed, reading it through first with no help from commentaries, then with the seminal 1944 *Skeleton Key to Finnegans Wake* by Joseph Campbell and Henry Morton Robinson, and soon was making theories and corrections of her own. Von Phul, who never finished college, was for a long time considered an unorthodox Joyce scholar, but she slowly worked her way into Joycean inner circles, publishing articles in journals like the *James Joyce Quarterly* and *A Wake Newslitter.*

As a Joycean, von Phul shone when making the kinds of associations that help an excellent crossword solver: a simultaneous joy in sleuthing for persnickety details with the instinct to juxtapose highbrow and lowbrow connections. Her most delightful contribution to Joycean studies was her discovery of the connection between James Joyce and John Lennon. "I Am the Walrus" was, per von Phul, "a lapidary memento of *Ulysses.*" Lennon's "yellow matter custard," for example, translated as a version of Stephen's vision of Parisian cocottes, "their mouths yellowed with the *pus* of *flan breton.*" "In transmuting the 'pus' ingested by bitch mouths into matter exuded from a dead dog's eye," von Phul noted, "Lennon is skillfully using one of Joyce's habitual devices, the reversed mirror image, and I suspect is quite consciously alluding to *Ulysses*, and to Stephen, blind, jaundiced with envy, dead with existential or neurotic angst."

She became a fangirl as well as a fanatic, regularly making "the usual pilgrimages" to Dublin and keeping up lively correspondences with other Joyceans. Her travel agent once booked her a non-*Ulysses*-themed trip with an archaeological group, but von Phul felt out of place: "I couldn't wait to get back to Joyce." In Joyce, von Phul's talent for crosswords found its permanent home. "There is obviously a connection between my interest in crosswords and cryptography and my fascination with Joyce," she noted. "When you're solving puzzles, you let your mind float with respect to words. It's very Freudian, dealing with puns and tricky word associations, and you almost have to know several languages."

A 1976 *New Yorker* "Talk of the Town" piece revisited von Phul fifty years after her original appearance in the magazine, interviewing the recent widow and great-grandmother in her Park Avenue apartment. "I don't do crosswords much anymore," she admitted, because it had grown hard for her to see the small numbers—but she far preferred the cryptics to the American ones. "I loathe the *New York Times* Sunday puzzle. Too easy, for one thing. And then all that cuteness. Ugh."

Despite eschewing the cuteness, Ruth von Phul never completely left games. In 1957, she made an appearance on *The $64,000 Challenge* and, "without having to cheat or anything," made it to the eight-thousand-going-on-sixteen question before "I stumbled over the meaning of the word 'rescissible.'" In the December 1973 issue of *Harper's*, the magazine invited readers to submit their original poetry to "Hip Haiku," with the best entries printed in the "Game" column in February 1974. One of the runners-up: Ruth von Phul. Her submission:

> What a paradox
> Is an unbending person
> Who cannot unbend.

On January 26, 1978, a *New York Times* editorial lampooned the use of the word *chair* for *chairman*. "Everyone has had her/his fun," the *Times* noted, sneaking in a snarky use of the alphabetical pronoun slash in place of the more conventional *his/her* order "with such locutions as Ethel Merperson or personopause." According to the *Times*, people would not be able to differentiate through context clues whether the "chair" in any given scenario is a synecdoche for a person, or a literal chair. "Women, wishing not to be regarded as sex objects, end up being described as something to sit on." (It's not mentioned whether the editorial board interrogated the use of the term *board* as potentially confusing: Could one mistake the decisions of a group of editors for those of an inanimate piece of lumber? Worse, what if someone heard the homonym and grew bored of the board?)

Von Phul noticed. A few days later, the *Times* printed her letter to the editor about the piece. Other respondents to the article raised an eyebrow at the *Times*'s inability to tell the chairman from the chair—a retiring chair of an academic department wrote that he was stepping down solely because of his "inability to come up with an all-around acceptable title"—but von Phul sidestepped sexism and relied on etymology for her rebuttal. Quoting from the *Oxford English Dictionary*, entry 6b, under "chair," she noted that the use of *chair* for *chairman* was hardly "a ludicrous women's lib neologism" but rather dated back to the seventeenth century.

Even though she left the puzzle world in her early twenties, Ruth von Phul would never escape her identity as the crossword ingénue. In the contributors' notes for an academic journal, in lieu of credentials, the editor described von Phul as "the 'retired undefeated crossword-puzzle champion of the world.'" Ruth von Phul died in 1986 at age eighty-two. Her obituary in the *New York Times* called her a "crossword puzzle composer and champion."

HOW TO CONSTRUCT A CROSSWORD

Mycroft Holmes, Sherlock's older brother, had a mind like a crossword constructor. He was even more skilled in the art of deduction than the famed detective himself. As Sherlock explained to Dr. Watson, his biographer and crime-solving assistant, "All other men are specialists, but Mycroft's specialism is omniscience." When Sherlock was stumped—it happened rarely, but it did happen—he took the facts to his brother. No matter how baffling the case, Mycroft could deduce the solution at once without budging from his armchair.

Unlike his brother, Mycroft had no lust for physical adventure. Every day, he walked down the block from his lodgings to the government building where he worked; in the evenings, he went around the corner to the Diogenes Club, London's premier establishment for antisocial gentlemen, where he sat in his favorite chair until retiring back home. (The club, which stocked its quarters with the latest periodicals but forbade conversation, resembled the quiet car on a train, but one moving precisely nowhere.) Mycroft had made up a job for himself at the central exchange of the British government. When a minister needed to know how a delicate scenario involving ten different subdepartments and several nations might play out, he would ask Mycroft, since only Mycroft could simultaneously hold every particular detail in his head while synthesizing the whole. "In that great brain of his," Sherlock said, "everything is pigeon-holed and can be handed out in an instant."

What did it feel like to take ideas from all directions into a room by yourself, where you had to balance details and ideas from all sides and make them fit into a square? How could you make all the elements cohere into a grid, without using any narrative connections, but get the whole thing to click into place?

Could I do it?

□ ▪ ▪ ▪

If the crosswords were to have a summer home, it would be the Berkshires. For centuries, New Yorkers and Bostonians have escaped city heat and grime to bask in the lush, green, lake-studded countryside that western Massachusetts affords. For generations, the Berkshires has also been synonymous with American literature: Herman Melville, Nathaniel Hawthorne, Henry Wadsworth Longfellow, Edith Wharton, Henry James, W. E. B. DuBois, Edna St. Vincent Millay—the list of authors associated with the area went on. The Berkshires are saturated with arts and leisure: jewel box museums, summer-stock theater, dance troupes. On the Fourth of July, the morning's parades yield to the evening fireworks display, where, from your pontoon boat at the center of the lake, you can watch each village orchestrating its burst into the sky.

When I decided to try constructing a crossword, I was living in the Berkshires on a writing residency for the month of July. I'd recently finished my dissertation, and I was about to move to New Jersey to begin a lectureship at Princeton, but for that one month, I was completely free. The five of us at the residency shared a house with one shower and no air conditioning. At night, we grilled burgers and played poker, using Life Savers as chips. My room, by far the coolest in the house, was in the basement, usually the owners' children's haunt, which I could tell from the lavishly bright puppet theater; it was also home to a locked cabinet of fancy wines, which I knew because I peeked behind the curtain that said *For Owner's Use Only*.

During that month, each resident got a private studio: a tiny, minimalist, perfectly crafted wooden black box with no electricity. Stained on the outside with black pine tar, the same stuff that had originally been used to waterproof Viking ships, the studios were surprisingly airy on the inside, with light wood walls, window slats, and skylights. The architects drew inspiration for each studio from a Berkshires author. Mine was Longfellow, motivated particularly by the Longfellow poem "The Old Clock on the Stairs" (the best bit is the refrain the clock sings: "Forever—Never! Never—Forever!"). The studio didn't have a clock or stairs, but it did have a square window with a ledge that served as a chair and a sundial; in the afternoon, when the sun was brightest, I'd lie under the ledge and nap.

The studios were portable, and every season, with the help of dollies and cranes, the little black fleet got transported somewhere new in the Berkshires. That month, all five were situated on the grounds at Arrowhead, the estate in Pittsfield, Massachusetts, where Herman Melville wrote *Moby-Dick*. Arrowhead is a stiff, elegant, rectangular yellow farmhouse. Melville co-opted the biggest bedroom in the house as his study, not only because it had the best light and the most room but because it afforded him a clear view of Mount Greylock, the profile of which supposedly reminded him of a sperm whale leaping out of the ocean. Melville's study also featured a little guest bedroom, accessible only through the big room, which Melville kept exclusively as Nathaniel Hawthorne's dedicated chamber. The rest of the family—Melville's wife and their four children—slept in the two small bedrooms across the hall.

Every day, I biked the mile or so from the residents' house in Pittsfield to Arrowhead, helped myself to a huge fistful of raspberries from the best raspberry patch in western Massachusetts, and trekked through the meadow to my studio, where I stared across the grounds to the window where Melville had stared at Greylock. A beaver family sometimes huffed outside my door, though maybe they were groundhogs. On my last day, I saw two deer camouflaged in the unmown grass, translucent eyes wide.

▢ ▪ ▪ ▢

I set myself ground rules. If I was going to try my hand at this, I'd go for the American gold standard: a *New York Times* daily, fifteen squares by fifteen.

Everyone who sends a puzzle to the *Times*, from newbies like me to constructors like Brendan Emmett Quigley with hundreds of published grids, follows the exact same submission method. (Variety puzzles, which appear every Sunday, are a different matter—there's a regular stable of freelance constructors who make these.) Cruciverbalists set up the crossword file in a specific order: first, a page with the empty grid; next, a page with the filled grid; then, two columns, one listing the clues in numbered order (Across, then Down), the other with their corresponding answers. You print out your puzzle, and you mail this hard copy to the Crossword Editor, c/o *The New York Times*.

The puzzle operates on a onetime, flat-fee freelance basis for all its contributors, and the rates, though not high, have been rising. As of 2019, the going rate for a daily puzzle was $500, with a larger Sunday puzzle earning the constructor $1,500. Once you'd published ten puzzles with the *Times*, you got a 50 percent pay bump: $750 for a daily, $2,250 for a Sunday. No one earns a regular salary to make puzzles, except the editors. *Times* puzzles must not have been previously published anywhere else. All rights revert to the *Times* upon publication. Constructors don't get royalties for reprinted puzzles.

The *Times* gives its would-be constructors both technical and aesthetic specifications. There are two main types of daily crosswords in the *Times*: themed puzzles, which appear Monday through Thursday; and themeless puzzles, which get published on Fridays and Saturdays. Daily puzzles are fifteen-by-fifteen grids, with few exceptions (innovative themes can push the rules a little bit). Sunday puzzles, also themed, are typically twenty-one-by-twenty-one squares. Monday's puzzles are the easiest of the week. Fridays and Saturdays, the themeless ones, are the most challenging. Sundays are about the same level as Thursdays, the hardest of the themed dailies.

Themed puzzles have a set of answers, usually three to six, anchored around a particular topic or bit of wordplay. Themes create a leitmotif throughout the puzzle, with unrelated clues often looping back to the main idea.

Themed puzzles can contain seventy-eight words maximum for a daily puzzle; themeless ones can have up to seventy-two words. Unlike Wynne's first Word-Cross, in which DOVE appears twice, in a *Times* puzzle, answers can't repeat themselves. TUNE would rule out TUNED and INTUNE and TUNEUP, and would make the clue "Sad tune" a tough sell. Themes, the guidelines continue, should be innovative, lively, and consistently applied throughout the puzzle. If you start your theme as a "continental breakfast" (BELGIAN WAFFLE, ENGLISH MUFFIN, FRENCH TOAST) don't switch it midstream to one in which breakfast foods get hidden inside words (PEGGY, BREADWINNER) or become sound-based jokes (CEREAL KILLER).

The fill—that is, all the answers that aren't part of the puzzle's theme—should be lively and contemporary. This hasn't always been the case. Eugene Maleska, who edited the *Times* crossword from 1977 until his death in 1993, rejected clues that relied on pop culture or used overly colloquial phrases.

These days, everyday words and phrases, even if they haven't yet made the dictionary, are encouraged. Avoid, as the *Times* put it, "uninteresting obscurity (a Bulgarian village, a water bug genus)." Crosswordese (ESNE, ESTE, YSER) should be kept "to a minimum," and no two extremely tricky answers should cross each other.

My ambition was to create a completely, innocuously, perfectly normal crossword. If you mixed my crossword into a month's stack of crosswords, I hoped, you would never question its place in the crossword canon.

▯▮▮▮

I searched for a how-to manual. The first one I found was *A Pleasure in Words* (1981), Eugene Maleska's memoir-cum-manual of his life in word puzzles, which contains a special section on how to construct a crossword. Maleska paints his process of crossword construction as a lexicographical fantasia on the joys of puzzling. In his naïve youth, Maleska narrates, for four days straight, he went to the library and armed himself with every unabridged dictionary to try to compile a master reverse dictionary—only to discover that such a thing already existed.

Maleska offers his pearls to would-be cruciverbalists. Be as clever as you can be—but not *so* clever that nobody else would understand you—and not *cliché* clever, because nobody wants to do a puzzle that's been done before. Don't use extremely common or extremely uncommon references. Avoid crosswordese. Maleska also meticulously reviews the strengths and weaknesses of every dictionary as a crossword construction tool, including ones that were so thorough as to be less helpful than the ones calibrated to contemporary usage. Mostly, the advice I took away was to have infinite, Mycroftian time, with no financial responsibility, or responsibilities to anyone else.

I needed nuts-and-bolts advice about what construction actually looked like on the ground. Luckily for me, some more recent guides offered the granular information I needed. *Crossword Puzzle Challenges for Dummies* (2004), the crossword guide in the notorious "for Dummies" series, is somewhat surprisingly one of the most authoritative and comprehensive resources, since it's by Patrick Berry, one of the top constructors alive. (Though the "for Dummies" version is currently out of print, Berry has the rights to the PDF, which he's reti-tled the *Crossword Constructor's Handbook*, and which he now sells for would-be constructors to download.) Also, around the crossword's centenary in 2013, T. Campbell compiled an exhaustive monograph, *On Crosswords: Thoughts, Studies, Facts, and Snark about a 100-Year-Old Pastime*, that presents a taxonomy of basically every kind of themed and themeless puzzle in existence.

Fortuitously for me, in near-eerie parallel timing with my adven-ture in crossword construction, the *Times*'s *Wordplay* blog ran a series called "How to Make a Crossword" in 2018. The series was divided into four parts, with a pair of veteran constructors annotating the thought process behind a sample puzzle in real time. In April, con-structors Finn Vigeland and Ben Tausig riffed to come up with the theme: two-word phrases with the last word a synonym for *song* (PUZZLE PIECE, TENURE TRACK, CALL NUMBER, MACBOOK AIR). The theme answers were nicely sized at ten or eleven letters apiece, to fit snugly in a fifteen-by-fifteen grid. In May, another set of experts designed the grid; in June, a third pair filled the rest of the grid with the clues beyond the theme answers; and finally, in July, the puzzle was handed over to the editor for judgment, revision, and publication.

▪▪▪

There are two ways to begin a puzzle: themed, with the major answers constellating around a mini-riddle; or themeless, usually with longer clues, and no help from a little internal narrative. If I were going to create a themeless puzzle, I'd start with what constructors call a "seed patch." Seeds are the two or three ne-plus-ultra answers of the theme-less, the ones that inspired the whole thing, and without which the puzzle would have no reason to exist. A seed might be a triple or qua-druple stack of fifteen-letter words. Or a seed patch might be a few somewhat unrelated but buzzy bits of a recent news cycle. Prolific con-structor Brendan Emmett Quigley publishes a new themeless puzzle on his website every Monday, mostly aimed at crossword junkies for whom the easy *Times* Mondays don't cut it. Quigley's themelesses often serve as something of a digest of the latest memes. For a few weeks in early 2018, for example, a Tide Pod Challenge fad flared online. As the most extreme kind of New Year's cleanse, some Twitter pundits posted jokes about eating Tide Pods, a laundry detergent pack-aged in bite-sized candy-colored gel pouches. Soon, a few intrepid YouTube personalities consummated the joke by stage-popping the pods, leading to a mini-outbreak of viewers who tried the stunt at home, with disastrous results. During the same news cycle, but in an unrelated story, Pepsi's CEO described that company's vision of a ver-sion of Doritos marketed to women, advertising a less noisy chip that was also less prone to leaving orange dust on one's fingertips. "Lady Doritos" quickly became mocked en masse on social media. Synthe-sizing both, Quigley published a themeless seeded with TIDE PODS ("'Challenging' things to eat?") and LADY DORITOS ("Tone-deaf snack proposed by Pepsi last week"). The idea was for the fruits of his seed patch to be consumed quickly—"last week" as a clue immedi-ately begs to become obsolete—and then discarded, as readers moved on to the next puzzle. (Other clues for the fill reinforce the disposabil-ity of Quigley's puzzle: RIOTER is "Fan of the team that just won the Super Bowl, maybe," referring to the rowdy jubilance of Philadelphia Eagles fans.)

A great themeless doesn't necessarily rely on weird central words.

Lack of ostentation can be equally impressive. In *On Crosswords*, T. Campbell classified smooth themelesses as "puddings": perfectly crafted fill with no awkward crosswordy quirks, the Japanese Zen gardens of the crossword biodome.

Like most first-time constructors, though, I decided to try my hand at a theme. Theme puzzles are the gateway drug for most constructors. Amateurs have often discovered the same theme over and over. In *A Pleasure in Words*, Maleska describes several "fool's gold" rites of passage among constructors: first, for instance, the eureka that ERNEST HEMINGWAY | THE SUN ALSO RISES | A FAREWELL TO ARMS were each fifteen-letter grid-spanners; then, the despair upon realizing that nearly every crossword constructor since 1950 had also landed on this coincidence. When Will Weng took over from Margaret Farrar to become the second-ever crossword editor at the *New York Times*, he banished what he called the "Bermuda onion" school of crosswords, or, as he put it, the "early 1950s custom of featuring clues that combined countries and foods in what had originally seemed a clever manner."

Themes were everywhere. I could make what Campbell called a "string" theme: **FIRST** AID STATION, **SECOND**HAND SMOKE, **THIRD** BASE UMPIRE, **FOURTH** CLASS MAIL. I could use puns. Maura Jacobson, one of the great constructors of the twentieth century, wrote over fourteen hundred pun-filled crosswords for *New York* magazine, perfecting the form of the deceptively light and easy puzzle that's extremely difficult to pull off effectively. Some clues from Jacobson's final *New York Times* Sunday puzzle, "The Lady Changes Her Name," are examples, to wit: "Columnist reacted angrily": ANN SNARLED (Landers, snarled up); "Novelist-critic dances": SUSAN

TANGOS (Sontag); "1942 Oscar winner reacts to a bad pun": GREER GROANS (Garson).

But I had to focus and find my theme somewhere.

So I started exactly where I was: in the Berkshires.

The crossword, like the Berkshires, hasn't always represented everyone.

If you were a middle- to upper-class British child sometime in the past two centuries, and you'd been packed away to a posh boarding school in the south of England, chances are, no matter where you'd grown up, you'd emerge postpuberty speaking BBC English: a crisp, posh accent that signaled a certain level of education and culture. In the middle of the twentieth century, the *New York Times* crossword became America's version of BBC English. Being able to complete the crossword signaled that you'd arrived in a certain echelon of education, and no matter your background, you could maneuver in a specific aspirational cultural milieu.

But that was a problem. The crossword catered to people in that tiny socioeconomic sliver. Rather than expanding people's horizons, the crossword gave them what they already knew, narrowing who could and wanted to enter the grid.

For instance, one of the most common midcentury crossword varietals was the quote puzzle. The grid turned into a graveyard, prophetic pedagogy arising from the squares. The basic form of a quote puzzle was to take a quotation that chunked nicely into three equal segments and use those as your three primary theme answers, like the crossword-famous Oscar Wilde potent quotable "TO LOVE ONSELF IS / THE BEGINNING OF A / LIFELONG ROMANCE" that breaks into three crossword-primed fifteen-letter segments. In the 1960s, constructor and, later, *Times* editor Maleska canonized the stepquote: a quotation broken into answers that looked like gobbledygook on their own, creating a meaningful phrase only when connected through the whole. Each clue in the stepquote had no hint beyond "Stepquote: Part One," and so on. (A typical Maleskan stepquote's theme answer might read: THEFA / ASHIO / ONWEAR / RSOUTMOREAPPA / ARELTH / HANTH / HEMAN: "The fashion wears out more apparel than the man.")

Quote puzzles were a secret handshake. Stepquotes made the difference between those in the club and the uninitiated even more apparent—either you got the code and could solve smoothly, or you had to grope for building blocks around the quote until you could scrabble together enough context to cobble your way to a solution. And the voices speaking from the quote puzzles overwhelmingly belonged to dead white men: Artemus Ward ("I'm not a politician and my other habits are good"); Henry Wadsworth Longfellow ("Learn to labor and to wait"); John F. Kennedy ("The achievement of justice is an endless process"); Mark Twain ("Nothing so needs reforming as other people's habits"); Thomas Fuller ("There is more pleasure in loving than in being beloved").

If I'd been a midcentury-era American constructor, submitting to the *Times* before the Shortz era, I'd have known exactly how to build my Berkshire crossword. I'd make a short list of American Renaissance authors, the ones burned into the collective imagination of this place. I'd find a quotation that I could break into clue-length segments— TIME FLIES OVER US / BUT LEAVES ITS / SHADOW BEHIND (15/12/12)—and artfully braid it through the puzzle. Without cluing them in any way related to my theme, I'd bury Berkshire nuggets throughout my fill—TWICE TOLD, for Hawthorne's *Twice-Told Tales*, ARCHER for the protagonist in Edith Wharton's *The Age of Innocence*— to the delight of my in-the-know solvers, who'd pick up these under- tones the way an oenophile lingers on the fruity or peppery notes of a pinot.

Happily, the crossword moved on from boat shoes and Whif- fenpoofs. After Will Shortz took the *Times* crossword's helm in 1993, the puzzle began to shift, consciously opening up to more contempo- rary references and wordplay-based clues that included rather than excluded solvers. The crossword was transforming from a beacon of a tiny fraction of the population's idea of intellectualism into a chorus that culled from everywhere: not a gatekeeper but a mirror.

And in the age of Google, the consensus was that a quote's payoff was usually more *pfft* than *pow*. "I know a lot of solvers aren't generally thrilled with them as the long entries (for the most part) go unchecked throughout the solving process," wrote Brendan Emmett Quigley, "and if there's any 'aha' moment, it's at the 'punch line' instead of repeatedly throughout the grid." "There's just not a lot to say about quote puz- zles," quoth crossword critic Rex Parker, author of a daily blog critiqu- ing the *Times* puzzle. "There's the quote. It's a quote, alright. The End."

I had grand designs for what my puzzle could look like.

I'd long admired visual grids, a cross between a Mondrian and latte art. Shaped puzzles had been a thing since the early days of cross- words. Charles Layng's *Cross-Word Puzzles: First Book*, published in 1924, featured a cornucopia of objects co-opted into crosswords like cookie cutters, from a butterfly to a maple leaf to a cabin featuring a pert little chimney square, dubbed "The House That Jack Built." In the 1920s, the Coca-Cola Company's in-house monthly publication, *Red Barrel Magazine*,* held a crossword contest: a $2.00 prize for the best original crossword puzzle containing words pertaining to Coca-Cola. The winning crossword in the March 1925 issue took the shape of a Coca-Cola bottle.† Though the answer words on their own had little to do with soda, the clues monomaniacally twisted each one to signify something Coca-Cola specific. 3-Across: "Too bad Noah didn't have a supply of Coca-Cola when he built this" (ARK). 12-Across: "The best time to drink Coca-Cola" (ANY). 6-Down: "On a trip through the desert, we would gladly pay this many dollars for the sparkling, delicious and refreshing thirst quencher" (TEN).

Grid art has only gotten better over time. In a *Times* crossword from 2009 by Elizabeth Gorski, the black squares at the grid's center formed a spiral, with THE SOLOMON R GUGGENHEIM / MUSEUM as answers spanning the top of the spiral, and—for the geometrically impaired—SPIRAL SHAPE across the bottom. Eight artworks hanging in the spiral-shaped Guggenheim museum appeared as clues, with each artist hung as an answer in the puzzle.

What if I made visual puns? TANGLEWOOD, the music performance space, screamed to have the letters W-O-O-D tangled throughout the answers. ARROWHEAD, Melville's estate, could feature A-R-R-O-W in an arrow, pointing to a HEAD across the grid. GREY-

---

*Though the soda's now-ubiquitous nickname might have seemed natural for inclusion in the grid, *Coke* was not yet an accepted moniker for Coca-Cola; Frank O'Hara's poem "Having a Coke with You" was written four decades later.
†What's black and white and red all over?

M	A	N	E	T		A	L	I	E	N	A	T	E	D		N	O	I	R	E
O	C	E	A	N		P	A	T	R	O	N	A	G	E		O	S	K	A	R
T	H	E	S	O	L	O	M	O	N	R	G	U	G	G	E	N	H	E	I	M
H	E	R	E	T	I	C					S	A	N	T	A	A	N	A		
		S	E	T		M	U	S	E	U	M		S	T	R					
H	I	F	I	S		S	O	P	R	A	N	O	S		R	A	F	F	L	E
O	N	I	N		P	I	A	N	O	T	U	N	E	R		D	A	R	T	S
T	E	N		P	O	S	T			M	D	V	I		I	B	A	R	S	
T	V	A		I	T	S		A	B	A		R	I	G		T	E	N	S	E
A	I	L		C	A	Y		B	E	G	U	I	L	E		I	R	K		
M	T	M		A	T	S		C	H	A	G	A	L	L		O	G	L	E	S
A	A	A		S	I	P		D	A	P	H	N	E		O	N	E	L	A	P
L	B	J		S	O	A	S		R	E	S		G	M	A		O	R	R	
E	L	O		O	N	C	U	E		V	I	R	A	L		Y	E	A		
S	E	R	B		S	E	M	I	T	R	A	I	L	E	R		E	D	D	Y
		W	A	N		K	A	N	D	I	N	S	K	Y		T	R	W		
S	P	O	U	S	E		C	E	S	S	N	A	S		S	E	U	R	A	T
E	A	R	H	A	R	T					D	E	E	D	I	D	O		
A	S	K	A		N	A	T	A	L	I	E	W	O	O	D		I	G	O	R
T	H	O	U		S	P	I	R	A	L	S	H	A	P	E		T	H	R	U
O	A	F	S		T	A	X	P	R	E	P	A	R	E	R		E	T	E	S

Elizabeth Gorski © 2009 *The New York Times*

LOCK, the mountain famously shaped like a whale that Melville looked at while writing *Moby-Dick*, could diagonally bookend the puzzle, with 1-Across as GREY and the final Down clue LOCKing it together.

The "Berserkshires."

▫▪▪▪▫

On a fine Sunday morning, I biked out to Arrowhead, filled a mug with Melville's raspberries, trudged through the meadow, set up my laptop with Longfellow, and settled in to make my crossword.

I prepared myself for the task by setting out my tools. Within the past few decades, crossword construction software has become ubiquitous among constructors. Although a few still make their own grids using Excel spreadsheets, and still fewer on graph paper alone, almost everyone uses a crossword-specific grid generator. I downloaded a construction program called CrossFire, the industry standard for Macintosh-using constructors, which set up the template of a blank grid and empty clue list for me. The program maintained rotational symmetry for my grid, so once I added a black square in one spot, CrossFire filled the equal and opposite space across the grid. Cross-Fire has a huge database of words baked into its system. If I wanted it to, CrossFire could not only complete the right symmetry of blank squares, but fill in letters that technically functioned in the space. It's pretty easy to tell when CrossFire has auto-filled a section, though, because CrossFire tends toward awkward, crossword-y words. For my own pride, I tried to keep the auto-fill to a minimum.

Morning changed to afternoon, evening, Monday. Eventually, I wrangled together something that functioned in a symmetrical grid, but no one would mistake it for a crossword. The visual puns made no sense outside my head—the arrow resembled an arrow the way Canis Major resembled the winner of the Westminster Dog Show, and the WOODs weren't TANGLEd around anything.

On Tuesday morning, instead of biking out to Arrowhead, I went the opposite direction, into the town of Pittsfield, to visit the library. The librarian at the Berkshire Athenaeum was a gem, a slight, elflike figure who not only knew everything about every book but everything about everyone. "I'm constructing a crossword," I told the librarian, who arranged his face in what I assumed to be an impressed expression. "But my theme isn't really working." I explained the "Berserk-shires" concept, my voice fading as his forehead wrinkled. "Oh!" he said. "When you said TANGLE WOOD, I thought, maybe it was a direction—ODDFELLOW, something where the letters in WOOD are TANGLEd in the word. Or, one of those ones where you have the letters WOOD all in one square—HOLLYWOOD, WOODROW WILSON, WOODY GUTHRIE." "A rebus!" I said.

I abandoned the "Berserkshires" on the spot, a new theme blossoming before me: IN THE WOODS.

▭ ▮ ▮ ▭

I jumped on my bike, pedaled back to the studio, and reopened Cross-Fire. Though I stuck to CrossFire's prepopulated word database, seasoned constructors often load custom word-hoards into the program, which they guard as jealously as dragons protecting treasure. Constructors beef up custom word lists with inventive fifteeners, or create algorithms to minimize crosswordese, or add little handy combinations (I GET, ARE I), to help them make their puzzles the most interesting around.

I enlisted a couple of sherpas to guide me through the world of word combinations. One was OneLook, a combination reverse dictionary and thesaurus site. When I typed a string of letters, OneLook found words that began with, contained, or ended with that string. I could also give OneLook gap-toothed strings, that is, combinations of letters and blanks, and OneLook would find possible combinations: all seven-letter words, say, that have A as their second letter and end with C.

But my primary helper was XWord Info, which mines data from the entire *New York Times* crossword archives. XWord Info provides helpful options like bite-sized fragments of common speech that

Home Reverse Dictionary Customize Browse Dictionaries Help

OneLook *Dictionary Search*

wood   Search

wood
wood duck
wood tick   ...monness, Length
wood mouse   ...n words and phrases, Common words
dead wood   ...n nouns, proper names, adjectives, verbs, adverbs
wood violet
wood nymph
wood grain
wood sorrel
wood louse

Words and phrases matching your patt...

1. a. baldwin wood
2. a harold wood
3. a. j. r. russell-wood
4. a. j. wood
5. a.j. wood
6. a baldwin wood
7. a harold wood
8. a j r russell wood
9. a j wood
10. a walk in wolf wood
11. abbey wood
12. abbey wood railway station
13. abbey wood sssi
14. abbots wood
15. abiel wood
16. abraham wood
17. abram wood

26. ag...
27. ag...
28. ah...
29. air...
30. aj...
31. ak...
32. al...
33. ala...
34. alan wood
35. alba plena wood anemone
36. albans wood
37. albert beaumont wood
38. albert wood
39. alex wood
40. alexander wood
41. alexander wood renton
42. alexandra wood

59. aloes wood
60. alone in the dark wood
61. alpheus field wood
62. alphonso wood
63. alson wood
64. amboina wood
65. amboyna wood
66. america wood
67. american wood council

76. andrew wood
77. andrew wood of largo
78. andrews wood
79. andy wood
80. angelina wood tattinger
81. animals of farthing wood
82. anita wood
83. ann wood
84. ann wood-kelly
85. ann wood henry
86. ann wood kelly
87. anna lomax wood
88. anna wood
89. anna wood brown
90. anne wood
91. annie wood
92. annie wood besant

Find clues or match patterns

See all the clues for any answer word, or all answers that match a specified pattern

Show instructions

Pattern matching options:

Sort items: ○ alphabetically   ○ by frequency

Answer length: ○ any length   ○ only length: [15]

Enter a word or pattern:

[WOOD|]   Standard search   RegEx

77 results for WOOD

29 Shortz Era entries found. Click any date for context. Repeated clues show (number of Shortz Era occurrences). See the dictionary definition for WOOD.

Date	Grid	Clue	Author
Thu May 24, 2018	23A	Walnut, for one	Erik Agard and Andy Kravis
Wed May 24, 2017	34A	Choice for a par 5 hole, often	Michael Hawkins
Wed Jul 30, 2014	45D	Pinocchio material	Jean O'Conor
Wed Apr 16, 2014	6D	Lumber (2)	Michael Dewey
Tue Jan 21, 2014	5A	Beech and birch	Todd Gross
Tue Nov 26, 2013	67A	Covered club, usually	Don Gagliardo and Zhouqin Burnikel
Thu Nov 21, 2013	14A	Makeup of one of the homes of the Three Little Pigs	Jules P. Markey
Wed Jan 16, 2013	1A	[5]	Michael David
Mon Feb 20, 2012	12D	Lumber (2)	Samuel A. Donaldson
Tue Jun 15, 2010	7D	Alternative to an iron	Jill Winslow

wouldn't necessarily appear in a dictionary list (ARE TOO, AM SO, OR NOT). XWord Info also knows every clue that has been used for every answer to every past *Times* puzzle ever published, save a handful that were lost to posterity after newspaper strikes in the 1940s.

According to corporate Zen wisdom, when you want to fill a jar with rocks of many different sizes, you start with the big rocks first. In this case, my theme answers—the five or six words that would tie the puzzle together—were my big rocks. So I spaced these throughout the blank grid, then added the necessary black squares around them to designate them as words. Since I knew the program wouldn't let me create an asymmetrical grid, I figured a pattern would emerge organically. But almost immediately, as I tested new fill, black squares started piling up helter-skelter, and the grid clumped into a crystalline mess.

I began again, this time with the spaces between the words. I went grid shopping on XWord Info, which provided a catalog of the most popular grids, showing my options from trendy to timeless. The *Times* prefers proportional, smooth-looking grids to those that are too densely scabbed with three- and four-letter pods. Grids tend toward a reverse staircase effect near the middle, or a crisscross revolving door at the center, creating an atrium that lets travelers move through the puzzle gracefully. Often, corners turn into isolated areas four or five letters wide, only reachable via a narrow strait. These semi-independent nations can be a boon to constructors; since they have their own bylaws, you can experiment in each area without having to dismantle the entire structure. On the other hand, island culture can be temperamental. Shift one letter in that section, and homeostasis goes haywire.

Grids often dictate difficulty. Patterns that skew early in the week tend toward a hedge maze aesthetic, with lots of interlocked small words and tidy corners. Friday and Saturday themeless puzzles feature minimalist pinwheels and grid-spanning blank white stacks, the Pangaea-like openness belying their difficulty.

Grid shopping was hypnotic. As I scrolled through the galleries of the most common *Times* puzzle grids, the shapes wavered between becoming nonsensical—try repeating the word *over* over and over and over until it becomes a set of two noises instead of anything containing content—and oversignifying. One of the most common grids in *New York Times* history featured four diagonal chains of black squares framing the puzzle's center. One of these grids might not look like anything, but when I saw them in formation, I realized I was face-to-face with scores of swastikas.

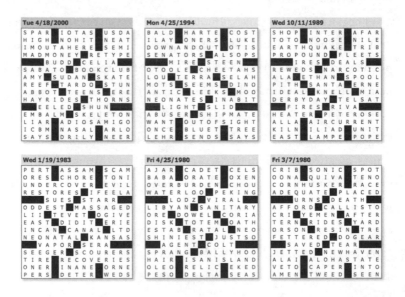

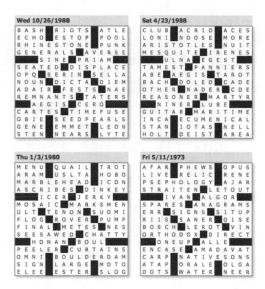

I kept scrolling until I found a pattern that seemed neutral yet flexible, something that had appeared in theme puzzles from easy Mondays to tricky Thursdays. It favored short-to-medium answers and featured a jaunty, off-center stairstep arrangement.

I opened a new file, set black squares painstakingly to re-create the pattern in CrossFire, and began to insert WOOD words. I plugged WOODROW WILSON in a horizontal slot, placing WOOD into a single rebus square, and invited CrossFire to suggest other words that might fit. WORMWOOD OIL emerged as a vertical crossing. Excellent. I had no idea what wormwood oil was, but apparently it was a thing. I created a little stand of trees with five rebus squares. With some swagger, I planted some trees—ASH, PINE, ELM, and OAK— inside longer answers, circling the squares in which they appeared.

I surveyed my theme answers, and the bubble of self-satisfaction dissolved into inadequacy. I knew that the WOOD answers relating to actual wood (WORMWOOD, etc.) weren't as clever as the idiomatic ones. Pun opportunities paraded around me. I felt like I was in a Busby Berkeley dance sequence, associations fanning out in fractals. I could do a Schrödinger—that is, an answer containing a square that could work with two letters clued in—that let HOLLYWOOD also be BOLLYWOOD! Circled tree-letters in concentric rings could radiate out from a cluster of WOOD rebus squares at the center. Geographic accuracy: REDWOOD in the puzzle's northwest quadrant, DRIFTWOOD along the coasts, BRAZILWOOD toward the south. I could snake the phrase *How much wood could a woodchuck chuck* in one direction through the grid and *As much wood as a woodchuck could chuck* in the other. *Are we out of the woods yet*: the WOOD rebuses making fences around parts of the grid. *Can't see the forest for the trees*: answers in which the letters TREE (SESAME STREET, MERYL STREEP) are replaced with types of trees. *No dead wood*: all the clues but none of the theme answers contain the letters DEAD, or the puzzle could be a lipogram, without the letters D, E, or A. How about, I thought, a connect-the-dots puzzle in which, when you drew a line joining the WOOD rebus squares, a log cabin diagram popped out.

▪▫▪▫▪

If setting the theme answers was pouring concrete, shaping my fill was blowing glass. At first, the pliable molten liquid seemed like it would bend to my will. But glass is finicky: I might have had a ewer in mind, but with the slightest shift or air bubble, that EWER became an APSE. And I couldn't play with the glass too much before it shattered.

CrossFire knew far more about how to create correct fill than I did—I could let it flood the whole field with a click—but its taste tilted heavily crosswordy (ESNA, ULNA, SSSS). I chose to go semi-Jeeves, asking it to only show me letters when forced. Using CrossFire's auto-fill at all felt like cheating, but I could only cheat if I was on the right track. If I'd goofed, unfillable sections of the grid flared red, instant eczema.

Every decision had consequences. A seemingly arbitrary choice between a C and an N—BACK versus BANK—made other decisions fall quickly into place. If C was the beginning of the word, a consonant could follow—H, L, R—while N would always prefer a vowel next. An N, though, could end a word with consonants directly in front—G, H, L, N, R—while a C-ending was fussier, almost certainly demanding an I or an A.

I began a longer string, which had to end in a C, to coincide with KNOCK ON WOOD, and the fifth letter had to work as the beginning of a four-letter word ending in ASH. When I checked for options,

OneLook bloomed with half the alphabet: BASH, CASH, DASH, GASH, HASH, LASH, MASH, NASH, RASH, SASH, WASH.

I became a mechanical god. I shifted gears; I tuned each letter individually. I was a perfumer, balancing a palette of scents to create the perfect nose. I was a chemist, titrating my micro-universe; a lepidopterist, shifting a butterfly's wing onto a pin. I built good old groups of T's and S's and R's and E's and A's. Some vowel and consonant clusters that worked beautifully at the ends of words made the balance extremely top-heavy at the beginnings: the clink of a K was a diva at the top of an area of the grid, demanding very particular letters, but at the bottom, K became a universal receiver, soaking up vowels and consonants. J, Q, and Z waltzed in, Anna Karenina–style, calling all the attention in the area. RAJAH and JOVE formed a royal crossing. But no matter how imperial I felt, eventually I had to compromise to make the grid function. CrossFire insisted that ISERE, basically pure crosswordese, was the only option for a particular southern central clue, but I couldn't fit anything else in without the whole region flaring scarlet.

Word definitions were optical illusions, now-you-see-'em, now-you-don't. A lexicographer at Merriam-Webster told me that she could spend weeks deep in the weeds of *bitch* or *ass* without thinking about what she was seeing. Yet just when I had forgotten that letters were anything other than turnstile blocks, meaning snuck back in. RACISM with ARAB underneath appeared in a corner, which felt like a sucker punch and suddenly brought meaning back into the letters. I flipped ARAB to AHAB. Done. I couldn't unsee the original, but at least no one else would have to.

My grid was neither catastrophic nor a work of genius: it was, maybe, barely, fine. My head ached.

By now, I'd spent over half my time at the residency making this crossword, and I was only halfway done. Three hundred dollars* for a daily puzzle isn't nothing, but at, say, six hours a day (inclusive of naps) for two weeks, puzzle making was roughly coming out to be a $3/hour enterprise—and that was assuming it was going to get accepted.

Although the grid is by far the most time-consuming element of the puzzle for a constructor to create, the clues were the only thing that every person who encountered my crossword would definitely read. Clues have to give some variety. If all the clues are simply definitional, the puzzle becomes pure pedagogy, but if every clue is an overly honed humdinger, the crossword is exhausting in a Pre-Raphaelite sort of way, jewel tone after jewel tone but nowhere to breathe. Clues provide navigation through the puzzle experience, guiding the solver

---

*The 2018 rate for a daily.

through potentially weird crossings. A particularly specific Down might be offset by an easier Across crossing it. Or clues can inject references from different worlds. If ALIA crosses words that all have to do with contemporary musicians and actors and artists, I might go with an "et alia" reference for contrast, rather than the actress Alia Shawkat; on the other hand, if we've suddenly waded into rivers of Africa and World War I battlegrounds and other overly precious mires, Shawkat could dust off the good-old-boys'-club cobwebs. Clues can deliberately withhold directions, like a recipe that has no measurements, lacks cooking time, and leads you to believe you're making something savory when you're actually concocting something sweet.

Clues determine a puzzle's difficulty, and editors might change up to 90 percent of a puzzle's clues to calibrate the solving experience. Consider BACON. For a Monday puzzle, BACON might be "Strips with fried eggs"; for a Wednesday, "Sir Francis"; Saturday, "Strips in a club." Note that the clues each refer to the same part of speech, grammatically, as the answer, but that Saturday's clue misdirects in two directions. "Strips in a club" suggests the verb *to strip*, which connotes a certain kind of "club," but when you realize that the "club" is a club sandwich, and "strips" is a noun, the answer is clear. On XWord Info, I found the cluing history of any given answer. Some words had only ever been clued one way in their entire history. BARM had only appeared as "Yeast," or "Brewer's yeast," or "Leaven." OBOE, on the other hand, had scores of options: "Woodwind able to provide an orchestra's tuning note," "Cousin of a bassoon," "Letter before Peter in the phonetic alphabet," "The duck in *Peter and the Wolf*," "High wind," "Light wind?"

I had no idea what to do with the combination AREI. CrossFire hated it, since it was neither a word nor a common phrase. But when I plugged the combination into XWord Info, I found that the string had been used in *Times* crosswords several times before, and, for my purposes, perfectly: "'Whose woods these __ think I know': Frost."

The real use of clues is to give the constructor the last gasp of control over the puzzle. If you aren't yet ready to relinquish your grid to the judgment of the world, you can keep fine-tuning the clues for your desired balance of subject matter, or the perfect ratio of straightforward to clever. OBOE, I turned into "Swan Lake theme instrument," and "Do I dare to __ peach?" justified EATA. Though when the word was truly, ultimately, just a crossword word, I didn't try to reinvent it. BARM: "Foam on fermenting liquor." ISERE: "Rhone feeder." I was pretty sure my more titillating definitions wouldn't last through the editing process. AHOLE, which I suggest as "Someone extremely irritating, euphemistically" would become "__ in one, in golf," and NETI's "Snot pot" would get bowdlerized to "Pot for nasal relief."

◻◼◼◻

I emailed the puzzle to my test solver—my mother. Fifteen minutes later, the phone rang. "Well, it took me twelve minutes to solve, which is about what a Wednesday puzzle usually takes me," she said. "I wasn't sure about BARM, but I got it from the crossings. And POLYHEDRIC, that was new to me."

"But did you get the theme? Did it work? Get it—all the WOOD, and also ASH, PINE."

"Oh—yes," said my mom, sort of thoughtfully, but sort of an

afterthought. "Yes, I got it. Very cute." She refused to speak about AHOLE, but she liked GRANT WOOD and WOODROW WILSON and "Actress Shawkat" for Alia.

I'd done it. We were having a normal conversation about a normal puzzle. I had a vision of myself in three to nine months, casually flipping open the Arts & Leisure section, and there I'd be, in tiny letters. *Puzzle By.* I pictured thousands of subway riders cursing me without even knowing me as they discovered I'd fooled them with my rebus. I'd conquered my Moby-Dick, the black-and-white whale.

I printed it out according to the *Times*'s style specifications, put it in an envelope, and mailed it to Will Shortz, Crossword Editor, *The New York Times*, 620 8th Ave., New York, NY 10018.

CHAPTER 4

PLEASANTVILLE, NEW YORK:
WILL SHORTZ

The fifty-two-story *New York Times* skyscraper rises out of the grid of midtown Manhattan like a steel fantasy of a crossword, a study in squares and frosted glass. The digital crossword lives in the *Times* building, and every day, the crossword gets beamed from these offices to millions of screens. But physical submissions don't stay in Midtown for long. Someone in the mailroom at the *Times* filed my submission into that week's batch—typically over 125 puzzles— loaded the stack into a FedEx box, and shipped it to Will Shortz's house in Pleasantville, New York, a fifty-five-minute train ride north from Grand Central Terminal.

Will Shortz was born in 1952 in Crawfordsville, Indiana, where he was raised on an Arabian horse farm. His mother, Wilma Shortz, wrote children's stories about horses. She was also a puzzler and won two cars and a vacation by entering corporate contests for jingles and slogans (like "Quint Mint," a gum brand). She helped Shortz refine

THINKING INSIDE THE BOX

and sell his first puzzle, at age fourteen, to a national Sunday school magazine. In 1965, Shortz encountered *Language on Vacation: An Olio of Orthographical Oddities* by Dmitri Borgmann, which he called "mold-breaking": this was the first book he'd ever seen dedicated to *logology*, or the art of describing and solving wordplay, rather than simply a collection of puzzles. Shortz wrote to Borgmann, asking him for advice on how to become a professional puzzler. "Borgmann's advice," said Shortz: "Don't."

Undeterred, for an eighth-grade assignment on what he wanted to be when he grew up, Shortz wrote an essay titled "Puzzles as a Profession." In neat, careful cursive loops, the essay describes the types of puzzles he'd already created and cites a *Newsweek* article about Borgmann to show precedent for such a career. Young Shortz reasons that the start-up costs of such a profession would be low—just a few books, reference materials, and pads of graph paper—and concludes, "Making puzzles is a great life from my point of view—easy life, fun and leisure[ly]." The essay received a B-plus. In the margin, his teacher wrote, "I thought you would connect this to the topic of becoming an adult. Obviously, you did not understand me."

Shortz attended Indiana University, where his mother had discovered a new individualized major program: students could craft their own majors from scratch. Shortz created a major he dubbed "enigmatology," that is, the study and science of puzzles. After graduating, Shortz went to law school at the University of Virginia, though he only intended to practice law before going into puzzles as a career. In 1978, he saw an ad in the *New York Times* for a puzzle editor at an unspecified publication. Certain that the ad was from *Games* magazine, in an uncharacteristically bold yet characteristically straightforward move,

Shortz waltzed into that publication's offices and announced that he was applying for the job. The ad wasn't from *Games*, but the magazine hired him anyway.

In August 1993, Eugene Maleska, who had been the *New York Times*'s crossword editor since 1977, passed away. Although Maleska retained his position as puzzle editor until the end of his life, constructor Mel Taub had already been occasionally ghost-editing for him. Taub, master of the "Puns and Anagrams"–style puzzle—a puzzle in which each clue contains a pun, an anagram, a rebus, or other wordplay—stepped in as interim editor later that month. But Taub didn't want the job permanently. (He later described the position as "hard work. You labored in a fishbowl, and even the slightest error would be magnified. Think of the gotcha gang.") Taub kept the section going through Maleska's backlog of accepted puzzles, and at the end of 1993, the *Times* hired Shortz for the role.

Like Dorothy waking up in Oz, when Shortz took over, the Gray Lady crossed into the black-and-white equivalent of Technicolor. The first Shortzian Sunday puzzle featured a rainbow rebus theme—each color in its own square, a wild synesthesia by the old standards—that included an efflorescence of pop culture references (AL GREEN, for example) of the kind that Maleska would have certainly eschewed.

Shortz canonized the gradient of crossword difficulty. Before Shortz, there was a slope throughout the week, with easier puzzles earlier and harder puzzles later, but under Shortz, this calendrical metric became more pronounced, with Monday easier than ever before, and Saturdays harder. The spectrum allowed for a balance between diehard crosswords, who took pride in joining an exclusive society, and casual solvers, who wanted to drop in on the puzzle but didn't want to commit to memorizing crosswordese like ORYX and ESNE and ALEE or the names of rivers in Siberia. Organizing puzzles by difficulty also gave the crossword the bandwidth to expand its own capacity and range without losing its identity. The *Times* crossword could be jokey on a Monday or brutal on a Friday, but on both days, it would still be the *Times* crossword.

Shortz's predecessors at the *Times* had confined their role to be steward of the crossword, but Shortz expanded the position; he has become the kingpin not only of crosswords but of the American puzzle world. Shortz is the "Puzzlemaster" on National Public Radio (NPR). There are hundreds of volumes of reprinted *Times* crosswords edited by Shortz.

Crosswords are Shortz's main career, but he has a robust side gig with another grid. Sudoku is a number puzzle in which the player gets a nine-by-nine square and is instructed to fill in all the numbers such that every row and every column contains the numbers one through nine precisely once each. The game isn't originally Japanese—there have been versions of such a grid in several games publications for decades—but it got its name in the 1980s, when it became wildly popular in Japan. Sudoku reached mainstream English-speaking audiences in 2004, when the *Times* of London printed its first number grid. The combination of the puzzle's easy learning curve but huge variations in difficulty make it addictive. It's also very easy to play online or on a phone. Unlike crosswords, most Sudoku are created by computer and can be generated in large quantities very quickly. In 2005, St. Martin's Press, which publishes anthologies of *Times* crosswords, asked Shortz to create three books of one hundred Sudoku each in ten days' time. Shortz engaged a computer programmer in the Netherlands and got the job done. By 2006, forty of the top fifty best-selling books in the "adult games" category were Sudoku, and a third of these were edited by Shortz.

Shortz is everyone's uncle. He carries himself with the formal politeness of a foreign affairs diplomat and the wholesomeness of a Midwestern tennis coach. He has a sheepish grin, boyish cheeks, and a trimmed mustache that defies trendiness; his eyes flicker on each blink between anxious to please and slyly ready to deceive. The piercing in his left earlobe is a shock—there is nothing else to suggest a rebellious past, present, or future—but on closer inspection, his ear isn't pierced; he has a mole exactly the size and shape of a stud.

Besides puzzles, Shortz's other passion is table tennis. In 2009, he used some of the money he had made from his puzzle empire to convert a warehouse a few blocks from his home into the Westchester Table Tennis Center, a fourteen-thousand-square-foot, world-class Ping-Pong facility. Shortz does not miss a day at the Ping-Pong table. When he travels for puzzle championships, he finds local clubs; he has played in all fifty states, Washington, D.C., Puerto Rico, and over thirty countries. In 2012, Kai Zhang, a fourteen-year-old table tennis player from Beijing, moved to Pleasantville to train for the Olympics at the Westchester facility. Shortz helped search for housing for Zhang, but eventually, the easiest solution seemed to be for Zhang to move in with Shortz. The Ping-Pong prodigy lived with the bachelor puzzlemaster for five years.

One blue-sky, crisp April afternoon, I took the fifty-five-minute train ride from Grand Central to Pleasantville. I wore my favorite dress, which had dark overlapping plaids; the crosshatching, I thought, was a subtle yet obvious nod. I had the same giddy feeling I'd felt when I got to meet the actors of a play I'd just seen backstage: both starstruck and more than a little scared that the dazzle would fizzle.

The train arrived exactly on time to the train station, where Shortz was waiting for me, just as we'd arranged. We drove the few short blocks to his house, during which he introduced the village to me: the largest Pleasantville in the country, Shortz said, it's still a hamlet of less than ten thousand people.

If he can help it, Shortz enters the *Times* offices fewer times a year than he could count on his fingers. Instead, he works on the puzzles from his Tudor-style house, which is a perfect architectural model of Will Shortz's brain, as though Shortz had been perfecting his ideal puzzle-themed dollhouse for the past forty years. The house is a museum of the crossword.

Shortz showed me a glimpse of his vast collection of puzzle-related ephemera. The living room features a glass curio tower displaying some of the highlights of Shortz's crossword collection. One cabinet contains, among other cruciverbal trophies, a vintage crossword-themed enamel bracelet from the 1920s, crossword cuff links, and a promotional crossword on a box of Kellogg's Corn Flakes from the 1950s, with a crossword grid in the shape of a K. As Shortz passed the K, he subconsciously paused to solve it.

Shortz also keeps photo albums stuffed with crossword event–related mementos: antique programs for special crossword-themed parties, banquets, and tournaments; novelty occasional puzzles for a wedding or a birthday party; one-off holiday card puzzles. We peeked into the basement, where there is, in pristine working condition, a crossword-themed pinball machine. The kitchen was one of the only puzzle-free spaces, save for a few refrigerator magnets.

Shortz led me up to his office on the second floor, which contained a giant desktop monitor, a couple of assorted tablets, and floor-to-ceiling bookshelves. In the library, also on the second floor, some bookshelves held volumes of Will's own puzzles, but most held oddly specific reference books—opera, chemistry, sports, a reverse dictionary—as well as outdated complete encyclopedia sets from the twentieth century. Pens and pencils studded the space strategically, as though each room were receiving constant acupuncture from writing implements, or as though some secretarial squirrel had adopted the house as its hoarding zone. Small mechanical puzzles mushroomed in nearly every unfilled corner. At any moment, someone could be solving something.

▭ ▪ ▪ ▭

Shortz edited the puzzle solo for over a decade. In 2000, he began hiring an intern each summer to work for him. Then he hired a fresh college graduate to work for him full-time for the academic year, creating a tiny one-on-one Juilliard of the crossword. The Shortz alumni roster—including Caleb Madison, editor of puzzles for the *Observer*, *BuzzFeed*, and the *Atlantic*; Natan Last and Anna Shechtman, constructors for the *New Yorker*'s crossword as well as myriad others—became a murderers' row of some of the top millennial puzzle talent. Not only do Shortz's assistants help him get through the submissions backlog, they keep him honest to the way language is being used outside Pleasantville, bringing in answers like AIGHT and clues like "Preppy, party-loving, egotistical male, in modern lingo" for BRO.

Joel Fagliano is compact and neat, with dark hair and an occasional beard (out of laziness, he says). Like so many millennial cruciverbalists, he became obsessed with crosswords after seeing Patrick Creadon's documentary *Wordplay*, the 2006 film about the world of competitive crosswords that became one of the highest-grossing documentaries of all time. Fagliano published his first *Times* puzzle as a junior in high school—prodigious, though not unprecedented. In 2011, after Fagliano's freshman year at Pomona College, he interned for the *Times* crossword. He returned to Pleasantville the following three summers, stayed on after college to work for Shortz, and never left. By 2015, Fagliano had become the digital editor of the puzzle. He acts as liaison between Shortz's living room and Eighth Avenue, building new content for the crossword app while making sure that the puzzles they are editing will translate perfectly online. Fagliano got his own assistant in 2017, when Shortz hired Sam Ezersky, a recent UVA graduate and already a prolific constructor.

Though they circulate submissions among themselves all the time, about once a week, Shortz, Fagliano, and Ezersky gather in Shortz's dark dining room, which has become the mail room, for a dedicated mail day. All three look at every submission. Ezersky and Fagliano sit across from each other in the dining room with pencils; Shortz stations himself and his blue pen in the living room. Their proudly antiquated system (as Ezersky has dubbed it, "old-fogey-ish") relies on physical copies. Each editor opens an envelope, skims through the grid and clues, slides the puzzle back inside, and writes a brief note about the submission on the front. Once the first reader has finished, he puts it in a different pile, to signal that it's ready for its second pass. Most conversations happen on the back of the envelope. "Theme is good, but the fill needs work." "TDEME": Theme Didn't Excite Me Enough.

▭▮▮▯

Most puzzles get rejected on the level of the theme: uninteresting wordplay, confusing wordplay, overly simple wordplay, clichéd word-play, jejune puns. Quote puzzles—a crossword with a quotation snak-ing its way through the theme clues—used to be popular, but over the past several decades, they've fallen out of favor with readers, as the *Times*'s audience has come to expect more than trivia from their themes. For most submissions, an editor opened the envelope, looked at a puzzle's theme answers, wasn't impressed, took a cursory glance at the grid to confirm the underwhelm, and slipped the puzzle back inside. TDEME.

For a puzzle to make it past TDEME, the editors have to deem it "enjoyable." *Enjoyable* is the ne plus ultra of any crossword, the "I-know-it-when-I-see-it" barometer that any submission with half a shot of acceptance has to hit. *Enjoyable* typically meant exciting wordplay: *how did they think of that, why didn't I think of that, why didn't I see that.* The kind of thing that you'd never thought of before, but once you'd seen it, you couldn't unsee it. For a rebus, the Where's Waldo factor is critical. In a Sunday puzzle by Hal Moore, "Love-Hate

Relationship," the LOVE in BATTING GLOVES and FOUR LEAF CLOVER crossed the HATE in CALIPHATE and WORDS TO THAT EFFECT, respectively. Each LOVE and HATE shared a rebus square, so for one of the crossings, solvers read LOVE; the other, HATE.

Enjoyable also means fun, lively, the kind of pattern that puts an involuntary smile on the editors' faces. Not only did the singsongy themes in a Peter Gordon puzzle—OODLES OF NOODLES, ABBY CADABBY, EVEL KNIEVEL, INIT TO WINIT—feature beginnings and endings that precisely repeated each other, but the puzzle had left-right symmetry, rather than standard rotational symmetry, to echo the mirroring trick in the clues. *Enjoyable* can also mean simple and elegant. Caitlin Reid debuted FIDGET SPINNER in the *Times* crossword by pairing it with three other two-word phrases that happened to end in a word related to fishing, though none had anything to do with that sport: TELEPHONE POLE, SLIDE TACKLE, and BLOOPER REEL. The fishing expedition made Ezersky smile. *Enjoyable* also has to remain enjoyable over time, and that means ensuring a balance between puzzles featuring contemporary cleverness and ones with evergreen wordplay.

Themeless puzzles are even more prone to one-upmanship than themed ones. In the 1990s, Frank Gehry changed what architects thought a building could do. He wanted to construct a building that writhed like the carp in his grandmother's bathtub, waiting for its turn to become gefilte fish. With traditional two-dimensional construction tools, designing and executing such a structure wasn't possible. But Gehry's team began using parametric design and three-dimensional surface algorithms to model their buildings digitally, and by moving from 2D to 3D, they could bypass huge swaths of the old process and tell contractors exactly how to make cutting paths and tools. 3D modeling brought designs like daredevil parabolic curves and helices, previously the stuff of fantasy, into reality.

Similarly, construction technology made complicated designs within the confines of a fifteen-by-fifteen or a twenty-one-by-twenty-one grid even easier to pull off. Gridding technology and word bank compilers raised the bar. And with greater power came greater competition. In 2009, the *Times* published its first themeless featuring a stack of four fifteen-word answers; a few months later, constructor Kevin G. Der responded with a puzzle that included two quadruple stacks, plus one grid-spanner across the center as an extra bingo.

G	E	O	M	E	T	R	I	C	S	E	R	I	E	S
A	C	T	I	V	E	I	N	T	E	R	E	S	T	S
T	H	E	D	E	S	C	E	N	T	O	F	M	A	N
S	T	A	I	N	L	E	S	S	S	T	E	E	L	S
■	■	■	T	A	R	■	F	I	R	■	■	■	■	■
R	A	J	A	H	S	■	L	A	R	C	■	O	W	S
O	Z	O	N	E	■	E	A	S	E	■	T	R	A	P
Y	O	U	K	N	O	W	T	H	E	D	R	I	L	L
A	L	L	A	■	P	O	K	Y	■	A	I	O	L	I
L	E	E	■	J	A	K	E	■	C	Y	G	N	E	T
■	■	■	J	A	R	■	■	F	O	B	■	■	■	■
E	S	S	E	N	T	I	A	L	O	R	G	A	N	S
T	E	L	L	S	I	T	L	I	K	E	I	T	I	S
R	E	A	L	E	S	T	A	T	E	A	G	E	N	T
E	D	M	O	N	T	O	N	E	S	K	I	M	O	S

Kevin G. Der © 2010 *The New York Times*

So the "enjoyable" heuristic has to also keep the crossword from becoming an arms race. The editors want to push the envelope, but they recognize that their solvers aren't always looking for the spiffiest puzzle on the block. Sometimes, a solid, quiet entry can be just as revolutionary as the pyrotechnic whiz. If each published themeless featured Jenga-esque triple stacks of fifteen-letter answers, jam-packed with as many J's and Q's in as few letters as possible, the category itself would have to be changed from themeless to show-off.

⬜️▪️▪️▪️

At Shortz HQ, if a puzzle made it past TDEME, the next stage was examining the grid. A check mark next to an answer meant that it was particularly good. A minus stood for a nose wrinkle, usually from a particular bit of crosswordese—INE, ESTE—not a death knell, but not ideal. Arrows pointed to crosswordy regions of the grid. CK meant "check," as in, look up—a geographical term, a music reference. A question mark meant a question mark. Exclamation points stood for something especially bonkers, like ZZZQUIL. "New to me" flagged a gut-check: although the phrase in question might seem unfamiliar to that editor, the others might think it was perfectly normal. Ezersky might miss an opera reference that Shortz could assure him most solvers of a certain age would know. Shortz might flag NOOB as "New to me," but Fagliano would affirm it was a thing.

Once they accept a puzzle, Shortz and one of his assistants edit it. Unlike reading submissions, editing is pretty strictly a two-person job. I watched Shortz and Fagliano edit a Sunday puzzle titled "Literary Circles." The constructor, Jacob Stulberg,* had embedded an

---

*Not only was I tickled that Shortz and Fagliano were working on a poetry puzzle on the day I visited, but by pure coincidence, I knew Stulberg—we were in the same doctoral program at the time. When I asked him about the puzzle, he told me that he'd buried some personal Easter eggs: he used ALBRIGHT, for example, to hide the word

entire poem, "The Locust Tree in Flower" by William Carlos Williams, into the puzzle, in order. The poem's thirteen words were buried within longer words (*among*, the first, nests inside CUCAMONGA, for example). THE LOCUST TREE IN FLOWER and WILLIAM CARLOS WILLIAMS were also answers: each of these phrases was, conveniently, twenty-one letters long, spanning a full Sunday grid. (Later, puzzle blogs complained that the poem was an overly esoteric Williams, and I sort of agreed: even though I'd recently taken a seminar devoted to William Carlos Williams, I hadn't come across it.)

Editing a puzzle, by and large, meant rewriting its clues. Shortz used a red pencil stamped with *American Crossword Puzzle Tournament*; Fagliano was on a large Mac desktop. Stulberg had clued MASTIFF as "Guard in many a yard." I liked the rhyme: after all, this was a poetry-centered puzzle. But the clue didn't ring right to Shortz and Fagliano. As though simultaneously interpreting a Rorschach test, they both announced their first associations with the word: Shortz, Sherlock Holmes; Fagliano, Harry Potter. Eventually, after riffling through Wikipedia and the American Kennel Club, they settled on "Relative of a Great Dane."

To clue ANT, Shortz and Fagliano turned to XWord Info. ANT has appeared in several hundred *New York Times* crossword puzzles, and it has had nearly that many clues, from the workhorse "Aardvark's morsel" to the colorful "Picnic schnorrer" to the clever "Queen's pawn?" to Shortz's new favorite, from June 2014, "Crawler on an

---

"BRIGHT" in the Williams poem, as tribute to a dearly beloved professor of that surname who'd recently died.

M. C. Escher Möbius Strip." Stulberg had clued ANT as "Hill dweller," which seemed too familiar to Shortz and Fagliano. "Marcher in a trail," suggested Fagliano. "One on a jungle trail," declared Shortz. "It's not a classic, but it'll do."

"We're all so different," Ezersky said of himself, Fagliano, and Shortz. I thought he was joking. Ezersky was talking crossword differences— his particular fields of knowledge intersected with those of Fagliano more than either one's did with Shortz, though Shortz was the transparent all-knowing eyeball of the bunch. But by most demographic measures, they could have been mistaken for, if not BROs, certainly members of the same family: white, college-educated, socioeconomically similar, preppy, and male.

They knew they had to watch for blind spots. One puzzle clued SIR as "Military term of address," which they realized wasn't exactly correct, as MAAM was just as accurate. But since the clue didn't specify that SIR was the only term of address, they felt comfortable leaving it as it was. To find where blind spots were, the editors often gut-checked with Deb Amlen, the editor of the *Times*'s crossword blog *Wordplay*, as well as several test solvers from different backgrounds.

That October, almost exactly three months after I'd sent in my puzzle, I got an email with the subject line: "Crossword." My stomach dropped. Ezersky, writing from Shortz's email account, broke the news to me: I hadn't made it past the dining room.

We must pass on your WOOD 15x submission, as the theme itself felt a bit too scattershot; having wordplay involving both hidden words and rebus answers is a lot for the solver to take in, and a straightforward revealer of just WOOD doesn't really hint at everything precisely enough. Also, with rebus puzzles in particular, we especially like there to be 1) a crystal-clear revealer that suggests a rebus theme specifically, and 2) exciting, surprising answers that hide the rebus squares elegantly.

TDEME.

¹C H A P T E R ²5

THE CROSSWORD HYACINTH: ENGLAND AND THE CRYPTIC CROSSWORD

During the first half of the eighteenth century, London entered a state of constant, extreme drunkenness. Gin was cheap, and people were getting soused on the regular. Parliament passed a series of escalating censures against gin, culminating in the Gin Act of 1751, which prohibited distillers from selling to unlicensed merchants. The act also encouraged men to drink more beer.* In 1751, to promote the Gin Act, English artist William Hogarth issued two contrasting prints, *Beer Street* and *Gin Lane*. *Beer Street* depicts a prosperous and plump citizenry: "Here all is joyous and thriving. Industry and jollity go hand in hand." *Gin Lane*, in contrast, features a boozy mother letting her child slip from her arms, crowds rioting behind her. The only thriving business on Gin Lane is the pawnbroker, whose

---

*In 1995, fast-food chain Chick-fil-A used a similar tactic, with an ad campaign depicting cows painting a billboard encouraging passersby to "EAT MOR CHIKIN."

cross-shaped sign dangles like an overgrown hangnail and blocks the view of the church, so that it looks like the steeple.

For British hand-wringers nearly three hundred years later, crosswords had become the new gin. America, the papers warned, had turned into a wasteland of crossword addicts wasting precious time on this wanton activity. In a December 1924 article titled "AN ENSLAVED AMERICA," the *Tamworth Herald* described the crossword as an epidemic plaguing America: "In a few short weeks it has grown from the pastime of a few ingenious idlers into a national institution: a menace because it is making devastating inroads on the working hours of every rank of society." The article escalated toward a conclusion of rhapsodic melancholy: "Many years ago, a misguided person thought to beautify some ugly stretches of shallow southern rivers by planting them with wild hyacinths. The plan succeeded beyond all expectation. The hyacinths spread with amazing rapidity, choking the rivers at last and putting the authorities to enormous expense to clear out their channels again. The cross-word puzzle threatens to be the wild hyacinth of American industry."

The British press luxuriated in its hysteria over the hyacinths.* There was a prurient delight to these hysteria-documenting articles,

---

*Cultivating a combination of mass superiority and mass fear is neither a new nor a unique tactic, and it persists in popular culture. In Meredith Willson's 1957 musical *The Music Man*, when salesman Harold Hill comes to River City, Iowa, the first thing he tells the good citizens of that town is that the latest fad to hit their town—the pool hall—is a time-wasting, morally decrepit menace: "Well, ya got trouble my friend, I say, trouble right here in River City. . . . The first big step on the road to deg-ra-day—I say, first: medicinal wine from a teaspoon, then beer from a bottle! . . . Trouble with a capital T and that rhymes with P and that stands for Pool. . . . Friends, the idle brain is the devil's playground! Trouble! . . . That game with the fifteen numbered balls is the devil's tool."

which thoroughly enjoyed their doomsday depiction of all America trapped in crossword hell. The reader got to feel immensely superior, envisioning an entire nation trapped in a grid like fish in a tank frenetically swimming around and around but getting nowhere. Pity the bettas across the pond.

The rhetoric of British backlash against the crossword stemmed from a firm moralistic streak. To be an upstanding member of society, newspapers admonished readers, you should be productive and should be attempting to maximize your time to its full potential. "AN ENSLAVED AMERICA" was sandwiched between "A FEW COOKING HINTS" and an article on missionary schools.

Time and industry got equated with morality in these anticrossword articles. Sanctimonious naysayers had the bossy-cum-savior mentality that, nearly a century later, would propel Lynne Truss's grammar-gotcha book *Eats, Shoots and Leaves* to the *New York Times* bestseller list. The real sin of the crossword was that it flagrantly advertised its uselessness. Those hours filled by filling in squares were hours of work, to be sure, but useless work, and therefore all the more poignant for being squandered, since they could have been squeezed into something useful. "It is estimated," the *Herald* article suggested, "that not less than 10,000,000 people have caught the infection, and that they spend half an hour daily, on the average, with the insidious pastime; that is to say 5,000,000 hours daily of the American people's time—most of nominally working hours—are being used up in unprofitable trifling." (How the author calculated these numbers, or how much time the *Herald* took to arrive at these statistics, was not revealed.)

The crossword was the perfect symbol of wasted time in modern life. The crossword aped productivity. You were greeted with an empty grid and told to fill it in, which, on the surface of it, seemed the gold standard of what it meant to do work. But the labor that the crossword required was purely a leisure activity, not one of industry. The crossword demanded the same attention and focus as productive labor, yet solving the puzzle produced nothing new. As soon as the crossword was completed, it was rendered useless. And the crossword did not need its solvers; all the answers were already there.

The ability to do the crossword required a workday with a certain amount, and certain type, of nonwork time scheduled into it. The farmhand who must rise before dawn and works in the field until dusk might have a break in his day, but he was less likely to have a newspaper and pencil readily on hand than the commuter taking the subway from the Bronx to Wall Street, with time to fill that couldn't be productive time yet was still part of the working day. The crossword geared the commuter up to produce: it created the simulacrum of work without the product of industry. Just as putting on business attire puts the person in the body of a worker, the crossword puts his or her mind in the grid of the office.

Moral guilt crossed with a superiority complex was also a cocktail for curiosity. The crossword became more appealing than ever for its shock factor. Suddenly, a mildly boring pastime acquired the power and allure of a dangerous demon. Who could resist the pull of an illicit pursuit?

British publishers shrewdly capitalized on antipuzzle hysteria to promote the crossword. The preface to the 1924 British edition of *The Cross Word Puzzle Book* gave instructions as officious as a surgeon general's warning:

THIS IS NOT A TOY!

TO FATHERS, MOTHERS, UNCLES AND AUNTS:

It is just possible you may pick this book up thinking of it as a present for younger children. Will you please do us this one favour—in the name of humanity? Just solve half a dozen of the puzzles, taken at random, *yourself*, before you pass it on. It's a small thing to ask—you'll be able to go back to your work in about a week.

By 1925, the crossword hyacinth had spread across Britain. Established leisure activities were being abandoned to pore over the puzzle. The *Nottingham Evening Post* announced, "The picture theaters are also complaining that the crosswords keep people at home. They get immersed in a problem and forget all about Gloria Swanson, Lillian Gish, and the other stars of the film constellation." (In an earlier decade, the very films heralded as pinnacles of society were the scourges of culture, drawing people away from more virtuous pursuits with their addictive allure. The new kid on the block is always blamed.)

British libraries, like American ones, were pestered with dictionary seekers. The *Western Times* of England reported in February 1925 that the damage to the dictionaries in Wimbledon's library, due to people trying to solve the crossword, "has been so great that the committee has withdrawn all the volumes." Dulwich Library began blacking out white squares in the crosswords to prevent people from hogging newspapers for hours on end: too many people were loitering to pore over the puzzle, so the library had to take action to make the puzzle less addictive.

Libraries weren't the only resources taxed. Zookeepers in Nottingham reported being beleaguered by questions about crosswordese species: "What is a word with three letters meaning a female swan? What is a female kangaroo, or a fragile creature in six letters ending in TO?" Ernie Bushmiller mocked the zoological crossword craze in a May 1925 *Cross Word Cal* strip, where the animals are labeled by crossword definition: a fluffy "Three Letter Dromaeus" pokes out its beak from behind the bars, a "Three Letter Boidae" coils around a branch, and a "Five Letter Bactrianus" (though we can see only one of its humps) leans its head through the bars to nibble from a bucket of "Alphabet Soup." The world had been retooled as a reference for the crossword.*

British superiority as expressed through the medium of the cross-word shifted, from stoic resistance of the grid's temptation to muscular

---

*Seeing the world as your own personal crossword dictionary lies somewhere between the Baader-Meinhof phenomenon—seeing one thing then thinking it appears everywhere—and pareidolia, or the tendency to interpret a vague shape as something familiar, like a face in a cloud.

proclamations of intellect. If British crosswords were harder to solve, they were therefore more virtuous endeavors. Early British crosswords frequently featured Latin in the clues: a 1929 "Virgil Bi-Millenary Crossword" in the *Listener* featured macaronic clues that not only leapt between English and Latin but embedded further puzzles into the Latin clues. (50-Down: *Et patrio Andromachen iterum—marito [anag. of first five letters only].*) When the *Times* of London finally caved to popular demand and began publishing its daily crossword in 1930, the paper published a Latin puzzle that same year, to reassure its readers that all hell had not broken loose.

▢▮▮▢

The grand poobah of the cryptic set the hardest crosswords in the world while cross-legged in pajamas. Edward Powys Mathers was born in 1892 in Forest Hill, South London, to the son of a newspaper proprietor. Mathers attended Oxford and became a poet and translator; in 1923, he published a well-received translation of Jean-Charles Mardrus's French version of *One Thousand and One Nights*. Mathers was also an expert in detective fiction and reviewed many detective stories for the *Guardian*. Mathers discovered crosswords in 1924, soon after puzzles crossed the ocean from America, but he was dissatisfied with the straightforward cluing style. In 1925, Mathers presented a crossword in the Saturday *Westminster Gazette* under the name Torquemada, the first Spanish Grand Inquisitor. (He also established the tradition that cryptic setters publish using a pseudonym.) Torquemada was the first crossword compiler to use entirely cryptic clues, that is, clues built on complex wordplay rather than definitions. (In America, a crossword creator is typically referred to as its *constructor*, whereas in Britain, the terms *setter* and *compiler* are more common.) By 1926, Mathers had switched to the *Observer*, which published his crosswords until Mathers's death in 1939.

In a foreword to a collection of Torquemada puzzles, Mathers's widow created a romantic portrait of the great setter composing in bed, like a cruciverbal Proust. "I see him sitting cross-legged in bed," she wrote, "with a puzzle in front of him, looking very like a somewhat relaxed Buddha, a cigarette between his fingers and eyes fixed in the distance—until something clicks and, with a contented smile or discontented shrug, he writes on the list in front of him, and ticks off the word in gaily coloured chalk."

Mathers typically wrote his clues in verse form and often created mini-narratives through the puzzles. One puzzle, for example, featured clues in the form of knock-knock jokes. Mathers's clues favored literary or biblical references. Though his puzzles were notoriously fiendishly difficult, they had a rabid fan base. One solver wrote in to the *Observer* to say that she'd memorized several of Mathers's rhyme puzzles. The *Observer* offered a prize for the first three correct solutions received each week, and it typically received over seven thousand qualifying entries. Solvers from all corners of the globe—West Africa, India, Alaska—sent in solutions. Many solvers worked together, either in person or over the telephone.

Upon Mathers's death, constructor D. S. Macnutt took over the *Observer*'s puzzle, writing under the pen name Ximenes, one of the original Torquemada's successors in the Inquisition. In 1966, Macnutt published *Ximenes on the Art of the Crossword*, a style guide and rulebook for the elements that should be present in all good cryptic crosswords. Macnutt based his rules on the guidelines that Torquemada had laid down and passed on to him. For a clue to pass the Ximenean bar, it must be absolutely clean and precise in its ambiguity: the clue must provide some sort of deception that the reader must enter and actively decode, but the clue should also not provide the reader with inaccurate information. Macnutt was not afraid of wordplay thickets, but he prized elegance and efficiency in cluing. The Rube Goldberg machines he created for the reader to arrive inevitably at a particular word might require twenty steps where two would do, but those extra eighteen steps were what made the puzzle worth entering. Macnutt loathed cluing clichés or tics of compilers and found himself bored with conventions: if a way of cluing a certain word did not feel fresh, it would not titillate the solver. There was not one logic that drove a Ximenean clue; on the contrary, Macnutt provided an astonishing array of ways of getting from A to B.

Yet even with the pseudonyms and pyrotechnic wordplay, cryptics don't erase the human behind the puzzle. Rev. John Galbraith Graham, a crossword constructor who wrote as Araucaria, broke the fourth wall between himself and his solvers through clues. The crossword was introduced with the preamble "Araucaria has 18 down of the 19." 18-Down read "Sign of growth (6)": Araucaria has CANCER. A longer preamble, which could be decoded once readers had filled in the grid, read: "I have CANCER of the OESOPHAGUS; no CHEMO-THERAPY, just PALLIATIVE CARE; no NARCOTIC or STENT or MACMILLAN NURSE yet—plenty of MERRIMENT, though I wouldn't have chosen the timing."

"There are crossword puzzles** and crossword puzzles," declared Stephen Sondheim, the eminent composer, in a 1968 article for *New York* magazine, in which he gave American readers a primer in the art of the British-style cryptic crossword. "To call the composer of [an American] crossword an author may seem to be dignifying a gnat," he quipped, but cryptics were different. The mannerisms of each cryptic displayed the constructor's specific style, unlike in a trivia-based American puzzle, where "a 'Bantu hartebeest' remains a 'Bantu hartebeest' whether it's in *The New York Times* or *The Daily News*." Sondheim wrote several cryptics and variations on cryptic puzzles for *New York* magazine, riffing on his predilections to form clues: "Does she stick on one note in *La Boheme*?"* "Successor to *The Sound of Music*"† "Entertain and wind again?"‡ Sondheim was respected across the pond for his prowess. Apex,§ a notorious cryptic constructor, constructed a Christmas cryptic (ApeXmas) every year, which he mailed to a select few; Sondheim and Leonard Bernstein were among the only Americans in the coterie.

I wrote to Sondheim to ask if he was still involved with crosswords. I slaved over that letter—this was *Sondheim*. His cow-themed triple pun "While her withers wither with her" in *Into the Woods* is one of the wonders of the modern world. After I printed it out and sent it via snail mail to a literary agent I'd found online, I expected nothing.

A few weeks later, I received, *deus ex machina*–style, a typewritten note on *Stephen Sondheim*–stamped square stationery. No word, space, or piece of punctuation was wasted. He replied that the only crosswords he did were the cryptic kind; he didn't have a "crossword

---

*MIMI (mi, mi)
†HEIR (air)
‡REGALE (re-gale)
§"Ape X," that is, ape-ing Ximenes.

coterie" (my words, not his), nor any particular solving routine. He was, however, proud that he'd essentially introduced America to cryptics, as they'd only been available in small publications in the United States before his *New York* magazine compositions.

▯▮▮▯

Despite Sondheim's efforts, the cryptic remained niche in America. In the 1990s, the *New Yorker* launched a cryptic crossword puzzle. According to *The New Yorker's Guide to Solving Cryptic Crosswords*, which the magazine would send to interested readers, the cryptic might have seemed foreign to American readers, but the guide predicted it would soon catch on, like "sushi or cappuccino or acupuncture." It didn't, and the magazine languished puzzleless until 2018, when literary editor David Haglund and web editor Liz Maynes-Aminzade established a regular puzzle feature for the website—though not a cryptic. The cryptic hyacinth had rooted in England, but the American-style hyacinth was also here to stay.

WORLD WAR II AND THE GRAY LADY

The Eccentric Club of London, or the Illustrious Society of Eccentrics, or the Everlasting Society of Eccentrics, was founded in the 1780s.* The club's motto, *Nil nisi bonum*, is an abbreviation of the Latin phrase *De mortuis nil nisi bonum dicendum*: "Say nothing if not good of the dead." Its members have included playwright Richard Brinsley Sheridan; Lord Melbourne, Queen Victoria's mentor; professional snooker player Joe Davis; Lord Edward John Barrington Douglas-Scott-Montagu, founder of the National Motor Museum and a key figure in British decriminalization of homosexuality; and Prince Philip, Duke of Edinburgh. In 1914, the club moved into the Dieudonné's Hotel near St. James's Square (a stone's throw from the Ritz), where its members convened until 1986, when the club

---

*Nearly all *New York Times* clues for ECCENTRIC give "Odd" or "An odd fellow," though Eileen Lexau's Monday, May 26, 1997, puzzle clued it as "Like a three-dollar bill."

was forced to liquidate. In the mid-2000s, with the financial support of Prince Philip, enthusiasts reincarnated the club and revived such traditions as the Friday the Thirteenth feast, in which members parade under ladders, unfurl umbrellas indoors, and embrace black cats. Throughout its history, the club has never come to a clear definition of what it means to be "eccentric": bedazzled fezzes, tartan slacks, and the propensity to burst into song at any moment are common features among members at its gatherings, but the club's eccentricities can veer far from your garden-variety self-stylized oddball.

In late 1941, the *Telegraph* posed a challenge to its crossword solvers from a "Mr. W. A. J. Gavin, Chairman of the Eccentric Club." Gavin, the *Telegraph* reported, had sent a £100 banknote to the *Telegraph*, and if a reader succeeded in solving the puzzle under controlled conditions in fewer than twelve minutes, the newspaper was authorized to donate that banknote to the "Eccentric Club Minesweepers' Fund." For the past few years, solvers had been writing letters haranguing the *Telegraph* that the crossword had gotten too easy, and Gavin's test appeared to be a gauntlet for complainers—if solvers found the *Telegraph*'s puzzle such a snooze, they'd have to prove their prowess.

Stanley Sedgewick, a managing clerk for a London accounting firm, was intrigued. He regularly did crosswords to pass the time on his commute and had become fairly expert, so he decided to take up the challenge. On a chilly Saturday in January 1942, Sedgewick joined over two dozen aspiring speed solvers in the *Telegraph* newsroom on Fleet Street. The contestants sat at individual tables facing a panel of judges that included the newspaper editor, a timekeeper, and chairman W. A. J. Gavin himself. The editor pulled a sealed envelope from a stack containing the puzzles due to appear the following week. Five contestants beat the deadline, although the fastest was disqualified for misspelling a word. The quickest correct solver, a Mr. Hawes of Dagenham, received a cigarette lighter as his trophy. Sedgewick was one word short. He was a bit deflated by the narrow loss. But the chairman treated the contestants to tea afterward in his dining room, and a mollified Sedgewick returned home, thinking nothing more of the event than as a pleasant way to spend a Saturday afternoon.

The Eccentric Club was a red herring. "Imagine my surprise," Sedgewick later recalled, "when several weeks later I received a letter marked 'Confidential' inviting me, as a consequence of taking part in 'the *Daily Telegraph* Crossword Time Test,' to make an appointment to see Colonel Nicholls of the General Staff who 'would very much like to see you on a matter of national importance.'" Colonel Nicholls was the head of MI8, a branch of the military intelligence service. Sedgewick was told that "chaps with twisted brains like mine might be suitable for a particular type of work as a contribution to the war effort." Along with a small coterie of fellow puzzle experts, Sedgewick was first sent to a "spy school" in Bedford and then to Bletchley Park, home of the British wartime code-breaking operations. Only years later, long after World War II was over, did Sedgewick learn that the "German weather codes" he'd worked on had been a crucial part of cracking the Enigma machine, used by Nazi Germany to protect military communications. The operation was so top-secret that even the puzzlers themselves weren't allowed to know what they were solving.

Many children's books riff on the fantasy of an exam that, unbeknownst to the test taker, is actually a trial for something entirely different. In Trenton Lee Stewart's 2007 novel *The Mysterious Benedict*

Society, Reynard* Muldoon sees an advertisement in the newspaper directing "gifted children looking for special opportunities" to present themselves at an office building to take a series of tests, which consist of hidden puzzles and codes: the children have to figure out the solution, but must first discern what the puzzle is, and then what the puzzle is asking them to do. They're also tests of honor. Muldoon is offered the right answers early in the process, but he refuses the opportunity to cheat, making him doubly qualified to serve. Muldoon and three other eccentric, brainy children pass the test and are promptly sequestered to a hidden area, where they meet a Mr. Benedict, who tells them that cryptic messages are being broadcast into people's brain waves by nefarious forces. The quartet become spies to crack the codes, infiltrate the evildoers, and save the day—and all because they are expert puzzlers.

But if crosswords could find heroes, they could also find traitors.

Leonard Dawe was an English amateur footballer most notorious for playing while wearing glasses. Born and raised in west London, Dawe played football at Cambridge, and upon graduating in 1912, he signed on to Southampton's amateur team. In 1912, Dawe was a member of the squad representing the United Kingdom in that summer's Olympics

---

Reynard, French, "fox." Foxes have a special literary affinity for puzzles and have been associated with cleverness for centuries. The anthropomorphic fox Reynard is the main character in an allegorical cycle of literary fables from the Middle Ages. Reynard is wily and not always ethical, and his adventures consist of him deceiving both the good guys and the bad guys.

in Stockholm, Sweden. The team took the gold, though Dawe himself didn't actually play in the Games. Dawe did make one appearance for the English amateur national football team in 1912, when he played for England against Ireland.* Famously bespectacled Dawe found more success as a schoolteacher than a footballer. He taught at several prestigious institutions before settling down as the headmaster of the Strand School, a boys' grammar school in London. Dawe, a firm but fair disciplinarian, became known as "Moneybags" because of his initials (LSD = pounds, shillings, and pence).†

Dawe was also part of the first generation of British crossword setters. In 1925, he began publishing puzzles for the *Telegraph*'s then-nascent crossword, and over the following four decades, he would contribute nearly five thousand puzzles to the paper. Dawe was one of the first setters to use cryptic clues. Under Dawe's watch, the puzzle became more standardized and rigorous, with streamlined clues and no two-word answers. Sometimes, Dawe would leave a blank crossword grid on a table and invite students to fill in the squares with words, both as a mental exercise for the pupils and a convenient pre-software mechanism to help save Dawe some time. Once the students had placed the letters in the grid, Dawe would set clues and send it to the paper.

During World War II, the Strand School was evacuated to Surrey, in a building next door to a camp of American and Canadian troops. Whenever they were on breaks, the schoolboys crept as close as they

---

*England lost, 2–3.
†Forty years later, a quartet of Liverpudlians would make the initials LSD more famous for different reasons; "Lucy in the Sky with Diamonds" does not refer to coinage.

could to the fences to eavesdrop on the soldiers. In the months leading up to D-Day, GOLD, SWORD, and JUNO, three code names for beaches assigned to Allied troops, popped up in various *Telegraph* puzzles, but since these were relatively common words, and they were spaced fairly far apart, intelligence offices chalked the concurrence up to chance. But in May 1944, more unusual code words started appearing in puzzles: UTAH and OMAHA, two more beaches; MULBERRY, the operation's floating harbors; NEPTUNE, the naval-assault stage; and OVERLORD, the name for D-Day itself. Dawe's clues had nothing to do with military operations; OMAHA, for example, was "Red Indian on the Missouri," and OVERLORD appeared with the clue "[common] ... but some bigwig like this has stolen some of it at times." But the coincidence was now too strong for the government to overlook, though Dawe had no idea that he was being a disloyal citizen.

MI5 officials arrived at the bewildered Dawe's house and made him burn the notebooks that he used to work on crossword clues. MI5 couldn't find any evidence that Dawe was using the crossword to leak information to the enemy, so they didn't arrest him. Eventually, Dawe figured out that the code names had appeared thanks to his co-setters. In 1984, Ronald French, one of Dawe's former students, told the *Telegraph* that he'd helped fill the grid with the code names. He, like many students at the school, hung out around the soldiers' camp, and he filled notebooks with any stray words and bits of information that they could glean. "I told [Dawe] all I knew and he asked to see my notebooks," said French. "He was horrified and said the books must be burned at once. He made me swear on the Bible I would tell no one about it. I have kept that oath until now."

On November 7, 1924, seven months after Simon & Schuster had published its first crossword collection, the *New York Times* ran two editorial columns side by side. The first described the Bolshevist Russian concept of "economic espionage," or the knowledge at any time in one's life of precepts other than those espoused by the Communist Party. The second, "A Familiar Form of Madness," painted a slightly different form of economic psychological danger. "Scarcely recovered from the form of temporary madness that made so many people pay enormous prices for mahjong sets," the *Times* reported, "about the same persons now are committing the same sinful waste in the utterly futile finding of words the letter of which will fit into a prearranged pattern, more or less complex."*

Although nearly every major metropolitan newspaper had embraced the crossword by the mid-1920s, the *Times* staunchly refused. Over the next several years, the *Times* persisted in declaring the crossword dead. In March 1925, the paper proclaimed, "Fortunately, the question of whether the puzzles are beneficial or harmful is in no urgent need of an answer. The craze evidently is dying out fast and in a few months it will be forgotten." By 1929, the *Times* was still trying to quash the crossword: "The cross-word puzzle, it seems, has gone the way of all fads," claimed an article titled "All About the Insidious Game of Anagrams."

---

*The author must not be immune to the crossword, as the writer seems to be highly familiar with the form: this half-sentence description of the crossword itself is admirably succinct yet precise.

Readers assured the *Times* that the crossword was still highly relevant. In a letter to the editor from Friday, February 1, 1930, the inaugural date of the *Times* of London's crossword puzzle, a Richard H. Tingley of Port Chester, New York, writes, "From the viewpoint of one who has constructed and published more than 2,000 of these mental teasers, and is still making them at the rate of seven a week, I can assure you that there is little warrant for your editorial assumption that their end is near. The craze—the fad—stage has passed, but there are still people numbering into the millions who look for their daily crossword puzzle as regularly as for the weather predictions, and who would be sorely disappointed should the supply be cut off." Tingley's argument was hardly unbiased, but he also was on to something. The puzzle had gone mainstream; the crossword had settled from its madcap youth into a comfortable position as a staple ritual of the leisure class. By 1941, the *Times* was the last major metropolitan daily newspaper in America that didn't offer a crossword puzzle.

On the morning of December 7, 1941, the Japanese Navy Air Service launched its military strike against the U.S. naval base at Pearl Harbor in Hawaii. On December 18, 1941, Lester Markel, the Sunday editor of the *Times*, sent a memo to its publisher, Arthur Hays Sulzberger: "We ought to proceed with the puzzle, especially in view of the fact it is possible there will now be bleak blackout hours—or if not that then certainly a need for relaxation of some kind or other." Sulzberger hardly needed to be convinced. A surreptitious crossword addict, he'd taken to buying the rival *New York Herald Tribune* in secret to devour its puzzle. Sulzberger justified the addition of the crossword for the comfort of his readers, but he made the call based on the bottom line.

Why skulk in stealth to pay competitors when you could print the money yourself?

Attached to the memo was a note from Farrar, addressed directly to Sulzberger. "I don't think I have to sell you on the increased demand for this type of pastime in an increasingly worried world," she wrote. "You can't think of your troubles while solving a crossword."

If the *Times* was going to have a puzzle, it was going to take that puzzle seriously. Whether or not Farrar had sent that memo to insinuate that she knew just the woman to help usher the puzzle into the *Times*, it worked; the *Times* hired Farrar as its crossword editor, and on February 15, 1942, the paper's first puzzle appeared.

The *Times* heralded the occasion with a scrupulous lack of fanfare, more funereal than FUN: "Beginning today," it announced, "*The New York Times* inaugurates a puzzle page. There will be two puzzles each Sunday—one with a flavor of current events and general information, and one varied in theme, ranging from puzzles in a lighter vein, like today's smaller one, to diagramless puzzles of a general nature." The *Times* would not lower itself to the status of cheap diversion. If the *Times* was going to embrace the crossword, it would create the nation's premier crossword.

The main crossword each week, with its "flavor of current events," was more closely related to a social studies pop quiz than to the giraffe riddles and quackery advertisements around the *World*'s crossword. The first Sunday *Times* crossword, by Charles Erlenkotter and titled "Headlines and Footnotes," was a twenty-three-by-twenty-three grid—an unusual size, since the Sunday puzzle would soon come to be standardized at twenty-one by twenty-one—and the average word length was 5.36; there were fourteen nine-letter answers, which were the longest entries. The clues were dry, more dictionary than whimsy, and had a militaristic bent: "Famous one-eyed general" (WAVELL); "Flier lost in Pacific, 1937" (AMELIA); "Native Hindu in a British Army" (SEPOY). Though the puzzle was conceived as an antidote to the news, this was an escape within the paper, not an escapist fantasy. For the crossword to sustain itself as a ritual that would appeal to *Times* readers, the crossword had to appeal to its loyal customers, and so it made sense for the puzzle to match the style and substance of the rest of the paper.

Crosswords have always had a complex relationship with the publications that house them. On the one hand, the crossword is an independent entity that can essentially be located anywhere. Many crosswords get syndicated across hundreds of newspapers nationally and internationally. Solvers in Tuscaloosa might be reading something entirely different on the front page than solvers in Ottawa, but when they arrive at the crossword, they'll tackle the exact same puzzle. But editors also generally agree that a publication's crossword should reflect its readership. *Soap Opera Digest*'s crossword has a very different target audience, and thus a very different set of priorities, than the puzzle in the *Los Angeles Times* or *New York* magazine. The borders around the crossword are neither the walls of Jericho nor a wholly permeable membrane.

▪▪▪

Under Farrar's guidance, the *Times* crossword became the gold standard for crosswords in America. Like Xerox or Kleenex, the *New York Times* crossword is often thought of not as a brand but as the thing itself. Farrar's mandates about grid design, which she arrived at by trial and error through the need to develop some sort of weeding-out rubric to wade through submissions, became industry standards for American-style crosswords.

- Boxes in a single answer have to be contiguous.
- Grids cannot contain unchecked squares; that is, all the white squares of a crossword puzzle must interlock, without singletons dangling into the void of black squares.
- No one- or two-letter answers. (Answers can contain one-letter and two-letter words, but they have to be part of a larger phrase.)
- Grids must have rotational symmetry: if you flip a crossword grid 180 degrees, it will be exactly the same pattern.
- A puzzle cannot have repeated words in the grid. (Wynne's first Word-Cross, with its doubled DOVE, would never fly in the Farrar era.)
- Diagrams must be a square, and must have an odd number of letters on each side, so that there is an exact center to the square. The standard *Times* daily puzzle size is fifteen-by-fifteen squares, and the Sunday puzzle is typically twenty-one by twenty-one.
- Black squares should occupy no more than one sixth of the total diagram.

In addition to architectural aesthetics for the grid itself, Farrar also instated regulations for the content of the clues and answers, which become a bit fuzzier.

- Answers should not be obscure.
- Clues do not have to be dictionary definitions.
- The crossword should pass the Sunday Breakfast Test; that is, its clues and answers should be appropriate for all ages. Its clues should

also not stray into emotionally or psychologically uncomfortable terrain. (If one must use CANCER, a useful combination of vowels and consonants, the clue should always refer to the Tropic of Cancer, or the sign of the zodiac, not the disease.)

- Crossword answers can be more than one word.

For each of Farrar's rules, there were, of course, exceptions. One April Fools' Day puzzle repeated every word in the grid. A puzzle about the Guggenheim museum mimicked the spiral shape of the museum, and constructors often experiment with bilateral instead of rotational symmetry. Before Will Shortz's editorial era, the *Times* had not published any nonsquare puzzles. But even the Shortzian exceptions are still exceptions, and each rebel has a cause. For example, Jacob Stulberg's sixteen-by-fifteen puzzle of Wednesday, May 4, 2016, embeds the phrase INTO EACH LIFE SOME RAIN MUST FALL diagonally across the grid, and the pattern requires an extra column.

Farrar remained at the helm of the *Times* crossword until 1969, when she turned seventy-two and, under the *Times*'s then-mandatory retirement policy, had to step down from her post.

CHAPTER 7

THE OREO WAR: RACE, GENDER, AND THE PUZZLE

When Margaret Farrar left the *New York Times* in 1969, Will Weng became the puzzle editor. Originally from Terre Haute, Indiana, Weng moved to New York at age twenty, joined the *Times* at twenty-three, and had become chief of the Metropolitan news desk when he took over for Farrar. Weng remained in this role until he retired in 1977, and during his relatively brief reign, he maintained the puzzle noncontroversially. Weng claimed that one of the main reasons he liked his job was that none of the highest executives at the *Times* did the puzzle, so he didn't face the scrutiny felt by his peers editing other sections. Weng's laid-back, democratic spirit prevailed in the puzzles themselves. Even though the clues themselves might be tricky, barrier for entry was low, because the puzzles relied more heavily on wordplay and groaners than esoteric cultural knowledge.

If Farrar was the doyenne of the Sunday Breakfast Test, Weng was the master of the dad joke. Weng embraced gags, aiming for the clever twist rather than the wonkish factoid. Typical Weng-ish wags included answers such as EYELOVEU for "Optometrist's cherished alma mater" and DELIVERED for "Removed a chicken part." 1971's April Fools' Day puzzle sprinkles a phrase through the puzzle that turns out to be a commentary on the puzzle itself: the clue for 1-Across reads "An old saw, with 31, 40, 46, 51, 57, 66 and 67 Across"; those answers, respectively, are FOOL MEONCE SHAMEON THEE FOOL METWICE SHAME ONME. (Note that the puzzle flouts one of Farrar's rules—a puzzle should never use the same answer twice—but that this rule-flouting is the heart of the puzzle.) The Weng aesthetic skewed less Woodstock and more *Mister Rogers' Neighborhood*:* his puzzles were freewheeling in that puns and wordplay ran rampant, but the formulas and essential crossword status quo that Farrar had set in motion remained firmly in place.

In a 1966 interview with *Boys' Life,* the magazine of the Boy Scouts of America, Margaret Farrar described some of her ace constructors. Nearly all of them, she said, had full-time careers and wrote their puzzles on the side. She cited Eugene Maleska of Cresskill, New Jersey, a prominent figure in the New York City Department of Education, as one of her most prolific and reliable constructors. "He started in his teens," Farrar reported, "and now even his children are constructing puzzles."

From the beginning, Maleska showed a certain disregard for universal accessibility in his clueing style. Born and raised in northern

---

Mister Rogers' Neighborhood—the public-access children's television show in which Fred Rogers takes viewers on field trips and visits Make-Believe, the puppet neighborhood-within-a-neighborhood—made its national debut in 1968.

New Jersey, Maleska created his first puzzle in 1933, while an under-graduate at Montclair State University, to get the girl. 1-Across, "Most beautiful girl on campus," led to JEAN, the co-ed Maleska was dating and would later marry.

When Jean showed her roommate the romantic puzzles Maleska had been making for her, the roommate took the enterprise pragmati-cally, telling Maleska that he could earn five dollars per puzzle if he published them professionally. Maleska began submitting crosswords to the *New York Herald Tribune* (the *Times* did not yet have a puzzle) and received over forty rejections in two years, until the editor finally accepted one, and Maleska became a regular contributor. Maleska later learned that the editor suspected the newcomer of plagiarism because the grids that were coming from this unknown constructor were per-fectly made, whereas normally a rookie's puzzles would be riddled with errors—too many black squares, unkeyed clues, and so on. Many of the puzzles Maleska initially saw rejected were later printed.

After college, Maleska took a job as a Latin and English teacher in Manhattan and rose through the ranks of New York City's education administration, eventually becoming superintendent of a school dis-trict in the Bronx, but he continued to construct at a voluminous clip, and his aggressively clever puzzles appeared regularly in the *Times*, by then the most prominent newspaper puzzle in the city. He invented forms such as the stepquote, which embedded a quotation diagonally throughout the puzzle. Maleska retired from education in 1973 but continued to create puzzles, and his side life became his second career. When Weng stepped down in 1978, the *Times* hired Maleska to replace him. During Maleska's regime, mandatory age-based retirement at the *Times* ended. The crossword-puzzle editor's tenure would now end with the death of the newspaper or the death of the editor, whichever came first.

Maleska's *Times* crossword flew the flag of its breed of erudition proudly. To be able to solve a Maleska-era *Times* crossword meant knowing that you had to become fluent in very specific crossword language. The veneer of democracy that pervaded Weng's puzzles changed to a proud hierarchy, and completing the crossword became conceived as a marker of a certain elite cultural status: largely white, upper-middle-class, groomed in the kind of education most easily achieved in ivy-covered fortresses of higher learning. The name Maleska became a metonym of a certain cultural aspiration: as crossword enthusiast Marc Romano put it, "If you were of a certain age or a cultural snob or raised in or around New York City (or, ideally, all three), [Maleska] was your hero."

During Maleska's reign, a rebellion stirred. Crossword makers divided into the old guard—constructors who proudly rely on crosswordese, arcane trivia, and genteel puns—and a self-proclaimed New Wave, who thought that crosswords should reflect the way people use language currently. Traditionalist Maura Jacobson, crossword constructor at *New York* magazine, exemplified the type of wordplay the old guard relied on, with puns that easily sailed through the Sunday Breakfast Test. ("What results from embassy vaccinations? DIPLOMATIC IMMUNITY.") Merl Reagle, in contrast, who wrote crosswords for papers such as the *Los Angeles Times* and the *San Francisco Examiner*, was a leader of the New Wave, with puzzles that regularly defied the old rules, such as one that embedded S-E-X throughout the clues ("Expensive job for Jimmy Durante: NOSE XRAY").

The New Wavers found a hub in *Games* magazine, which debuted in 1977. Published by *Playboy**—which had not previously been known for its puzzle offerings, with the exception of jiggling "jigsaws" in which customers put together images of cover girls—*Games* received, perhaps for the better, little to no oversight from its owners. The magazine very quickly hit a six-figure circulation, and readers spent, on average, five and a half hours on every issue. In 1978, *Games* hired a recent law school graduate, Will Shortz, to be its associate editor, and the magazine became a place for young crossworders to hone their chops and experiment with the form. Emily Cox and Henry Rathvon,† for example, created grids with no black squares and a few seemingly random letters scattered throughout; solvers had to figure out where the black squares were, as well as the correct answers, relying on the letters provided like climbers clutching grips to scale a rock wall. Constructors peppered their puzzles freely with the pop culture references and racy humor that Maleska eschewed.

The battle between the ancien régime and the New Wave culminated in the Oreo War. OREO is a terrific crossword word. Four-letter words are the bread and butter of crossword grids: in a typical fifteen-by-fifteen layout, over a quarter of the answers will probably be four-letter words. Ever since 1912, when Nabisco first offered its splittable, dunkable, crème-filled black-and-white sandwich cookie, the word has had a prominent connotation in American culture. But under traditional crossword conventions, brand names were not permitted as

---

Games was started independently, purchased by *Playboy* in 1980, and sold a few years later.
†Cox and Rathvon became crossword-famous for their cryptic crosswords, which they started publishing in *The Atlantic* in 1977.

clues. To those on the traditionalists' side—including Maleska, Jacobson, Weng, and William Lutwiniak, co-editor of the *Washington Post*'s Sunday puzzle and former National Security Agency cryptologist—OREO should always be clued with reference to the prefix meaning "mountain," as in *oreortyx*, a mountain quail. But to the Young Turks—Shortz, Reagle, Stanley Newman* at *Newsday*, Henry Hook at the *Boston Globe*—Oreo was a cookie.

Things were reaching an impasse in 1986, when Robert Guilbert, a former ad copywriter from Milwaukee who enjoyed spending his retirement doing the puzzle, invented a game called Pago Pago, an infinite crossword on a Möbius strip, and began to peddle it around to crossword fans. Pago Pago was never a go, but when Guilbert discovered how devoted puzzlers were to their pastime, he saw a new business opportunity. Guilbert wanted to create a Crossword Puzzle Academy, with its crown jewel a Crossword Hall of Fame that would celebrate all things crossword. But Guilbert had no idea the hornet's nest he was getting into. He later told the *Times*, "While these constructors are a close-knit fraternity, there's not much unanimity there." In 1988, both the old and new factions convened at the Harvard Club in New York City to discuss the academy's foundation. Traditionalists Maleska and Weng were president and chairman; New Wavers Shortz and Newman were vice president and secretary. Shortz was tasked with picking a Pantheon of Immortals, extraordinary cruciverbalists recognized for their contributions to the

---

*Newman livened up the crossword in other ways, including organizing annual crossword-themed cruises.

field. Other honorees were inducted into the academy, such as Merv Griffin, the television producer. The end of the proclamation lauding Griffin reads:

WHEREAS, [*Wheel of Fortune*] inspires an interest in words, in spelling, and in word-play games, and from its inception has sustained and nourished the public's fascination for the American phenomenon known as the Crossword Puzzle,

THEREFORE, we proclaim that **M E R V G R I F F I N** from this time forward is **FELLOW**, the American Crossword Puzzle Academy's **HALL OF FAME**.

Guilbert died in 1990, before the Crossword Puzzle Academy could come to fruition, and the plans were abandoned. But the seeds of reconciliation had been planted.

When Shortz took over the *Times* puzzle in 1993, he put a definitive end to the Oreo War. Before Shortz's era, OREO appeared as an answer in 106 *Times* puzzles, always clued in one of two ways: "Mountain: Prefix" or "Mountain: Comb. form." (The sole exception came in a 1992 puzzle by Tap Osborn: "Mountainous cookie?") Shortz came down firmly for Team Cookie. The snack took a variety of clues, from straightforward to persnickety. OREO on a Monday might be "Cookie with a crème center"; on a Saturday, "It's 29% cream." And even though the OREO was a cookie, that didn't mean that it couldn't also be a status symbol for serious cruciverbalists: "Dessert item that was clued as 'Mountain: Comb. form' in old crosswords" appeared one Wednesday.

The crossword is black and white, but it's very, very white. This mono-culture seeps into the types of clues that appear in the puzzle, and into the way that words get clued. BLACK first appeared in the *Times* clued as "African-American" in 2000; before that, it was almost always "Supreme Court Justice," with the occasional "ebon" or "Anna Sewell's 'Beauty.'"

The Oreo War ignores a third definition of the word. In 1974, Fran Ross published *Oreo*, a story of a biracial daughter searching for her identity. The title character gets called an "Oreo" because she looks like a black person but "acts white." As writer Danzy Senna puts it, to be considered an "oreo" meant "too black to be white, or too white to be black, or too mixed to be anything."

People who write about the crossword, such as English professor Michael Sharp blogging as Rex Parker, have flagged the *Times*'s racial lacunae. In response to THUGS clued as "Gangsta rap characters," Parker wrote that he "just stared at the grid, wondering how the NYT can continue to not know that it has a race problem. And a glaring one, at that." Parker bemoaned clues' blindnesses. The *Times* puzzle, he said, was "a white-produced puzzle for a largely white middle/upper-middle-class audience" that not only "barely acknowledges black people exist[ed]," but when it did, it only did so "via clues gleaned from a cursory (and often dated) understanding of rap and hip-hop." Parker pointed out that however necessary it was to remain timeless, "going to 'gangsta rap' for a THUGS clue, however defensible from a strictly lit-eral standpoint, is fucking terrible in the age of #BlackLivesMatter."

In an article for the *Outline* titled "The NYT Crossword Is Old and

Kind of Racist," writer Adrianne Jeffries took the puzzle to task for refusing to update its vocabulary. "Oriental" still appeared in clues as late as 2005, though the *Times*'s official style guide had outlawed it in the rest of the paper by 1999. ESOS is "Those, to José" or "Those, to Juan." And when the puzzle does try to stay woke, it often falls flat. CRIBS is the cringeworthy "Homies' homes." ILLEGAL appeared as "One caught by the border patrol" in 2012. AFRO and DORAG count as diversity.

Mangesh Ghogre, the first Indian national to have a byline in the *Times*'s puzzle, started doing crosswords to boost his English skills and soon became obsessed. "Every morning," he wrote, "I have virtually visited the US through the bioscope of the American crossword." Ghogre loved immersing himself in American culture through this peculiarly efficient slice of life; nowhere else, he concluded, would he have been able to get so rigorously miscellaneous a grounding in what daily life in the United States looked and sounded like. (Ghogre learned about Oreos from crosswords.) Yet Ghogre also learned about what his own culture looked like from the crossword's perspective. "It was amusing to find fills which were associated with India in the crossword. Nan, raja, rani, sari, delhi, sitar, ravi, Nehru are usual suspects by now. But as an Indian, I always felt there was much more to India than just these words."

Shortz isn't entirely to blame. On any given day, a crossword will most likely be by a white male, but of the several hundred constructors who submitted, not many are not white. The core audience for the puzzle does still skew white, older, and upper-middle-class. In her article, Jeffries pointed to a comment on Rex Parker's blog about the *Times* crossword, in which a commenter wrote, "This puzzle had too many proper names, computer lingo, and black pop culture to be enjoyable for me."

In June 2018, a *Times* crossword featured a theme that riffed on the phrase TRIGGER WARNING, with various puns on SHOOT and RIFLE and other gun-related words. In isolation, the theme is a piece of wordplay like any other Tuesday, juggling literal and figurative layers in a newsworthy phrase. But the puzzle was published right after an epidemic of school shootings had shaken America. Deb Amlen, the *Times*'s in-house crossword columnist, stepped aside from her regular write-up of the day's puzzle, excusing herself because she believed that the *Times* shouldn't have published it, that all the guns were literally too triggering for the sanctuary of the crossword. Shortz acknowledged the point, but, to him, a puzzle was a puzzle was a puzzle. The wordplay worked nicely, the fill was smooth, and the puzzle was a fresh take on a contemporary phrase that the *Times* crossword page hadn't seen before. Besides, if this were a political statement, it could be argued that the TRIGGER WARNING was the only possible way for the crossword to respond to current events. If the crossword hid from the news, it wouldn't be taking any creative risks. Responding to TRIGGER WARNING purely on the level of language might help defuse the tension, rather than continue to amplify fear.

When the *Times* used the term BEANER in a puzzle in 2019, online backlash was strong and swift. As Jeff Chen, editor of XWord Info, wrote, "I respect Will's viewpoint that people will see what they want to see in any entry ... [BEANER] feels so, so, so very wrong, considering that the alternate definition isn't much in real usage these days. Puzzles ought to be enjoyable, a smile-inducing diversion from the daily struggles of life. Even if BEANER punches just a small number of solvers, that makes it worth changing—especially since the fix is super easy." Shortz soon issued an apology.

And the puzzle's rapidly trending in a diverse direction. The *Times* has been expanding its puzzle team to bring on a new co-editor and test solver, with the goal to keep pushing diversity of both solvers and constructors. Mentors such as Andrea Carla Michaels work with young constructors to encourage the next generation of voices to join in. Cruciverbalist Erik Agard and others encourage young, minority voices through online networks.

⬜⬛⬛⬜

One Tuesday, the answer HAREM appeared at the direct center of a *New York Times* grid, where the free space on a bingo card goes. HAREM wasn't a completely random fulcrum for this grid. Several clues are spider-related, and the word LEG appears eight times in circled letters that run through the grid in a symmetrical star. The center of the spider's web is a female space tinged with seduction and danger. But getting to the HAREM proved problematic. The clue—"Decidedly non-feminist women's group"—irritated several solvers, who called the clue sexist, awful, and demeaning. "Harem-gate," as moniker-happy wonks labeled the kerfuffle, pointed to a far murkier issue than one tone-deaf clue: Since when have crosswords become a boys' club?

Crosswords haven't always been a culturally gendered activity. Amateur solvers divide roughly equally between men and women. Margaret Farrar wrote the rulebook for the American crossword. But once you start getting into the crossword expert level, the expectation shifts. The best crossworders, according to stereotype, tend to be male, geeky, and able to play a game but not carry on a conversation. The crossword ingénue is newsworthy not because she's good at crosswords but because she's good at crosswords *and* knows how to put on lipstick.

The gender gap in crossword construction has steadily worsened since the turn of the twenty-first century. In 1993, women constructed roughly one third of *New York Times* crossword puzzles. Nearly two decades later, that number was closer to 15 percent. Crossword-puzzle editorship is even more of an androcracy. On the one hand, crosswords seem as though they should be inherently gender-blind; the form necessitates abstraction from social context. But crosswords are not divorced from the world—as the complex history of women and the crossword demonstrates, the crossword is fundamentally porous as literary form. Though crosswords seem utopic, the assumptions you didn't know you were making continue to creep in.

The problem isn't that women have suddenly become less good at crosswords. Maura Jacobson, the longtime constructor of *New York* magazine's crosswords, was revered for her puns and endless wordplay. Liz Gorski is famous for grid art; musical notes and gingerbread men emerge in her elegant grids. For decades, Frances Hansen was one of the most prolific and certainly one of the quirkiest crossword constructors in the country. Hansen had a habit of putting her own poetry in grids. In one of her last puzzles for the *New York Times*, a 2002 Sunday Christmas-themed puzzle, she embedded a four-line poem with *abab* rhyme scheme and regular iambic trimeter, in which each of the lines was twenty-one characters long, the length of a typical Sunday grid:

HANG UP YOUR STOCKINGS DO /

BUT PLEASE DO NOT SUPPOSE /

THAT SANTA YEARNS TO VIEW /

SWEATSOCKS OR PANTYHOSE.

Yet almost all major crossword editors since Margaret Farrar's tenure have been male. Ben Tausig, an ethnomusicologist at the New School and a prominent independent crossword editor, suspects that this has caused subconscious gender bias. Tausig proposed that like attracts like. Once the gender balance had begun to skew toward male editors and constructors, they started constructing puzzles for each other, where the clues appealed to a certain aesthetic that was typically gendered male: obscure sports references, competing to get the most fifteen-letter words stacked on top of each other in a puzzle, arcane computer game culture. Of course, none of these things are necessarily male, and some of the most prolific constructors and solvers in the community were women, but as men tended to hold the positions of power, they tended to dominate the conversation.

As editor of the American Values Club crossword puzzle—a subscription-based weekly dedicated to intricate, wordplay-dense, carefully crafted puzzles—Tausig has actively fostered gender parity in his stable of writers, regularly publishing work by constructors like Aimee Lucido and Zoe Wheeler, both of whom were part of Brown University's Puzzling Association and made their *New York Times* debuts in 2010 as undergraduates; and Anna Shechtman, Shortz's second female intern. Tausig told me he'd once followed a teenage female constructor on social media, encouraging her to keep writing. And Tausig's model of encouragement extends beyond the American Values

Club: in other puzzle circles, veteran constructors, such as Erik Agard and Andrea Carla Michaels, regularly mentor new talent, encouraging voices from underrepresented groups.

The *New Yorker*'s online crossword puzzle launched in 2018 with a conscious eye toward providing some demographic balance. It began with constructors—three men, two women—rotating puzzle duties each week. Although two editors at the magazine (one male, one female) oversaw the crossword's operation, no single editorial voice prevailed, which means that each constructor had more freedom to establish authority over the puzzle, and there was no danger of implicit editorial gender bias. Of course, the co-op model has limitations—for one, the puzzle by nature will remain confined to fewer voices—but it does present a different way that crosswords can operate than the traditional top-down male-dominated hierarchy.

Even in the days of Margaret Farrar's editorship, female constructors created only about a third of the *Times*'s offerings. The female constructors who did submit to the *Times* tended to build for the "M-T ghetto," the less difficult Monday and Tuesday crosswords that some constructors sneer at, even though it's actually quite difficult to create an easy but elegant puzzle. The themeless world has almost exclusively become a boys' club. As crossword construction software has become more prevalent, it has become easier than ever to construct a themeless, and bragging rights go to the constructor who can put together the largest and most sophisticated word database, so that you can construct a grid with as few black spaces and as little crosswordese as possible. It's a pen-waving contest: My stack is bigger than your stack.

And even some female-sounding bylines turned out to be men. Marie Kelly and Alice Long, two constructors for the *Wall Street*

Journal, were both Mike Shenk, the puzzle's editor. Shenk wasn't trying to create a false veneer of more female constructors—"Marie Kelly" hides "Mike" inside; "Alice Long" is an anagram of Shenk's college newspaper, the *Collegian*—but the illusion was created nonetheless.

Pseudonyms are common in the construction world. In England, noms de plume are de rigueur. Ever since Edward Powys Mathers published the first cryptic as Torquemada, cryptic crossword compilers have traditionally masked themselves with a nom de plume. *Cryptonyte* twists Superman's nemesis Kryptonite into *cryptic* plus *Tony*, the setter's real name; *Araucaria* is from the Latin for "monkey-puzzle tree"; *Dumpynose* is an anagram of *pseudonym*. But cryptic compilers' pseudonymous puzzle identities are usually clearly falsified, and they often don't sound gendered.

In 2019, the *Wall Street Journal* announced that Shenk would publish solely under his real name, citing only the paper's policy not to use pseudonyms in journalism and the need for "transparency." But commentators sniffed out the larger issue. "In a perfectly equitable world, it would not matter. Hurray wordplay and crossword drag! But, yeah, no. We aren't there. Male editors shouldn't use female pseudonym [*sic*]. Masks the problem," wrote Rex Parker.

David Steinberg suggested another culprit in the twenty-first-century gender gap: computers. Steinberg, a teenage puzzle prodigy, published his first *Times* crossword at age fourteen. In June 2012, he launched the Pre-Shortzian Puzzle Project to digitize every crossword in the *New York Times* since the puzzle's debut in 1942, and by 2015, he had finished every available puzzle. Steinberg combed the Pre-Shortzian Puzzle Project and XWord Info for data on constructors and discovered that the decline of female constructors correlated exactly with the rise of crossword software. Before 2003, when crossword-constructing software became more prominent, women made up about 30 percent of constructors; from 2003 to 2015, that figure had slid toward 18 percent. The statistic reflects the proportion of submissions Shortz receives: in any given batch of ten, only one or two will be from a female constructor. Steinberg theorized that as puzzle making and programming became increasingly interwoven, the gender gap in construction widened in parallel with the gender gap in other tech fields.

Steinberg's "boysplained" theory, as Anna Shechtman described it in an essay for the *American Reader*, didn't cut it for Shechtman, Tausig, and others in the field. The cliché that women aren't interested in science and technology, or, worse, essentializing theories about innate difference in ability between genders, are just as false and just as infuriating in the crossword world as they are in other fields. Shechtman responded that the problem wasn't the technology itself but the culture surrounding it, writing that puzzle making was "remarkably well suited to the brogrammer culture skewered on shows like HBO's *Silicon Valley*—spaces buzzing with mental agility and free-floating virginity." The reason there were fewer female puzzle makers wasn't because women couldn't use the technology—it was a club they didn't want to join.

Crossword construction also suffered from lopsided economics. In the 1980s, then–*Times* editor Eugene Maleska wrote that although some of his stalwart writers had day jobs—a lawyer, a composer, a Texas millionaire with a secretary just for crossword puzzles—the typical constructors were, by his estimation, "housewives and retirees." The demographic has since expanded to include younger constructors, and gender politics, though still problematic, have woken up enough to move beyond the outdated "housewives." But it's still true that crossword construction is few people's main gig. A *Times* daily puzzle will, as of 2019, garner its creator $500, or $1,500 for a Sunday puzzle.* Although this rate is far better than it once was—when Shortz took over in 1993, contributors made $40 for a daily and $150 for a Sunday—constructors spend so much time crafting the work that the hourly wage is pretty much pennies.

For most constructors, it's a hobby that barely rises to the level of side hustle. The fact that crossword construction is so rarely a primary job shapes the nature of who tends to create puzzles. Constructors Tracy Bennett and Amy Reynaldo have openly discussed the problems of being a working mother and constructing crosswords: juggling career and family leaves little time for concentrating on grids.

▯▮▯▮▮▯

One constructor, however, has not only cracked the economic conundrum—he's shattered it.

Westchester Magazine, which covers local news and culture in Westchester County, New York, has over a quarter of a million readers each month. The magazine has done a few features on Westchester County denizen Will Shortz, mainly featuring his Westchester Table Tennis Club. But *Westchester Magazine*'s crossword-puzzle feature isn't written by Westchester's native son. It's done by the king of crosswords you've never heard of.

---

*For constructors who have published over ten crosswords with the *Times*, the rates increase to $750 for a daily and $2,250 for a Sunday.

When you meet Myles Mellor, the first thing he will tell you is that he has had a very happy life. He had been working in real estate for his whole career, making a decent income, content but not really fulfilled. After his mother died, his father grew depressed, so Mellor wrote him a crossword puzzle every day to cheer him up, mailing him grids drawn with felt-tip pen on rough paper. His dad loved them, and Mellor was hooked.

Mellor realized that he had the best chance of getting his crosswords published if he prioritized two things: jamming in theme content instead of achieving perfect rotational symmetry, and quantity over cleverness. Mellor pitched his theme puzzles to industry magazines to see if they wanted a crossword featuring on-brand clues. His first two gigs were *9-1-1 Magazine* and *Shotgun News*. (The clues to *9-1-1*'s puzzle probably didn't cure the answers in *Shotgun News*'s.) Mellor banked on the addictive quality of crosswords. Once he could establish himself in a magazine, he reasoned, readers would get hooked and demand a regular crossword feature, guaranteeing a steady income stream. For these gigs, the editor typically gives Mellor a brief containing lots of ideas for theme answers that they think will resonate with readers, and Mellor spends a couple of hours fleshing these themes into a full-blown puzzle.

Mellor has syndicated puzzles in newspapers across America. He has also developed a cushy bespoke crossword business, serving everything from a Canada-wide advertising campaign for MasterCard (Mellor developed giant crosswords, supposedly to fill the amount of time customers would save by switching to MasterCard) to a private corporate birthday party with the theme "Sexy at Sixty" (Mellor's puzzle is inside a numeral 6 and a numeral 0, as though engraved in birthday candles).

And crosswords, for Mellor, have paid off. Mellor garners a six-figure salary from his full-time puzzle empire. His wife, he likes to say, eventually told him, "You can quit your day job."

Mellor realized how much people cared about his puzzle when he made a mistake. For his first puzzle for the *Los Angeles Times*, he'd submitted a computer file in which the clues and answers didn't line up, and the paper printed the incorrect version. All day long, Mellor had to fend off angry solvers ranting about the terrible solve, but when he called his editor, he discovered that he'd gotten the easy end of the stick. "You have no idea what it's been like," she told him. "We've had hundreds of calls about the crossword." The editor was more bemused than angry, though. "We had great articles about the economy in this issue," she said. "We have very important political articles." She expected that any one of the more controversial, thoughtful news pieces might get a lot of calls that morning, but no: "The only thing we got calls about was the crossword puzzle!"

KROSSVORDS AND MOTS CROISÉS

Vladimir Nabokov thought in crosswords. "The pattern of the thing precedes the thing," Nabokov told the *Paris Review* in an interview describing his writing process. "I fill in the gaps of the crossword at any spot I happen to choose." For the trilingual author who loved macaronic wordplay, an A was never just an A. Nabokov had grapheme-color synesthesia, giving each letter its own texture and character, which made reading in black-and-white impossible. A fantasia of sights and sounds burbled just under what the words said they meant, making each sentence an explosion of associations. The long A of the English alphabet "has for me the tint of weathered wood, but a French A evokes polished ebony," Nabokov wrote in his memoir, *Speak, Memory.* "The word for rainbow, a primary, but decidedly muddy, rainbow is in my private language the hardly pronounceable: *kzspygv.*"

Nabokov began his career at the intersection between politics and puzzles. When he was growing up, his family was among the elite of

Russian society. His father was a prominent lawyer and statesman, and his mother was heiress to a gold mine fortune. While he was away at university in Cambridge, England, Nabokov's parents fled the Bolshevik Revolution, joining a surging Russian émigré population in Berlin. His father edited *Rul'*, a popular newspaper championing a pro-Western democratic government in Russia. In March 1922, Nabokov's father was assassinated during a rally. He leapt in front of the real target, the leader of the exiled Constitutional Democratic Party, to shield him from the bullet, and took the hit instead. Death by crossed wires surfaces time and time again in Nabokov's novels—in *Pale Fire*, for instance, an assassin kills the poet John Slade instead of his real target, a European monarch—as though if he reenacts his father's death, the ghost will finally cease haunting Nabokov's imagination.

A few months later, Nabokov graduated from Cambridge and moved to Berlin, where he assembled a smorgasbord of odd jobs to support his literary ambitions. "Deeply beloved of blurbists is the list of more or less earthy professions that a young author (writing about Life and Ideas—which are so much more important, of course, than mere 'art') has followed," Nabokov wrote in *Speak, Memory*: "newspaper boy, soda jerk, monk, wrestler, foreman in a steel mill, bus driver and so on. Alas, none of these callings has been mine." Nabokov's version of the steel mill and soda fountain was language and sports, of all kinds: he tutored English, gave tennis and boxing lessons, compiled a Russian grammar, translated *Alice in Wonderland* into German—and, in 1924, published the first crossword puzzle in Russian in *Rul'*.

Nabokov transliterated English to coin the term *kreslovitsa*—literally, "cross" plus "words"—for his puzzles, but under the secular

Bolshevik regime then in power, the word *krest* flirted too close to religion. Instead, the puzzles became dubbed *krossvords*, with the Anglicized spelling masking any etymological whiffs of a Christian cross. Like their English-language counterparts, Nabokov's *krossvords* appeared in the ephemera section of the newspaper, surrounded by advertisements, puzzles, and comics. And, like the first English crossword editors, Nabokov was careless. One day, there was a mismatched puzzle and solution; another puzzle attributed a Knut Hamsun character to Ibsen. Nabokov's grids were typically small to medium-sized, averaging about nine by nine squares, and the puzzles varied wildly in size, shape, and symmetry. Nabokov played with grid art—one puzzle's shaded squares spelled out руль [*Rul'*], while another was shaped like a pyramid.

Nabokov's crosswords in *Rul'*, like the rest of the newspaper, reflected the kaleidoscopic magpie culture of émigré Berlin in the 1920s. As translator Joseph Clayton Mills, who first published an English-language version of the puzzles, explains, Nabokov's puzzles created "a world that incongruously mingled high culture and low, East and West Czarist Russia and metropolitan Berlin. In Nabokov's puzzles, references to Pushkin sit alongside the names of department stores and movie starlets, and there are unmistakable political overtones throughout."

In 1940, Nabokov and his family fled the Nazis and emigrated to the United States, where he soon landed a position as a comparative literature professor at Wellesley College in Wellesley, Massachusetts. He also became the butterfly curator of Harvard's Museum of Comparative Zoology in nearby Cambridge (Massachusetts, this time). Nabokov and his wife, Véra, learned America through butterflies, taking long road trips crisscrossing the country to find new specimens for his collection. Nabokov was especially interested in "blues," a group of small butterflies found on every continent except Antarctica. Blues range the cool-toned spectrum from sky blue to cornflower to violet. In 1943, Nabokov identified the Karner blue as a distinct and rare subspecies of western blue, and though other midcentury lepidopterists doubted the classification, DNA evidence in 1999 verified Nabokov's claim. (The Karner male is lilac; the female, a pigeon-gray mauve. Its larvae eat only wild blue lupine, and if this periwinkle flower fades too fast or doesn't bloom in time, the Karner blue will perish.)

Between butterflies, Nabokov wrote novels. While Véra drove the car, he composed drafts on thousands of four-by-six index cards. Later, he arranged and rearranged the cards until arriving at the book's order. The process was travel-friendly, but more importantly, it matched his brain.

Nabokov was a restless man, possessed with demonic energy. Insomnia plagued him throughout his life. Barely in his twenties, Nabokov had launched into a whirlwind romance with Svetlana Siewert, a glamorous socialite. But in January 1923, Siewert's parents, dubious about the young poet's long-term prospects, broke off their engagement. Brokenhearted young Vladimir continued to publish poems in *Rul'* dedicated to his lost beloved for the next few months. In May 1923, however, while at a masked ball, an alluring figure in demi-mask presented herself to the mourning creature. His misery dissipated immediately. That June, Nabokov published a parting poem to Svetlana in *Rul'* and a besotted verse to the woman in demi-mask, Véra Slonim. By 1924, Nabokov and Véra were married.

In the summer of 1926, Véra Nabokov was unwell; a bout of severe anxiety and depression had rendered her physically as well as mentally weakened, and she was sent to two sanatoriums in the Schwarzwald, to gain weight and recuperate. Nabokov stayed behind in Berlin to continue tutoring the couple's regular pupils.

Véra made Nabokov promise to send her daily letters reporting on his activities—where he went, what he ate, what he wore, and so on. Nabokov obeyed faithfully, almost ostentatiously. He reported tennis matches in the broiling sun, and late suppers of eggs and cold cuts before insomniac nights, during which he described writing the very missives Véra read. The missives took on the tone of a newspaper, though a newspaper about a nation of one, a diary curated outward. Often, Nabokov began or ended his letters with some comment about *Rul'*, still the newspaper of record for Russian émigrés in Berlin. Nearly every sentence was punctuated with affection—a nickname, a sweet note—larding the missives with sweet intimacy. But he did not hide frustrations—money was always a concern—as pussyfooting around too much might have made her feel patronized and pushed her back into her depression.

As the reports continued, Nabokov started to vary them—just as newspapers historically slowly expanded beyond the daily news into culture pieces, advertisements, and games, Nabokov's newspaper of himself began to feature weather reports, advice, and a puzzle section. The games to help Véra escape were balanced with reports of the real world that she craved. And the games were just as much for Nabokov's benefit as for Véra's. It was Nabokov who lay awake night after night, lonely, reaching out to Véra; he was the one writing 80 percent of the missives. The games were presented as a gift to Véra, but the real gift was, to Nabokov, making them.

From July 1 through July 19, 1926, when Véra returned home, Nabokov added a puzzle nearly every day to his daily reports. The first of these puzzles was a crossword, which Nabokov apparently fore-shadowed in a "telegrammlet" to Véra the day before. Crosswords served as both a tool and a toy for convalescing Véra: a healing device to stimulate the recovering person's brain muscles, the way squeezing a stress ball might help stimulate the biceps, and a welcome distraction from other concerns. Nabokov's puzzles were also equal parts baubles for Véra's pleasure—a wealthier, less witty, lovesick partner might have enclosed a charm each day for Véra to add to a bracelet—and pleas for a response. The letters themselves were filled with teasing yet barbed jabs at the ratio of letters between them; if this were a tennis match, Nabokov would be winning several games at love.

In his letter of July 2, Nabokov begins with a little hand-drawn crossword puzzle, and when he arrives on the verso side where the puzzle has occurred on the recto, he interrupts his message to note the puzzle: "(here the word puzzle's showing through; I am curious whether you will solve it!)" The parenthetical reflection betrays the puzzle's true purpose; though the crossword is a gift to amuse the con-valescing Véra, its true purpose is to serve as a mechanism that will force a written reply. "Had we published a little book—a collection of your letters and mine—there would have been no more than 20% of your share, *my love* . . . I advise you to catch up—there's still time . . . I love you unspeakably today," Nabokov writes.

In this crossword to Véra, Nabokov enacts a crosshatching of imagery and form. He presents the crossword puzzle, five four-by-four word squares arranged in an X on the page; none of the squares touch each other, and Nabokov only gives clues to fill in the words vertically. After the crossword comes a description of his morning swim, under "a huge, hot sun. You squint at it, and a silver glitter trembles, a rainbow splinter. On the way back, I bought envelopes, ink (and, as always happens on the day I buy ink, I made a blot), sent off the letter." When you get to the spot in the paper where the puzzle shows through, faintly, on the other side, and Nabokov comments on the puzzle itself, you get a repetition of the effect he has enacted metaphorically. The image of the sun refracting against the water, glittering and splintering, is paired with the inkblot and the materiality of writing; then, the physical reflection of the crossword's letters through the page causes Nabokov's mental reflection on the state of the letters between himself and Véra. The crossword becomes an agent of rhetorical synesthesia, a window through which Nabokov describes the world.

On July 5, 1926, Vladimir drew Véra a moth, labeled *Jaspidea Celsia* (♂), its markings rendered freehand in careful detail. Nabokov had been observing butterflies since he was a boy; as he later recalled in *Speak, Memory*, "From the age of seven, everything I felt in connection with a rectangle of framed sunlight was dominated by a single passion. If my first glance of the morning was for the sun, my first thought was for the butterflies it would engender." The day appeared to Nabokov as a rectangle waiting to be filled in, like an index card, or a crossword square. Butterflies were hidden and everywhere.

On July 6, Vladimir drew Véra a butterfly, labeled *Crestos lovitxa Sirin*. The wings of the butterfly are divided in two halves; the upper half contains the crossword grid, while the lower half contains the clues. *Crestos lovitxa Sirin* is "Nabokov's crossword": *krestlovitska*, latinized to eliminate the *k* (not in the Roman alphabet); plus *Sirin*,

Nabokov's pen name (he frequently published in *Rul'* as V. Sirin, after the half-bird, half-woman of Russian mythology).

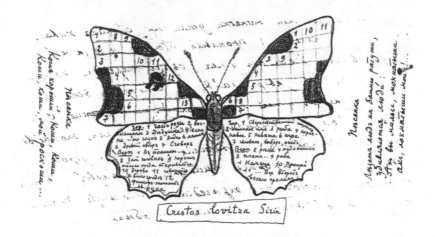

The crossword butterfly's deadpan taxonomy underscores the enigma underlying the surface-level puzzle in Nabokov's doodle. Was this a crossword-patterned butterfly, or was this a butterfly-shaped crossword? Was life imitating art, or art imitating life?

▢▪▪▪▢

One of the best places to see the crossword-puzzle mentality in action is in its relation to writing. Many authors use word puzzles as a scratch pad—the poet James Merrill doodled his own name in anagrams—but when the crossword becomes folded into the work itself, it reveals a basic paradoxical mental process: You have to tighten connections even more rigorously at the same time as you let a few screws loosen.

The crossword requires an automatic mind-set where you enter a Zen zone, but it also necessitates the sharpest awareness to detail.

Getting into the crossword mentality is like a human pretending to be an automaton pretending to be the world's best human.

[crossword graphic]

Nabokov's *krossvords* are hardly the only crosswords in languages besides English. Though arguably the most famous crosswords appear in English, the puzzle is by no means an English-language-specific phenomenon.

In 1960, Raymond Queneau and François Le Lionnais founded Oulipo, short for *Ouvroir de littérature potentielle* ("workshop of potential literature"), a group of mainly French-speaking writers and mathematicians who created work using constrained writing techniques. Writers in the Oulipian school combined the capacity for infinitely complex wordplay with a rabid appetite for detective novels. And Oulipian wordplay, though extravagant, is hardly devoid of emotions. Loss, trauma, repetition, joy, sadism, madness, revenge: the passions drive the invention of these language machines.

Georges Perec was one of the most prominent original members of Oulipo. *La Disparation*, translated into English as *A Void*, is a lipogrammatic novel that never uses the letter E.* In contrast, Perec's univocalic *The Exeter Text: Jewels, Secrets, Sex*, translated into English by Ian Monk,† depicts the "e's retern" via a successful jewel heist during an orgy in Exeter Cathedral. As Ian Monk writes, "Hence the *e*-text (glee engenders wretchedness) represents the *e*-less text's (wretchedness engenders glee) perfect reverse."

---

*Except the four in the author's name.
†Or "E. N. Menk."

Perec created complex *mots croisés*, challenging himself to build larger and larger squares with no blank spaces. (This is an easier task in French than in English; there are more words in French that use the same letters of the alphabet.) To Perec, the crossword is not a flattened version of a poem or story: the crossword is a petri dish of the creative process. In the introduction to his collected crosswords, Perec describes the process of creating a crossword as two tasks, entirely in opposition with each other, yet equally vital: "The filling of the diagram," he writes, is "a tedious, meticulous, maniacal task, a sort of letter-based arithmetic where all that matters is that words have this or that length." On the other hand, the search for clues requires loosening the brain into the "imprecise neighborhood" of a word's definition. The crossword marries an anal-retentive tendency with the mind-set that psychologists might call the "flow" state. Perec sets up the comparison between creating the grid and finding the clues for the words as though pitting these two acts in competition against each other. You'd expect to find one victorious over the other, superior in both the imagination it demands and the pleasure it provides. But though it's structured as a competition, there isn't a winner. The diagram might seem to exist merely as a backdrop to support clues, but this diagram provides the way that these associations can arrive at all. Without the clues, the crossword would be letters jailed on the page, but without the letters, the associations that give rise to the clues would never have existed. The mechanical act of diagramming might be maniacal, but this arithmetic is what creates inspiration.

Perec's 1978 novel *Life: A User's Manual* is based on a jigsaw puzzle, but crosswords make an essential cameo. The novel's plot proceeds spatially rather than narratively, leading the reader from apartment to apartment in the building. Upon entering one apartment, Perec walks readers through a still life of a dining room in slow panorama. The description gives each detail poised as though the inhabitants had just stood up, half-eaten canapés perched under the electric lights, the evening paper spread out under wine barrels to catch the wine before it starts to drip. "On one of the pages," writes Perec, "you can see a crossword puzzle . . . the grid has not been filled in completely, though progress has been made." Then he places the actual unfinished crossword grid into the book. That unfinished crossword becomes a meta-symbol for the novel itself. Though the characters receive the world jigsaw-style, one piece at a time, the grid of the unfinished crossword gives a structure for how the reader experiences the book's content: jumping back and forth, answering and erasing clues, eventually filling in space over time.

When translator David Bellos approached Perec's novel in 1987, he had to face the problem of making the crossword grid work in English. How do you translate an unfinished crossword grid? The grid entails certain letters; how do you achieve the same constellation of assumed words when you cross languages? Two of the clues in the French grid—ETONNEMENT and OIGNON—are critical to the novel's wordplay, so Bellos used ASTONISHED and ONION as the English cognates for these, but filled in the rest somewhat more freely. Bellos reorganized the spaces in the grid itself to be more friendly to English-language words, though he follows Perec in including two-letter words, and in indulging in an asymmetrical grid rather than constraining himself to a symmetrical space.

| C | H | A | P | T | E | R | | 9 |

TOURNAMENT OF CHAMPIONS

Stamford, Connecticut, is the seventh-largest city in New England and the first stop out of Manhattan on the express Metro-North train to New Haven. Nearly half the adults living in Stamford have a bachelor's degree or higher, one of the highest percentages for any city in the country. The town was originally a bedroom community for Manhattan. It's now dominated by office buildings and double-wide zebra crossings, where pedestrians can barely make it across in the time allotted by the walk signal.

Stamford is also the birthplace of word puzzles in America. In 1647, Stamford denizen Samuel Danforth, a Puritan minister and one of the founding fellows of Harvard College, published his *Almanack for the Year of Our Lord 1647*. In addition to the usual handy miscellany of an almanac—celestial tables, tides, court dates—Danforth decorated each month with a calendrically appropriate enigmatic verse, inviting readers to solve for the forecast.

When Will Shortz discovered Danforth's enigmas, he saw them as proof that puzzles had a rightful place at the center of American cultural history. As a senior at Indiana University, Shortz had to write a final project to fulfill the requirements of his individualized major in "enigmatology." In *The History of American Word Puzzles to 1860*, Shortz aimed to reclaim puzzles' reputation from mere "fun-fun-fun" and restore their place in the canon. "Today, puzzles have lost that aura of dignity which they rightly deserve," he declared. "Puzzles may be only an amusement, but they are an intellectual amusement, and their history is an important part of the history of literary and intellectual thought."

Shortz reasoned that the existence of Danforth's enigmas demonstrated that puzzles were already integral to American life before America was even America. Printed books themselves were a rarity, and, as Shortz explained, Puritans dedicated most of their free time to their religion. "In this social environment," wrote Shortz, "the fact that word puzzles were written and published at all only serves to show the appeal that puzzles in general hold for people." It is a truth universally acknowledged, Shortz argued, that people in search of intellectual and literary pursuits, no matter what other demands and devotions they have to attend to, will create word puzzles.

But even Shortz couldn't solve all of Danforth's enigmas. Take April:

That which hath neither tongue nor wings
This month how merrily it sings:
To see such, out for dead who lay

To cast their winding sheets away?

Friends! would you live? some pils then tak

When head and stomack both doe ake.

Shortz recorded the accepted answer as a brook thawing from winter, but Shortz's adviser, Dr. Fred Householder—a classicist and linguist most noted for challenging Noam Chomsky's belief that phonology could reveal universal meanings in sound and speech—penciled a skeptical comment in the margin: "I doubt this. More likely bulb opening or the like. And what's the last couplet?"

<hr />

After the publication of *The Cross Word Puzzle Book* in 1924, when the puzzle's popularity skyrocketed, crossword tournaments soon followed. That same year, the *New York Herald Tribune* hosted the inaugural National All Comers Cross Word Puzzle Tournament in Manhattan, where competitors solved onstage, oversized puzzle grids propped on enormous easels so the audience could watch the drama unfold. When Ruth von Phul, the crossword's first ingénue, won, she became a media sensation overnight.

In January 1925, an intercollegiate crossword-puzzle tournament at the Hotel Roosevelt in New York doubled as a battle of the sexes. Harvard, Yale, Princeton, and the City College of New York were on the men's side; Wellesley, Smith, Vassar, and Bryn Mawr, the women's. Wellesley and Yale won their respective divisions. In the championship round, they were neck and neck. Judges scrutinized the grids, determined that the Wellesley women had made a mistake in one of the final words, and declared Yale victorious.

But as the crossword fad shifted from spectacle sport to bespec-tacled private ritual, the crossword tournament fell out of fashion. By 1978, America hadn't seen a major organized crossword tournament in decades.

That's when Shortz started the American Crossword Puzzle Tournament, or ACPT, as a way for like-minded crossword enthusi-asts to once more celebrate their prowess in public. That year, 149 contestants gathered in Stamford, Connecticut, to do five puzzles on a Saturday afternoon. Judges stayed up all night to tally every letter in every grid. The grand finale was on Sunday morning, when Margaret Farrar herself presented the prize to the winner, Nancy Shuster, a housewife from Queens.

In 2006, filmmaker Patrick Creadon directed *Wordplay*, a love let-ter to the *New York Times* crossword. Creadon introduced moviegoers to constructors, celebrity solvers—Bill Clinton and Jon Stewart, among others, rhapsodized about the puzzle—and, of course, to Shortz. The second half of the film chronicled the ACPT, where Creadon fol-lowed top solvers as though trailing Olympic hopefuls. *Wordplay*, which Creadon produced for $100,000, generated over $3 million at the domestic box office, making it one of the most profitable documen-taries of all time.

After *Wordplay*, tournament attendance spiked, from five hun-dred contestants in 2006 to seven hundred in 2007. The crowds out-grew its traditional venue, the Stamford Marriott, and in 2008, the tournament migrated to Brooklyn. Eventually, "the Wordplay bump," as ACPT regulars called the swell in their ranks, tapered, and in 2015, the tournament returned home.

In March, things in Stamford were pretty dead. I walked down Main Street mid–Friday afternoon, where the only other people in sight were two men sitting in the traffic circle, a triangular strip of green serving as an ersatz park. One, an artist at an easel, was painting what appeared to be that street corner, blue work jacket slung across his shoulders in the sunshine. Closer to me, the second man sat on a bench, his hand leisurely stretched toward the dog lying at his feet. I approached warily—allergies and a Dalmatian-nipping incident at age two had cured me of any natural affinity with animals—but the creature remained thankfully still. Too still. *Excuse me*, I started to say, but as the words approached my tongue, I saw the plaque on the bench, announcing the sculpture's name and provenance. I went over to the painter, squinted, and tapped his shoulder. Bronze.

I walked the few empty blocks from Main Street to the Stamford Marriott Hotel & Spa, where the landscaping facing the sidewalk resembled a British garden gone brutalist. Thick hedges rose above hip height, and concrete lattice walls masked the small rectangle that allowed access from the sidewalk. The courtyard area, dark green and brown, had its own microclimate, perpetually a clammy fifty-five degrees and smelling of damp cinder block. The walkway to the front door had been terraced as though by Escher, with paths chopped into several different levels: I thought I was following one up to the door, but I turned the corner to find myself at the bottom again.

The Marriott was designed to be approached by car, not on foot.

A driveway swooped to the double-glass doors in a hotel parabola, where travelers put hazard lights on, unloaded suitcases onto a carpeted dolly with skinny brass columns, and handed over keys to a valet, who navigated the car somewhere into the spiraled kennel of the parking lot, where it would wake up on the other side of the weekend.

Once the automatic tinted-glass doors slid shut behind you, the lobby was window-free, with colorless carpet and gleaming wood-grained mahogany walls. The cavernous space had been scaffolded into several mini-levels. In a slightly sunken pit at the center, a large structural column was disguised as a chimney and pointed through the ceiling to somewhere, an electric fire perpetually burning in its grate like a television tuned to the image of "fire."

□■■□

I'm average at crosswords. I'm a hunt-and-peck solver. I comb the puzzle, find the answers I know, plop them in, and start sifting again. I admire cryptic crosswords from afar, like bonsai.

But games run in my blood. Both of my sets of grandparents are from Atlantic City, New Jersey, a town that has always made its legal and less-than-legal living through games. Back in the radio days, my great-grandmother Sara was once on a quiz show. The host asked her, "Is Mickey Mouse a dog or a cat?" "Cat," she'd snapped.* My mom's great-great-uncle Benny, according to family lore, took the rap for Nucky Johnson, the mobster who ruled Atlantic City in the twenties. On the other side of the family, as tiny girls, my grandmother and

---

*In the 1806 edition of Merriam-Webster's Dictionary, *cat* is defined as "a common domestic animal," and *dog* is defined as "a common domestic animal."

great-aunt used to run the numbers from their father's boardinghouse lobby to the bookies' back room in the corner candy store. They were the perfect criminals, since they had no idea they were doing anything wrong. By the time I knew them, my grandparents' gamesmanship had mellowed. My mom's parents timed breakfast to *The Price Is Right*; my dad's parents timed lunch to *The Newlywed Game*; and they often met for dinner and *Jeopardy!*

My family finds it difficult to enter willingly into competitions when we don't know if we'll be above average, but we're great at taking risks when we know we'll come out on top. We compete among each other to see which one of us is the most competitive. Like a slightly less fraught version of J. D. Salinger's Glass family, in which all the children receive scholarship money from the quiz show *It's a Wise Child*, my brother and I grew up in a game world. Dad turned daily life into a series of contests—the game of what to have for breakfast, the game of going to the drugstore to pick up the newspaper and cutting the line to put down the exact amount of money. (Things my dad likes: racket sports, bridge, solving math problems in his head. Things he hates: yoga, meditation, ice fishing.)

My mother is the best at crosswords, and my father is the most puzzle-oriented, but my brother, Ben, is the family's true games person. Ben, a data analyst by day, is a trivia host by night, working various pubs through a franchise called Geeks Who Drink. Ben memorized sports almanacs as a kid and could spit out facts about Super Bowl winners and baseball players' RBIs like a jukebox. When he was seven years old, Ben burst into tears on the Little League field when his team lost. My mother tried to console him by telling him that if he was so upset, he didn't have to compete. Ben turned his wet face to her and said, "But, Mommy, I love competition!" In fifth grade, Ben placed in the top ten of New Jersey's state geography bee; in high school, he captained the Scholars' Bowl team to a state victory. Ben has roped us all into the invitation-only online trivia contest LearnedLeague. I'm in the lowest possible tier, or "rundle."

At age thirty, Ben became a *Jeopardy!* champion. He also became an internet meme when clips of his extreme frustration with the buzzer—he pressed the button so rapidly and so often that the little joystick juddered in his hand, as though he were trying to drill his way through the lectern—landed on *The Tonight Show Starring Jimmy Fallon.*

My thing is Boggle, a rapid-fire word search, in which players shake a four-by-four* square, scribble the words they see over the course of three minutes, and then compare lists. You get points for words no one else has, and you get more points for longer words. There are two basic Boggle strategies. Either you blitz and write down everything, or you hunt for the Bantu wildebeests, the long words that will garner you many points, and assume that everyone else will cancel each other out on the little words and no one else will find your rare game. I once challenged Will Shortz to a Boggle match. Not to brag, but we tied.

□ ▪ □ ▪ □

A few weeks before the ACPT, I told my parents I was going to Connecticut for a crossword-puzzle tournament. I meant this as information. They saw it as an invitation.

"Ooh—is that the one in the movie?" my mother said. "I've always

---

*Big Boggle, my favorite, is a five-by-five square; there's also six-by-six Super Big Boggle.

wanted to go to that!" My mother was our family's best crossworder, a nightly solver who could regularly finish every day of the week. "Maybe we'll come too!"

"Can we go to a bridge tournament instead?" asked my father. "You should write a book about bridge."

"Neither one of you has to come," I said.

"You two go," Dad said. "I'd be in last place anyway."

They both came. My father and mother work together, running a consulting and publishing firm that my father inherited from his parents. Two decades ago, they moved our family from southern New Jersey to northern Vermont, installing their office on the top floor of our house. They share a cell phone.

Ben called me a few hours after I'd spoken to the parents. "Will Mom and Dad be mad if I don't come to your thing?" Ben fretted. "I think they're expecting me to go. But I have Geek Brunch that Sunday, and—I just don't know."

"I don't know why they're going," I said. "Why would they assume you're going? There's no reason anyone else has to go to this."

"Because it's games," said Ben.

On the train, I casually glanced at the fellow passengers, sizing them up to see if any of them were my competition. The crossword is a commuter's sport. Solvers can clock themselves by how many stops it takes to complete the grid. But the Amtrak from Boston to Stamford didn't prove to be a useful clock, since there was too much time between stations to measure prowess by cities.

I wasn't really going to the tournament to compete. I was going to interview, observe, soak in the atmosphere, become inaugurated into the crossword cult. But as I swanned down the Northeast Corridor, I couldn't help but get that spark that contests always give me. Somehow, improbably, with no Rocky-esque montage of training, I saw a vision of my Cinderella crossword story, that through some incredible osmosis or sheer luck, I'd magically be imbued with a prodigious talent and whiz past the others—or all my competitors would find themselves simultaneously struck with lethargy, Lotos-Eaters-style, and would loll about as I soared ahead. I knew—I *knew*—that I had less than zero percent chance of making it into the finals, that I was there to learn, not compete—but deep down, a tiny kernel of magical thinking whispered to me that maybe—*maybe*—I would win it all.

There are five skill-based divisions at the ACPT, from the top solvers in A through the pikers in E. The top three finalists in the A, B, and C categories solve their puzzles on huge whiteboards onstage. Puzzlers sift into several levels. In addition to the A through E rankings, plus a special category for rookies, there are divisions by age—twenty-five and under (Juniors); fifties, sixties, seventies, and eighty and up (Seniors); and by region—Connecticut, Other New England, New York City, Long Island, Westchester/Upstate New York, New Jersey, Other Mid-Atlantic, South, Midwest, West, and Canada/Foreign.

But solvers really divide into two basic kingdoms: speed solvers and the rest of us.

▭ ▮ ▮▭

At the turn of the twentieth century, mechanical engineer Frederick Winslow Taylor had an idea. Factory workers in America and Britain, he'd noticed, "soldiered," dialing production to a crawl to protect their own interests; moving too fast, they argued, would get them to finish tasks too quickly and thus put everyone out of a job. Taylor disagreed. In *Principles of Scientific Management,* the grandfather of how-to guides, Taylor argued that efficiency, not underworking, was the key to success. Taylor boiled management into a formula: turn complex jobs into a series of simple ones, measure everything, and make workers' earnings directly linked to performance. Taylor's streamlining has left a long legacy, from students taught to perform on standardized tests to Japanese lifestyle guru Marie Kondo's art of "tidying up." Taylorism was an instant success, but it had its drawbacks in the workplace. Charlie Chaplin satirized the system in his 1936 film *Modern Times*: As a factory worker, Charlie-Cog had to screw nuts onto a machine, but the machine kept speeding up, faster and faster, until he was working at such a breakneck pace that he finally snapped.

At the ACPT, Taylorism still thrived among speed solvers. There were various tricks to speed solving. Speed solvers typically started in one corner and worked their way toward the middle. For easy puzzles, they often read only the down clues and filled in one direction to avoid having to switch vectors and lose crucial moments. Most speed solvers used a lowercase *e*, even when writing in all capitals, because the single-motion *e* was much easier to inscribe than its three-pronged counterpart. Speed solving relies on muscle memory, like putting a Rubik's Cube together. Howard Barkin, the 2016 ACPT winner, could solve the Monday and Tuesday *Times* puzzles while carrying on a conversation, the way an expert knitter knits. A couple of minutes into the chat, he'd look down and the puzzle would have basically written itself. Dan Feyer, the ACPT champion from 2010 to 2015, and then again in

2017 and 2019, posted a YouTube video of himself solving a *Newsday* crossword puzzle in one minute and eight seconds: he begins with a long Across clue in each key quadrant, then flips and solves all the Downs rapid-fire. Some speed solvers psyched themselves into mental agility through athletic attire, like 2018 winner Erik Agard, who took the stage of that year's championship in a bright red basketball jersey and sweats.

Among the regular solvers, competitors had to differentiate their personalities off the grid. Though the bulk of solvers fell somewhere in the incognito spectrum, in street clothes and displaying only mild superstitions, each year, more and more solvers used the tournament as an opportunity to make a fashion statement.

In the winter of 1924, a shopkeeper in Paris noticed two American women working through a crossword puzzle. Inspired by the striking graphic, he created checkerboard-patterned angora stockings. The crossword craze had not yet arrived in France, and although the novelty item "found good customers among American women," according to the *New York Times*, French women declared it "hideous." A few years later, however, once *les mots croisés* had arrived in France, the ugly-chic seeped into Parisian fashion. A French advertisement for a masquerade costume featured a woman festooned with a crossword-adorned peplum dress, a crossword-emblazoned capelet and the pièce de résistance, a cube-shaped fez with grids painted on all sides.

The crossword has continued to lure designers. New York–based Lisa Perry's Pre-Fall 2015 collection featured several items in a crossword-motif tech-satin, including a swing dress ($895), a swingy jacket ($845), and a pillow ($150). But most contemporary crossword fashion has migrated from haute to handmade. On forums like Etsy, the site for handmade and vintage items, enthusiasts can buy crossword silk scarves, earrings, sweatshirts, and personalized ornaments.

At the ACPT, the reigning aesthetic was orthotics meets checkerboard. A man wearing a T-shirt with *TOTALLY CLUELESS* emblazoned across the back sat next to a woman whose T-shirt read *CLUED IN*. Several sported crossword-patterned baseball caps, silk scarves, and fleece vests. Another woman's hand-knitted cardigan featured grids on the sleeves and a pencil on the back, sewn next to the word *DOWN* where a designer's label might be. Jen, one of the tournament officials, wore a crossword-fleece vest; Emmy, her service dog, had a crossword bandanna with *JUDGE* drawn into some of the blank squares.

Some solvers took the crossword theme a little more loosely. One man entered the ballroom in billowing orange silk pants, two vuvuzelas tucked under his arm. A group of friends had nicknames à la professional wrestlers, which they'd displayed in placards propped inside their yellow dividers, visible only to themselves: *ACE IN THE HOLE, THE LEGEND SLAYER, THE PEOPLE'S CHAMPION, SUPER SOCK, THE CEREBRAL ASSASSIN.*

There were other kinds of solvers besides the costumed. Leisure-suit solvers treated each crossword slowly and steadily, like Miriam and Josephine, nonagenarians who had been solving puzzles for decades. Before every puzzle, Josephine nestled into her front-row corner, perched a second pair of spectacles atop her cat-eye frames, and arranged a crossword-patterned teddy bear next to her puzzles; a crossword-silkscreened tote rested at her feet. The leisure suiters had places of pride within the ballroom. They toiled diligently over each crossword, using the full amount of time for each puzzle, yet their grids often arrived at the judges' room with more empty squares than filled ones. Josephine's sheet for the hardest puzzle of the day resembled a *Tetris* board frozen midfall—the blocks had begun to accumulate from the bottom up, in mostly solid aggregate with a few gaps here and there, and there were a few vertical pieces falling into the grid, but the top was almost entirely blank.

□▪▐▌

Sir John Gielgud, the noted English actor whose many accolades included the celebrated Emmy, Grammy, Oscar, and Tony quadfecta, was also revered as a crossword solver, notorious for how quickly he demolished the *Times* of London's cryptic. However, accuracy wasn't exactly his goal. One day, apocryphally, a co-star peeked over his shoulder as he solved and asked, "Excuse me, John—what are Diddybums?" Gielgud, without missing a beat, replied that he had no idea, but that "it does fit awfully well." When he couldn't figure out a clue, he blithely filled in the grid with words that fit, even if they had nothing to do with anything.

Gielgud would be the nightmare solver for ACPT officials. Though most of his submission would be wrong, if Gielgud had happened to get any of the right letters, even by luck, those answers had to be highlighted so that the computer that organized the scoring could tabulate them. Gielgud might not have followed the spirit of the law, but the letter must be obeyed.

In the January before the ACPT, coordinator Michael Smith sent a BCC'd email to a group of crossword veterans, telling them only to arrive in the "back room" on Saturday morning at nine A.M. sharp.

Those tapped few—per the *Times*'s crossword columnist Deb Amlen, the "glitterati of the crossword world"—were the ACPT's officials.

If a grid-loathing assassin ever wanted to decimate the American crossword-puzzle brain trust in one swoop, she'd have to look no further than the Marriott mezzanine on the second-to-last weekend in March. The atmosphere in the back room felt like coffee hour after church, but where the entire congregation happened to be plainclothes CIA operatives on a crossword mission. Most of the crew, like Brad the librarian, had been officials for decades and knew everything about everybody: how was Florida, how old is Henry now, how's your knee feeling. They compared LearnedLeague stats. "I'm stuck in the A-ghetto," Brad said: "I'm not going to get knocked down to Rundle B, but I can't win my rundle." A few others nodded. I kept my mouth shut.

Veteran constructors made up the bulk of the glitterati. Brendan Emmett Quigley paced the back of the room in leather jacket and novelty T-shirt, arms folded, his red stubble already in a five-o'clock shadow. BEQ, author of puzzle compendia like *Drunk Crosswords* and *Sex, Drugs & Rock & Roll Crosswords,* favored current events and sharp-edged clues. Though he maintained an irreverent streak in his puzzles, Quigley's personal punk style had mellowed since he had become a father. I once met him for an interview in a dive bar (his pick), but he'd chosen it since it was the only place he could watch soccer while his kid napped.

Gumby-esque Mike Shenk, editor of the *Wall Street Journal*'s crossword, leaned against a doorjamb, with his trick of never quite standing in or out of a room, always hovering in three-quarter profile.

Shenk, like Shortz, grew up on a farm. When he was a kid, Shenk made labyrinths out of the hay bales and mazes through the chicken coop. Affable and shy, with rubbery jowls and a perpetual half-smile, Shenk spoke softly and stuttered slightly when he spoke, but his puzzles were among the crispest and filled with the most fiendish wordplay in the business. Shenk was also part of the team behind Puzzability, which generated puzzles that appeared in venues from the *Times*'s op-ed page to *Martha Stewart Living* to Snapple bottle caps.

Stanley Newman, guffawing too heartily for this hour on a Saturday, wore a loudly patterned shirt that, from afar, seemed to sport a crossword pattern but, on closer inspection, proved to be a black-and-white Hawaiian shirt. Newman, longtime editor of the *Newsday* crossword, always had a gaggle of old-timers around him, reminiscing about ACPTs of yore.

Programmer Matt Ginsberg explained how puzzle scoring worked, though most of the officials already knew. Every crossword at the ACPT got marked by hand. Scores used to be tabulated by hand, too, which meant that in previous years, after the final puzzles were in, the judges were still counting squares until about two A.M. Finally, in 2012, Ginsberg built a computerized program for grading crosswords, which chopped grading time in half. The software was "incredibly brittle," as Ginsberg warned officials each year, but it still worked, so he didn't want to monkey with it.

The system relied on highlighters. (Or *hilighters*—the instruction sheet Ginsberg distributed used both spellings interchangeably.) The computer could read only highlighter, so the officials translated the grids into a simplified language of colors. Humans were still better at recognizing handwriting, tight U versus sloppy V. The tournament's MVP, as awarded in the back room, was the competitor deemed to have the best handwriting of the weekend.

Officials got different names for different tasks. When officials worked in the ballroom, they became "ballroom referees." Each ballroom referee wielded a blue highlighter. They played zone defense crossed with Whac-A-Mole, scanning the lowered sea of heads to spot when hands popped up in their designated areas. The referee would scuttle to the finished contestant, collect the paper, and mark down the number of minutes remaining on the clock in official blue highlighter. The referee then handed the puzzle to one of the runners, who were a few of the officials' children. Like ball boys and ball girls at tennis tournaments, runners stood at alert at the edges of the room, sprinting forward when they needed to take a puzzle, then zooming back to their spots. Once the runners had gathered a substantial stack, they took them up to the scoring room.

The scoring room was amply stocked with simple sugars: Twizzlers, Capri Suns, Nutri-Grain bars. Here, officials were dubbed "judges." Judges started with the back side of the puzzle first, using a yellow highlighter to mark the time that the competitor had spent on the puzzle. Puzzlers got bonus points for every minute still left on the clock. Then, the judge flipped over the puzzle and wrote her initials in the corner using a regular pen—the initials were for the human record, not the computer; if a judge had poor highlighting techniques (not filling in the squares fully, etc.), a scorer could track her down to chastise her.

Judges could choose one of two scoring options: either mark any wrong squares in the grid in yellow, or mark any correct squares in blue. Puzzles that look like rotting jack-o'-lanterns, with more answers empty than filled, would get treated in blue. Though it was more tedious to check for right answers, after training the brain all day to scan for errors, the blue highlighter would became a godsend for the more difficult puzzles of the day, or for a competitor with a Gielgud-style grid who had filled in the blanks rather than solving the puzzle. The only thing a judge definitely could not do was alternate between marking in yellow and marking in blue on the same puzzle. That would make the machine go berserk.

Answer keys for the puzzles remained in the scoring room. To score, judges would read each puzzle left to right, like reading a book, ignoring the Downs. This created unintentionally striking coincidental images and phrases, as though the judges were building a memory palace. SIAMESE ASCENTS, in one puzzle: "I can't get the image of Siamese cats climbing mountains out of my head."

If a judge messed up while highlighting—coloring a correct square yellow, or a wrong square blue—she could correct herself by going over that square with a pink highlighter. Pink deliberately confused the computer, which would then ignore the square, which, in this case, would be exactly what the judge wanted it to do.

Once the puzzle sheets had been properly highlighted judges handed them over to the tech room, where the most seasoned officials fed them carefully into the brittle program. Solvers got a certain number of points for each answer correctly gridded, plus a bonus for a perfect puzzle. Points were docked for wrong answers.

"You will collectively examine over a million boxes this weekend," Ginsberg announced. The room burst into applause.

The ACPT always follows the same schedule. Friday night is the warm-up. Solvers do two rounds of "variety" puzzles. In both rounds, there are three different puzzles, and they can solve any one of them; the winner of each combination of puzzles, judged by accuracy and speed, gets entered into a raffle, with prizes revealed later that evening. Saturday is D-Day, the SATs meets the Super Bowl. Sunday is the Grand Finale. Everyone completes one last puzzle; then, after an interminable break and a more interminable awards presentation, the finalists compete onstage: first the C division, then the three best B's, and finally, the three top A's. The A division winner is crowned ACPT champion.

When contestants arrive at the Marriott on Friday night, they receive an official ACPT yellow folder containing the following: a printout of the tournament instructions, a narrative explanation of the Byzantine ranking system, a name badge, a set of labels for judging use, a few ads printed in color (a crossword-puzzle retreat, a *New York Times*–sponsored crossword-themed ocean crossing, a crossword magazine with calls for submissions), and some extra bonus crosswords.

More stacks of free puzzles mushroom in the hotel lobby. In addition to that day's *New York Times* and *Washington Post* puzzles, several constructors attending make special puzzles commemorating the occasion. There are also a few limp attempts at kid-friendly puzzles, decorated with hand-drawn suns, probably slid onto the table by a well-intentioned overzealous Marriott manager; most of the kids here with their parents have been solving the real puzzles for years.

Every year, too, something predictably different happens. In 2017, the Second Quinquennial World Palindrome Championship, nested inside the ACPT, creating a matryoshka doll of word competitions. Eight of the world's best palindromists ("pa-LIN-drom-ists") convened to vie for a $1,001 prize. Shortz presented the hopeful octet with a set of constraints, and they had the weekend to work their palindromic magic within those themes, scuttling throughout Marriott minibars like an *oozy rat in a sanitary zoo*. The crossworders would be the judge, and the crowd favorite would be crowned the winner.

Shortz, in sports-announcer mode, introduced each palindromist in front of the assembled Friday night crowd. A camera crew popped up to record the palindromists' introduction. "A Man, a Plan, a Palindrome," a short profile about 2012 winner Mark Saltveit, had successfully crowdfunded its expansion into a full-length documentary. "Legend says"—per the film's Kickstarter platform—"that the first words spoken by a human were a palindrome. Adam introduced himself to Eve saying: 'Madam, I'm Adam.'"

While the cruciverbalists worked their variety puzzles, the palindromists received a series of warm-up constraints—*Use a q not followed by a or u*, or, *Start or end with French or Spanish word(s)*—and scattered to pun it out. Jon Agee, author of such classics of the palindrome canon as *Go hang a salami, I'm a lasagna hog*, came up with my favorite: *007 saw Q's DNA. Lands! Q was 700.*

At Friday's social hour, after the variety puzzles, contestants mingled in the Marriott, noshing on ziggurats of cheese squares. My dad introduced me to a new friend. Sue, an attorney, wore what seemed from afar to be a full-on cow costume but turned out to be a crossword-fleece onesie, complete with footies. "My daughter-in-law made it for me!" Sue said. "I wear it to sporting events, sometimes, when it's outdoors and cold, because it's so warm and cozy." I asked Sue how people reacted. "They think I'm the mascot, sometimes. Or I get mistaken for that Chick-fil-A cow!"

▢▮▮▮▢

On Saturday morning, the ballroom had been filled with long tables, each featuring a flock of propped-up yellow folders to divide competitors into cubicles. Two stadium-screen-sized countdown clocks flanked the front of the ballroom sentry-like. The clocks were set to the amount of time allotted to solve the puzzle; when the puzzle began, they'd start ticking down to zero.

My parents and I got to the ballroom thirty minutes early, and we were lucky to snag three seats in the same row. As competitors entered, they milled in their pre-solve rituals, nervously chatting and arranging their name tags like runners pinning bibs on before a race. Some did hummingbird darts in and out of the room, fetching fuel and snacks. Others plonked down to protect their seats. The line at the lobby coffee shop snaked down the hall past the restrooms. A man with a polo shirt tucked into his pleated khakis, already settled between Dad and me, neatly fanned out seven pencils from a thick fistful. A woman in a tracksuit swilled a Muscle Milk. Sue arrived incognito; the crossword suit, she said, was too hot for actual competition. A few solvers opted for oversized headphones, while others packed earplugs into their ears.

Breakfast and coffee were not served in the ballroom. The only food was a container of Oreos on the back table, a true cruciverbalist's snack.

As in a boutique studio exercise class, the front-row solvers claimed their spots first. A woman with two pairs of reading glasses draped on her nose, crossword-themed teddy bear perched on a metal pencil box, was vigorously puzzling away, forty minutes before the first round. Josephine, age ninety-plus, had arranged her corner setup like a dollhouse: pencils, magnifying reading glasses, water.

My mother surveyed the room and narrowed her eyes. "They're seriously not taking advantage of their marketing opportunities," she said. Solvers had to plan their paraphernalia, as there was virtually no swag for sale at the ACPT. When we checked in, we didn't get free T-shirts or reading glasses. The extra pencils by the pencil-sharpening station were standard-issue pencils, unmonogrammed. The Oreos (a "black-and-white treat" provided by a puzzler) weren't ACPT-stamped.

All hope of merchandise wasn't lost. The ACPT's expo, housed in a small adjunct room, featured some crossword-related wares: mostly books, with a couple of booths of magazines and homemade jewelry. Mom and I decided to check it out while Dad guarded our seats. The sellers found themselves in a peculiar catch-22 of boredom: They couldn't compete, because someone needed to be watching the table, but no one would buy goods during the competition itself, so they'd have to wait out each round anyway. The vibe was more bake sale than professional convention. One man came from Massachusetts with a box of hand-stapled crossword newsletters. Once he ran out, he said, he'd go home. A jewelry designer presented retooled Scrabble-tile earrings and *I Survived Puzzle Five*–stamped keychains. The Village Bookstore from Pleasantville, New York, Shortz's hometown, featured a rack of crossword books bearing Shortz's face. They also had broadsides of an original crossword-themed poem: "The white and black squares / promise order," the poem began, and continued to describe, in semierotic particularity, the ritual of doing a crossword each morning over a steaming cup of tea.

Back in the ballroom, Shortz had entered, in his traditional polo and khakis. He shook hands with some of the front-row solvers and bent down to chat with Josephine. Eventually, he climbed the platform in the center of the room. "Welcome to the ACPT," he said. The crossworders burst into whoops and cheers before quickly hushing themselves.

Shortz explained how the day would go. Each puzzler would receive six identical puzzles, with an hour-long break between Puzzles Three and Four—longer, if you breezed through Puzzle Three—for lunch. The puzzles were all timed. If you finished a puzzle before time was up, you waved your puzzle in the air, and an official took it from you and recorded your time. Solving time was noted by the minute, not the second, so if you solved the puzzle with seven minutes and thirty-two seconds on the clock, you could use the next thirty-two seconds for free without dropping any points. The pocket of time right before each minute was crucial, and officials became extra alert during these tense moments.

The tournament puzzles didn't follow the *Times*'s Monday through Saturday calendar of difficulty. Puzzles One and Four, the warm-up and postlunch, were the easiest; Puzzles Two and Three, the steady climb; Puzzle Six, the cruise to the finish.

Puzzle Five was notoriously the hardest puzzle of the tournament. Setting Puzzle Five was an honor, since only the most seasoned constructors were typically trusted to create something clever enough to stump the experts. The constructor who created Puzzle Five each year became the tournament's de facto villain, cursed over many a Marriott lobby whiskey.

Solvers who finished puzzles early could leave the room to debrief with solvers going at similar paces. Some obsessively loaded and reloaded the tournament stats on their phones, checking how they compared and seeing where the top puzzlers had made mistakes. Others fluttered in nervous silence, immersed in ways of not talking.

Most crossworders simply pulled out another crossword to fill the gap between puzzle and puzzle, just as they would with any other slot of empty time. Ron, the seven-penciled puzzler next to me, finished each one with several minutes to spare, handed it to a volunteer, and placidly set in on one of the spare crosswords in his folder. After several years competing, Ron had worked his way up to the C division. He shrugged modestly when I praised him; he'll never really crack into the B's, he said, but as long as he stays above the halfway line, he'll be okay. He was, he confessed, blushing a little, thinking about starting a blog. *The View from C-Level.*

My father wasn't having a great time. By lunch, he was floating in the bottom 10 percent, hovering just above the no-shows in the rankings. But his competition lizard brain had been activated, and he was deep into crafting potential psychological warfare. He sized up the room. The strategy component of a crossword tournament—how to psych people out, how to size up the competition—was limited, since inside your yellow folder, it was solver against self. Dad managed to find a few psychosocial options to test. Once you finish, should you get up right away and flaunt your speed by walking out? Or should you sit in your spot and play possum with your prowess?

Dad took to the whole scoreboard thing instantly, cheering up a little when he realized he wasn't ever going to hit dead last, even counting the zeros. He switched to tracking the top solvers, mentally calculating how many words the fourth-place person could miss and stay in the top ten, how fast the thirtieth-place person would have to be to crack the top twenty. He intuitively understood the alphabetical divisions and the tournament bureaucrats. Dad, like Shortz, was a law school graduate who never really practiced law.

"I didn't bother to look my ranking up," said my mom airily, and my dad immediately told her that she was about two thirds down the list. She nodded, smirking, content to be comfortably above my father. My mom was competitive in the sense that she would happily do each puzzle as well as possible, and try to perfect her own skill—but she doesn't share the lizard brain inside my dad and me, jealously compelling her to be better than everyone else. She already knew, in her own way, she was.

Outside the ballroom, some of the volunteers were serving squares of one of those huge, white-iced supermarket sheet cakes for all the solvers celebrating a birthday over the weekend. Contestants dove into the sugar rush. But once solvers crossed the threshold from the bacterium-patterned carpeting outside the ballroom door to the different but equally complicated carpeting inside the ballroom, the mood shifted at once from genial to tense. It was time for Puzzle Five. Some hissed at the constructor. Others' faces grew pale. My dad rolled his eyes. My mom sat up a little straighter.

Shortz let the gentle booing proceed for an extra few seconds, relishing the moment, then blinked mildly and started the clock. With everyone's heads buried, Shortz slipped out to procure a square of birthday cake, the only thing I'd seen him eat all weekend. He ate it standing up as he walked back into the ballroom, digging into the white sponge with a plastic fork. Custard oozed out of the center, and the melting white icing stuck into his napkin so the whole thing became a sodden, crumbly mess, white frosting on white cake with white center custard pooling into the white napkin. Will kept walking as he poked his fork into the goop, and when he reached the front, he crumpled the napkin and threw it into a bin, somehow managing to wipe his palms clean in the process, as if the square had never existed. Without losing a beat, he resumed scanning the room for the top solvers to shoot their hands in the air.

Twenty minutes into Puzzle Five, I felt itchy, like I was wearing a turtleneck made of hair. I felt fidgety and a smidge ulcer-ridden. I was unable to stop doing the crossword but also couldn't tune out the world enough to melt completely into the game. I was caught between past and future. The crossword mimicked the way I constructed and solved problems so I wouldn't have to deal with my life, but since it wasn't an escape hatch of my own design, it didn't quite fit. The crosswords translated the world into grid and solution, but the solution only solved an answer to a problem that may or may not have ever been there.

▭▮▮▭

After the day's solves, the cruciverbalists packed back into the ball-room for the evening's crossword-themed entertainment. During the year of the Second Quinquennial World Palindrome Championship, they voted on the winning palindromes, which involved long recitations and baroque scoring, and by the end, no one could remember where each had begun, even though the end was the same as the beginning.

Matt Ginsberg presented "The View from Dr.Fill" [*sic*] (as Gins-berg explained, he took out the space between the period and "Fill" in his program's name to prevent autocorrect from turning it to "Dr.

Phil"). In 2011, Ginsberg first brought Dr.Fill, his crossword-solving software, to the ACPT, and it has competed every year since. It's become a ritual on Saturday evening to hear how Dr.Fill has been doing: what tweaks Ginsberg has made over the past year to improve his machine, and how constructors have failed or succeeded to thwart him again.

Computers* have bested humans in the majority of mental games: backgammon (BKG 9.8, in 1979), checkers (Chinook, 1994), chess (Deep Blue, 1997), Scrabble (Quackle, 2006), Go (AlphaGo, 2016), Texas Hold'em (DeepStack, 2017). According to Ginsberg, Watson, the artificial intelligence that won at *Jeopardy!*, has an asterisk next to its victory because it was allowed to vet the categories beforehand, and Dr.Fill can do no such thing with the puzzles. Humans, Ginsberg said, were still better at three games: bowling (the machine was too perfect, and wore the oil off the alley), contract bridge, and crosswords.

Ginsberg has stylized himself as the Jekyll to Dr.Fill's Hyde, mere custodian of the crossword world's nemesis. Dr.Fill was more villainous HAL than omniscient Siri, a nefarious force whose goal was to topple the crossword world. Ginsberg toted Dr.Fill in a briefcase around the Marriott like a Chihuahua in a purse. Whenever Ginsberg entered the tournament ballroom as Dr.Fill, he wore a special sweatshirt: the front read, *THIS IS YOUR BRAIN*; the back, *THIS IS MY VOLLEYBALL ON YOUR BRAIN*.

Ginsberg spoke about Dr.Fill with a healthy paranoia. "I'm just interested in whether a computer can consistently do better than an average human at an average crossword," Ginsberg claimed, "but

---

*With the exceptions of Deep Blue and Watson, which are hardware, the triumphant AI opponents are all programs.

that's not the game the crossword world wanted to play." According to Ginsberg, constructors and champion solvers would be satisfied only if Dr.Fill could best the nastiest curve balls. "The constructors throw howitzers at me every year," Ginsberg said, and try as he might to tweak the software endlessly to make Dr.Fill ready for any trick, the constructors' continued use of Dr.Fill as their personal target practice meant that the machine couldn't win. It had become a vendetta, according to Ginsberg. "But I don't take it personally," he said. "If that's the way I have to answer the question of whether a machine can defeat a human at a crossword, then so be it."

I asked Joel Fagliano if he was deliberately trying to trip Dr.Fill up the year he constructed Puzzle Five. "I'm trying to trip everyone up," he said.

▭▮▮▭

Later on Saturday night, the glitterati and regulars drifted back into the lobby, close to the bar. Solvers in the Seniors division wearing bucket hats indoors hogged the good couches around the fake fireplace, each doing crosswords alone, grim and silent in their labor. A determined octet of twenty- and thirty-somethings had set up a quiz game involving colored buttons and iPads. Speed solvers gripped electric blue drinks, the signature cocktail of the tournament, apparently.

One paced around the sunken area by the Marriott faux-fireplace, walking with a little skip-step. He had light, piercing eyes, no glasses, hair cut into some sort of dark unassuming bowl cut that didn't mask his cowlick. He tracked his own slightly elliptical yet purposeful orbit. This was Howard Barkin, the winner who'd upset seven-time champion Dan Feyer in 2016. By 2017's Saturday night, he was out of the running for top three—an error in Puzzle Five had sent him skittering down the rankings—and each ellipse he made around the lobby seemed to be retracing that clue.

Ross, an expert constructor but middle-of-the-pack solver, slid over to me as I watched. "The first year I came to the tournament," he said, "my first thought was: How many people are getting laid? I walked in, and I realized: zero percent." Then, he said, "There were the old stalwarts, but there was this group of people—*the pod*, I call them—these twenty-somethings, thirty-somethings, mostly male—people who wouldn't have ever been brought together, were it not for this thing, the crossword puzzle."

Tournament regulars are an extreme end of the bell curve, but all solvers have a story. When most people are asked how they'd begun to do the crossword, they overwhelmingly reply something along the lines of "My grandmother used to do it," or, "My father and I would do it together." The puzzle provides a triumphant moment each day, trapping yourself in the maze in order to escape victorious. Rather than getting out of your life, you could have the vicarious superhero sensation of getting in and out of the crossword. The crossword creates a shape around which your day can form itself actively. The Container Store is popular because it sells the promise of a busy and organized life. Similarly, the crossword takes a day and makes it into a day with purpose.

In the Richard Linklater film *Waking Life*, there's a scene where a man and a woman are in bed together. The man says: Imagine a population that's been given a crossword puzzle one week, and then another one that's been given the same puzzle a week later. The second one would be a lot better at it, because they've had the words seeded in conversation around them.

Linklater's theory might be true. Even the hardest puzzles are supposed to get very slightly easier over time, because the words that appeared in the grid have gradually made their way into the general conversation in very slightly higher-than-average proportions.

Ross, who told me about Linklater, believed this theory of collective heightened awareness. "I'll get a word in a puzzle," he said, "and I've never used that word before, and don't remember having read it, but I get it. And then I can usually trace it back. Like, oh, something my granddad said fifteen years ago. It usually has nothing to do with the clue that prompted that word in the first place.

"There's that frustrated feeling you have of being stuck—and then the satisfaction you have when you sleep on it and you wake up and you can finish the whole thing," added Ross. "Literally sleeping on it. There's your erotics for you."

The final puzzle before the championship round started at nine o'clock sharp on Sunday morning. My parents and I hustled to make it on time, but we could have hit snooze. It was a soft sharp, with crossworders bleary from overpunning. The last puzzle, the largest of the tournament and about the difficulty of a typical *Times* Sunday morning, was a ceremonial hoop, something to do between breakfast and the championships.

To give the judges time to score Puzzle Seven and determine the finalists, Shortz instituted a crossword-puzzle talent show: jugglers, crossword-themed improv, an a cappella rendition of Billy Joel's "We Didn't Start the Fire" recast as "We Didn't Solve the Puzzle."

After the talent show, the stage was cleared for the talent. Shortz read aloud each award winner from each category, from tenth-place Midwestern to seventh-place Junior, and allowed for applause after every name. Finally, Shortz made it to the championships in the C, B, and A divisions, and after he announced the nine finalists, all three groups marched into an anteroom to wait their turn. Each division solved the same grid, but there were three sets of clues: C, B, and A, in ascending order of difficulty. The audience got the puzzles so we could play along.

The C-group finalists took the stage first. Each stood in front of a large whiteboard, holding the clues in their hands, and strapped on the military-grade noise-canceling headphones that all finalists wore. Several years ago, a competitor had taken a recording of translators talking at the United Nations—hundreds of people in hundreds of different languages—and turned it into a custom white noise for the ACPT, so now the competitors listened to bastardized Babel as they solved.

The event's emcees, hosts of a word game show on NPR, provided a running stream of live-action commentary for the A division. ("Tyler's filled in ZEBRAFISH where it really should be BETTAFISH, when will he figure that one out, oh good, he's gotten into that tricky southwest corner; look, Dan has started from the bottom and worked his way up.")

The audience squinted at the whiteboards, trying to judge whether all the letters were correct, and whether a finalist had, in a fatal flaw, left a clue blank. Several audience members, done with the final puzzle, had already turned to a new one from the stacks in the lobby, or on their phones.

And as soon as the A finals ended, a million little boxes later, it was over.

◻◼◼◻

"We're not coming again next year," said my dad, who was at least pleased that he hadn't finished last. "I kind of liked it!" said my mom.

"The finals were boring," said my dad. "I couldn't see anything."

"I have an idea for how they could organize that last day," said my mother. "There's so much wasted time."

Crossword people who don't come to the ACPT are more numerous than those who do. Garden-variety crossworders are everywhere. Like a trick bookcase that is a door, or the rock in the flowerpot that opens in the back to hold the spare key, crossworders look like the rest of us.

In books, smart characters who get bored do crossword puzzles. When eccentric Henry translates *Paradise Lost* from English into Latin in *The Secret History*, Donna Tartt's novel set on an idyllic Vermont college campus, narrator Richard realizes that the project is "nothing more than a method of whiling away the early morning hours, much as other insomniacs do crossword puzzles." When the secretary in Mary Gaitskill's short story "Bad Behavior" quits her job after her boss abuses her, she lives at home and whiles away the productive part of her day doing crossword puzzles. Her mother also does crosswords— she is in the car doing puzzles when the secretary interviews for her job. It becomes a genetic act, the secretary turning into the mother when she is bored and frustrated, idle but not out of her own volition. Crosswords signal busy people idling, or idle people busying themselves.

My parents returned to their usual crossword patterns: my mom doing the puzzle every night, my dad looking at it occasionally before turning back to his bridge problems. Going home on the train, I was recycled into a loop. I was exhausted but not tired, invigorated but not excited, trepidatious without feeling tingly. There was a certain calm that comes from doing this test over and over without consequences, hot yoga of the mind.

The crossword creates stress to release it, getting you back to baseline frustration. It's a link to the past and future without needing to trouble the present. At the end of the day, an abandoned puzzle is the same as a completed puzzle. We tell ourselves games in order to live.

CHAPTER 10

DECODING THE CROSSWORD

A fter returning from Stamford, I start dreaming in puzzles.

CROSSWORDS IN CONNECTICUT:
A COZY MYSTERY.

A sloping white house in Connecticut, all cocoa and conviviality, oversized gingham sofas and a fireplace big enough for four people to stand inside side by side. Our host, Bill Tall, has invited the top crossworders in the country to his Connecticut house for a weekend of puzzling. Everyone will solve seven puzzles, but Puzzle Five is the crown jewel of the weekend: as solvers say, "Live and Die by Puzzle Five."

Snow is just starting to fall, barely visible pinpricks, but the sky is that hard, clear gray that means that we're in it for the long haul, and by the next morning, the entire landscape will be indistinguishable from itself, heaping drifts of white on white.

A., our hero, has joined the puzzle elite to observe the weekend's events. This is A.'s first time at this yearly ritual. Unlike everyone else, she's an Everywoman at the crossword, a truly average solver, which puts her at the bottom of this pack. A. isn't perturbed: she's here to learn what makes these crossword-puzzle people tick.

But what began as a lighthearted gathering of cruciverbalists in the countryside quickly becomes sinister when the snowstorm shuts off access to the outside world. The power goes out for a few minutes between Puzzles Four and Five, and when it comes back, last year's champion has mysteriously gone missing. Some of the crossworders start murmuring uneasily.

Nevertheless, Tall hands out Puzzle Five, the weekend's climax. Puzzle Five's title, H_NG_M_N: A., h_nged. You're supposed to drop every A from the theme clues, and the double twist is that the extra A's you've dropped find themselves "hanging" from various other answers. (SCARRED LETTER?)

Our hero, A., begins to suspect that something's amiss. Even with her limited knowledge of crosswords, she grows increasingly suspicious at the other puzzlers' apparent nonchalance. A man is missing! Should we solve Puzzle Five, or should we start a search? ("Femme fatale's fatal attraction?" reads a clue. Even A. can solve it: MANHUNT.)

The air around A. quickens. She senses she's not getting the double clue, though she can sense there's a double clue there. She can tell that the way to solve this mystery of the disappearing champ is in the crosswords: Has the champion been murdered, and is it up to A. to figure out the answer lurking somewhere in the clues?

Or is Puzzle Five a meta-puzzle to frame A. herself?

Crosswords and mysteries are yoked together: a set of elements that the solver must piece together. The crossword is made of clues and grids—but where do they come from, and how do they go together?

A clue is a ball of yarn. It came to mean "that which points the way" because of the Greek myth of the labyrinth: Theseus uses a ball of yarn, which Ariadne had given him, to find his way out of the Minotaur's labyrinth. Mystery writers used the clue as a way to untangle a narrative; a story ends in a denouement, or un-knotting, that resolves the knot of the plot. Many clues, in stories and in life, were made of cloth.

The rise of detectives in both fiction and real-life mysteries elevated the importance of the clue to near-fetish status. Detective fiction first emerged as a popular literary genre in the mid-nineteenth century. Edgar Allan Poe's 1841 short story "The Murders in the Rue Morgue" is widely considered to be the first detective story. The detective soon thereafter became a staple figure in real-life British and American police forces. In 1887, the first Sherlock Holmes novel, *A Study in Scarlet*, was published in *Beeton's Christmas Annual*, a yearly paperback magazine, after being rejected many times. Originally, the detective received little attention: *The Sign of Four*, the second Holmes novel, was published to the mildest of fanfare in 1890. But this indifference soon changed. In July 1891, *The Strand*, a new monthly magazine, published the first Holmes short story, "A Scandal in Bohemia." Readership soared. When *The Strand* serialized *The Hound of the Baskervilles* from 1901 to 1902, subscriptions increased by thirty thousand; people lined up around the block of the magazine's offices to get the next installment. What made Holmes Holmes—that is, what made Sherlock so popular amid the glut of detective fiction at the turn of the twentieth century—was his use of the clue to put together the pieces of the puzzle. And what made Doyle's writing about Holmes so addictive was the sense that all of the aspects of the case were baked* into the story: you, too, could solve the puzzle (provided, of course, that you had Holmes's astute intellectual prowess and hypersensitive powers of observation).

A straightforward clue demands a transaction of facts—the second-highest mountain in Nepal,† the winner of the 1957 Oscar for Best Picture‡—whereas more Byzantine clue operations require a decoding of all aspects of that phrase. With most clues, more than one answer is available, but the grid constricts the possibilities to a single correct response.§ Inside the grid, interlocked letters begin to yield words once clues are filled in. Grids with more letters joined together will reveal more words as the puzzle progresses, enabling the solver to cross-check between visual patterns and problem-solving logic to get

---

*221b Baked.

†Kangchenjunga (second-highest in Nepal, third-highest on Earth).

‡*Around the World in 80 Days.*

§Unless the crossword is a Schrödinger puzzle, that is, a puzzle featuring grids that can be filled using two letters in specific squares.

the answers. In grids with more black spaces, it's every clue for itself. Grids with fewer blank spaces aren't necessarily easier. "Stacks," or answers built without black spaces, can be extremely difficult to fill in, because constructors often have to resort to unfamiliar letter combinations to get them to function.

The beginning of the twentieth century was the renaissance of the grid. Artists and builders had used grids for millennia to create diagrams and build things. Chessboards and mosaics, checkered patterns and harlequins, have always abounded across aesthetics worldwide. But in the twentieth century, for the first time, the grid appeared on the outside, not the inside. The grid had been a background figure for centuries, a tool used to create perspective and to provide structure within a painting. Now, the grid was not the ground, but the figure itself. Think Piet Mondrian's 1943 *Broadway Boogie-Woogie*, for example, which pixelates Manhattan into essentially a primary-color crossword grid. As art critic Rosalind Krauss put it, "By 'discovering' the grid, cubism, de Stijl, Mondrian, Malevich . . . landed in a place that was out of reach of everything that went before. Which is to say, they landed in the present, and everything else was declared to be past."

▯▮▯

Where there's language, there will be language games. The relationship between arranging letters and thinking about language is hardwired. Visual puns and grids are an important part of wordplay. Children can babble verbally and visually. Deaf children babble in sign language. Long before he could read, my brother discovered that he could rearrange alphabet magnets into "word" combinations, which he then attempted to pronounce. Synesthetes with grapheme-color association—that is, those who relate a particular color to a particular letter of the alphabet in their minds—who were raised with a certain set of Fisher-Price alphabet magnets frequently have their synesthetic alphabets cued to those colors.

Anagrams, acrostics, and riddles saturate the Bible. Consider Genesis 6:8: "And Noah found grace"; "Grace" and "Noah" are anagrams in Hebrew. Ancient Romans loved the happy coincidence that "ROMA" and "AMOR" are anagrams. The SATOR square, or a five-by-five word square that can be read either across or down, was first discovered in the first century in Pompeii. The square has appeared engraved in masonry across the Roman Empire, from Pompeii to England. Medieval SATOR squares abound, carved in the buildings like a twelfth-century Kilroy Was Here, or engraved in amulets as a charm to ward off evil or cure illness. When written out in a sentence, the words form a palindrome: SATOR AREPO TENET OPERA ROTAS [The sower Arepo holds a plow].

S A T O R

A R E P O

T E N E T

O P E R A

R O T A S

In the third century AD, the Roman emperor Caracalla prescribed that people with malaria wear a magical amulet containing the word *Abracadabra* written in a descending triangle:

A — B — R — A — C — A — D — A — B — R — A

A — B — R — A — C — A — D — A — B — R

A — B — R — A — C — A — D — A — B

A — B — R — A — C — A — D — A

A — B — R — A — C — A — D

A — B — R — A — C — A

A — B — R — A — C

A — B — R — A

A — B — R

A — B

A

The late nineteenth century saw a boom in public interest in acrostics and word games. The double acrostic, or an acrostic that contains words running down both sides of the text, became popular in the 1850s. Queen Victoria was very fond of double acrostics, even constructing* one herself. In 1865, Lewis Carroll published *Alice's Adventures in Wonderland*, which was an immediate commercial success; indeed, Alice-mania continues to the present. *Alice's Adventures in Wonderland* was a revision of an 1864 manuscript called *Alice's Adventures Under Ground* that Carroll wrote for Alice Liddell. The revision from the 1864 to the 1865 version added most of the puzzles and wordplay to the original story, which was a more straightforward dream narrative. Word games might not have been the only element that

---

*Queen Victoria's "Windsor Enigma" brings coal to Newcastle: The left-hand side of the acrostic reads NEWCASTLE down the page, while the right-hand side, if you read from top to bottom, reads COAL MINES.

attracted readers to Alice, but playing with language has become an indelible part of Alice's world. Carroll also captivated the Victorian imagination through his popularization of such word games as a proto version of Scrabble and "doublets," or word ladders that change a letter at a time to transform one word into another.

□■■■□

Inspector Endeavour Morse buys the *Times* of London at a bookstall in Oxford, boards the express train to Paddington, and by Didcot, the railway town ten miles south of Oxford, he has solved the crossword—except for one damned clue. Morse is embarrassed. His identity is tied to finishing the crossword; after all, his first name was revealed to the public through a cryptic crossword clue: "My whole life's effort has revolved around Eve" is ENDEAVOUR, that is, an anagram of EVE + AROUND. With his dictionary, Morse assures the reader, he could have cracked the puzzle in no time. But Morse isn't thrown off for too long. As Colin Dexter, the British novelist who invented Inspector Morse, writes in *The Wench Is Dead*, the novel in which Morse's little hiccup takes place, he "quickly wrote in a couple of bogus letters (in case any of his fellow-passengers were waiting to be impressed) and then read the letters and the obituaries." Crossword solved—but more importantly, the illusion of the crossword has been solved.

Crosswords and mysteries have been yoked together since the crossword's inception. In detective-driven plots the solver has to use both clues and context to figure out the solution. Not only did the turn-of-the-century periodical *The Strand* regularly publish Holmes and other popular detective fiction, it was also known for its puzzles and brainteasers, printed in a regular column called "Perplexities." In *The Strand*, the clue and wordplay became physically bound together.

Inspector Morse symbolically struts his stuff with crosswords. Colin Dexter also uses the crossword as a space to establish the power, and class, dynamic between Inspector Morse and his partner, Sergeant Lewis. Morse and Lewis meet in *Last Bus to Woodstock*, Dexter's first Inspector Morse novel. Lewis initially encounters Morse as the latter is completing a cryptic crossword puzzle. Morse explains to Lewis the knot he's untangled to arrive at a titillating answer—BRA—but Lewis refuses to be embarrassed. He's impressed by Morse's skill, but, as Morse well knows, impatient with games. The crossword encapsulates their relationship: Morse is the one who solves the puzzles, but he also leaps to conclusions and likes to demonstrate his knowledge flamboyantly. Lewis is the sidekick, less intellectually gifted but more reliable, prone neither to leaps nor to flaunting his intelligence. Morse uses the crossword as barbell, flexing his intellect; his solving style shows that he's clever but also that he's a show-off.

Dexter's use of the crossword as a sign of both leisure-class intellect and detective prowess winks to Dorothy Sayers, a doyenne of British crime writing. Crosswords had arrived in England only a few years before Sayers's 1928 short story "The Fascinating Problem of Uncle Meleager's Will," but by then, the crossword was already as British as kippers. In Sayers's tale, the curmudgeon of the title has just died, and his new will apparently leaves everything to his suddenly much more marriageable niece, Miss Marryat. However, Old Moneybags Meleager has frustrated his would-be heirs: the new will is hidden, and the old one leaves everything to (gasp!) the ultra-Conservative Primrose League. If Miss Marryat can't find the new will, not only will she remain destitute, but her political nemesis—Miss Marryat is a Socialist—will gain at her expense.

Toward the end of his life, Meleager became a first-rate crossworder. ("'Cross-words?' said Hannah Marryat, knitting her heavy brows. 'Oh, those puzzle things! Poor old man, he went mad over them. He had every newspaper sent him, and in his last illness he'd be trying to fill the wretched things in.'") Now, Meleager's created a meta-puzzle for his will-seekers. The key to the will's location is hidden in a crossword, and the crossword itself is hidden across the house.

But Meleager can't beleaguer our hero. Lord Wimsey, Sayers's detective, is not only an A-1 sleuth but an ace cruciverbalist. All the clues are in rhymed couplets, and they read as one long poem, so, unlike with most crosswords, you get to play along by reading the clues as though they are a continuous block of text. Wimsey and the others unpack the whimsical poetic clues—"Your expectation to be rich / Here will reach its highest pitch"—to solve the grid. There are four darker tiles in the house's impluvium, which lead the team to a chapter and verse in the Bible, which finally brings them to the will. The crossword itself isn't the will, but the key that points everyone to the hideaway under the stairs where the will has been secreted in a panel in the wall.*

---

*Children's book author Ellen Raskin also used the puzzle-in-the-will-solution for her 1978 Newbery Medal–winning book *The Westing Game*. Sixteen potential heirs of businessman Sam Westing have to crack the wordplay in his will if they want to win his

"The Fascinating Problem of Uncle Meleager's Will" uses the crossword to show some of the paradoxes of the British class system. The crossword is both democratic and hierarchical, since the butler gets to reveal his intellectual chops, but the aristocrat still asserts his cultural dominance. The story ends where it began, with Bunter asking Wimsey for help with a crossword clue: "'If your lordship would be so kind,' said Mr. Bunter, producing a small paper from his pocket, 'I should be grateful if you could favour me with a South African quadruped in six letters, beginning with Q.'" The crossword simultaneously brings upstairs and downstairs together while cementing the distance between them.

Just as Sayers uses the crossword to both trouble and reinforce the relationship between Wimsey and his valet, satirist P. G. Wodehouse also uses the crossword as a metonym for intelligence—but instead of affirming the balance of mental power in favor of those who hold financial heft, Wodehouse deploys the crossword as a mechanism to reveal the daftness of the upper class and the intellectual superiority of the economically inferior.

In Wodehouse's 1937 novel *Summer Moonshine*, wealthy, bored Lady Abbott, languidly lounging on a settee, is stumped. A cooling evening breeze, Wodehouse writes, conveniently fans "a brain which had become a little heated as it sought to discover the identity of an Italian composer in nine letters beginning with p." Lady Abbott rejects

---

$200 million inheritance. Each pair of would-be heirs knows that they have to figure out clues and solve a puzzle to earn the prize, but they don't know what the clues stand for or what type of puzzle they're solving: the reader, in the catbird seat, gets to see all the clues unfurl, but even the reader isn't given full access to the story until the end.

Irving Berlin "because, despite his other merits, too numerous to mention here, he had twelve letters, began with an i, and was not an Italian composer." Galumphing footsteps foretell Sir Buckstone, who bursts through the door and triumphantly mansplains: snatching Lady A.'s pencil, in a firm hand, he writes "Pagliacci." *Pagliacci*, an Italian opera by the composer Leoncavallo, is no more right than Irving Berlin, but if Lady Abbott and Sir Buckstone are satisfied, then the crossword has done its job: placating the upper classes while poking fun at them under their very noses.

Twenty years later, Wodehouse's aristocrats had gotten no better at solving the puzzle. At the beginning of *Something Fishy,* published in 1957, Lord Uffenham is in distress. He barks to his niece, Jane, to go ask the valet for a crossword answer, with no intention of solving the puzzle on his own: the point is to have the butler come in to solve it, but clue by clue, so that Uffenham can *pretend* he is solving it. He tries to reap all the self-congratulatory and social benefits of having a completed crossword puzzle while doing none of the actual labor himself. The crossword symbolizes society—a token of the leisure class accomplished by the actual engine, that is, the servant class.

Lord Uffenham represents the English aristocracy of a bygone era, clinging to prewar customs while the rest of the world has zoomed by, as though, in the twenty-first century, he exclusively used a landline rather than a cell phone. He laments the "sound old tradition of the Sun God Ra" and resents the wordplay now dominating the form. Sun God Ra–style crosswords favored a certain breed of education, knowledge that one could achieve only through a particular pedigree. Lord Uffenham loves crosswordese because it signals an elite club, but the crossword now reflects a meritocracy. The cryptic requires an elite status, but one born out of cleverness, not out of knowledge available only to people with access to a certain education.

⬛⬛⬜⬛⬛

These days, the crossword has become its own satire. Amy Santiago, a police officer in the comedy television show *Brooklyn Nine-Nine*, shows off her chops by doing the crossword, and, in one episode, solves a crossword-related crime. In crossword cozy mysteries, not only do readers get to solve the mystery itself, they get to solve actual puzzles. There are typically crosswords included in the plotline, or as extra bonus material, or both. The Crossword Mysteries series by Nero Blanc— titles include *Death on the Diagonal* and *Two Down*—chronicle Anna-bella Graham's anagrammatic adventures in crime busting. Parnell Hall's Puzzle Lady series features the "Puzzle Lady," Cora Felton, in titles such as *You Have the Right to Remain Puzzled* and *Arsenic and Old Puzzle*. Whenever a crossword-related crime turns up—*A Purloined Puzzle*, for example, features a stolen crossword puzzle, with a bloody knife left in its stead—our heroine gets called in. (The real scandal: Cora hates crosswords.) *The Crossword Mystery*, a Hall-mark original series, stars a brilliant, beautiful puzzle editor whose crosswords have become linked to unsolved crimes. She's forced to team up with the rugged, handsome police detective to help crack the cases.

In 2013, the *Guardian* ran a contest to solve the six still unsolved cryptic clues in Wodehouse's *Something Fishy*; with varying degrees of confidence, entrants succeeded. As with the deliberately bungled clues in *Summer Moonshine*, the unsolved cryptic clues in *Something Fishy* aren't voids that thrust readers out of the novel, but enigmas that invite you in. The unsolved crossword generates frustration for characters in the book, but it's fanfic catnip, a way for the reader to know more than the characters will ever learn.

Crosswords are escape hatches for writers as well as for their readers. Kirchstetten, Austria, fifty-four minutes by train outside Vienna, is a hamlet best described in fairy-tale adjectives: sleepy, bucolic, backwater. At age fifty, poet W. H. Auden bought a farmhouse—the first house he'd ever owned—and lived there every subsequent April through October (he wintered in New York) with his partner, librettist Chester Kallman, until Auden's death in 1973.

When guests visited the poet on Audenstrasse—the town renamed his street, though Auden retained the original *Hinterholz* on his garden gate—they were swept into the old master's routine. Auden rose every morning at six thirty A.M.; climbed an outside staircase to his study, which was next to a large loft with a warning sign that proclaimed, in German, *BE CAREFUL! RAT POISON!*; and sequestered himself to write. Guests wanting breakfast would have to fend for themselves until midmorning, when Auden would emerge for his errands, cramming his large frame into a VW Beetle. At eleven A.M., Auden went to the local gasthaus for beer and a sandwich, and to make any necessary telephone calls. By one P.M. precisely, Auden would be back at home for his prelunch vermouth and the crossword.

Auden kept the puzzle on the table and filled it in during lulls in the conversation.

"The Common Life," Auden's final poem in the Kirchstetten-set sequence "Thanksgiving for a Habitat," paints the poet and Kallman in their living room doing "British cross-word puzzles." "I'm glad the builder gave / our common-room small windows," he writes, "through which no observed outsider can observe us: / every home should be a fortress." Not only is the crossword a touching sign of domestic contentment, it's a symbol for coded behavior. Auden and Kallman knew that their conservative hamlet would welcome a pair of old bachelors chummily but platonically doing the crossword, not a pair of male lovers.

Note "British" puzzles. Auden disdained American crosswords. "The Americans are so inaccurate," he grumbled. "A five-letter word for 'irreligious person; answer 'pagan!' But if the pagans were anything, they were overreligious." Auden accepted a position as poet-in-residence at Christ Church college, Oxford, in 1972, just a year before his death, and left the East Village apartment he'd had for years. Once he'd sold his books and his belongings; the only thing remaining for posterity was a thick flotsam of completed cryptics.

If Inspector Morse uses the crossword as a way to strut his own intellect, the crossword can also be a way to solve the world. During an episode in the first season of *Sex and the City*, the late 1990s to early 2000s television show about single women in their thirties living in New York, the narrator, sex columnist Carrie Bradshaw, compares men in their forties to the Sunday *New York Times* crossword puzzle: "tricky, complicated, and you're never quite sure if you've gotten the right answer." Later that episode, Carrie's strolling down Madison Avenue with a shopping bag when she spies Mr. Big, her on-again-off-again love interest throughout the entire series, having an uptown Sunday brunch al fresco. Carrie tosses a glance at his table. "Hinge," she says, pointing to the half-completed crossword folded next to him. "That's the answer. It brings two things together." Carrie saunters on, but Big chases her down. "I would have gotten 'hinge,'" he says. He asks her out to dinner. Carrie pauses, pointedly nonchalant. "I'm good at crossword puzzles. I'm not so good at people puzzles." She struts off but turns over her shoulder with a come-hither glance. He's still watching her strut.

The crossword here serves many functions.

Crossword as foreplay. The crossword gives Carrie the opportunity to flirt with both words and action. As she leans across the table to write the answer, she brushes her arm ever so slightly against Big, displaying a hint of décolletage.

Crossword as intelligence. In the half-second between when the viewer sees the crossword puzzle on the table and Carrie picks up Big's pen, Carrie has already had time to read the clues, scan the grid, know how many boxes are available, possibly see if any letters have already been filled in, and arrive at the answer. Carrie leverages the crossword as a power dynamic between herself and Big. He's got a lot of societal advantages—male, wealthy, taller, older—but Carrie isn't milquetoast, and she wants to keep Big in a state of uncertainty as well. If he can play the game, so can she. Carrie's a wordsmith by trade, and verbal acuity is her trump card. Once she has the advantage intellectually, she's got him on his toes both mentally and physically. As Big runs after her, he says that he would have figured out the answer. It's a thin, petulant, and entirely indemonstrable claim.

Crossword as pretext. At this point in the season's arc, Carrie and Mr. Big keep running into each other by coincidence, but when they plan to meet, circumstances pull them asunder. Carrie wants to make it clear that she'd like to be with Big, but she also wants to play the game correctly. An absurdly apt answer to a crossword puzzle is perfect: all the obvious innuendo with none of the risk of a direct statement. Casually offering a crossword solution, apropos of nothing, connotes a sort of superabundance of cleverness. If the situation backfires and Big doesn't get the hint, Carrie still maintains the upper hand, as she can pretend she's simply radiating brilliance on her Sunday morning walk. But Big takes the bait; after all, he's looking for pretext too. By claiming that he would have figured out that clue, he's not just talking about the puzzle—like Carrie, he's also referring to their mutual desire to be together.

Crossword as status symbol. The crossword is shorthand for a particular constellation of social markers. Carrie associates the crossword with people slightly older than herself, giving the crossword both gravitas and a distinct whiff of boredom. During the episode, Carrie walks the viewer through the differences between men in their forties and men in their twenties. If you're classified as a crossword, you've crossed into a world of respectability, but you're also kind of dull: you leave the party early, sober. On the other hand, you're a lot more attractive the morning after than that twentysomething stud; while the hot young thing is making coffee using toilet paper as a filter, the crossword man is breakfasting on Madison Avenue.

Crossword as bromide. Carrie knows that using the crossword as a metonym for the enigmatic object of her romantic obsession is profoundly cheesy: as symbols go, you can't get much more obvious than this. So Carrie pushes the analogy into fable. Her initial comparison between men in their forties and the crossword is purely rhetorical, but then the figure of speech becomes reality when the crossword itself appears before their eyes on the table. The metaphor's forced to begin with, which Carrie cheerfully acknowledges by plunking the crossword itself into the scene. The physical crossword plays a slightly different, though just as cheesy, role. In Carrie's initial account, Big is the crossword puzzle. But when the crossword itself makes a cameo, it serves as a piece of technology in its own right, a device that Carrie and Big use to talk with subtext that's actually clearer than their attempts at straightforward communication.

Crossword as city life. Like bialys and Barneys, the crossword as symbolic form belongs to a certain New York mythos. The *Times* crossword creates a reality effect; it's a seemingly banal but iconic detail that the viewer can latch onto and use to extrapolate an entire world. Having the education, leisure, and desire to do a Sunday *Times* puzzle creates one level of society, but copies of the *Times* crossword are also ubiquitous. Mr. Big's breed of puzzle is very particular, but sex is everywhere.

*Crossword as sex.** But the crossword is also unconsummated

---

*Once you start finding innuendos, as any hormonal teenager or thirty-something sex columnist will corroborate, it's impossible to see almost anything without it becoming erotic—pepper mills, traffic signs reading *DON'T BLOCK THE BOX*—and crosswords are hardly immune.

desire. It's boring yet tantalizing, predictable yet unknowable, an isolated ritual yet a tool for innuendo. At this point in the season, Carrie and Big have yet to make out, let alone go further. The crossword is foreplay but frustration, too, an invitation as well as a barricade.

CHAPTER 11

THIS IS NOT A CROSSWORD

S urrealist artist René Magritte was born in Belgium in 1898. When he was thirteen, his mother, a milliner, leapt off a bridge and drowned herself in the River Sambre, her dress covering her face. Magritte studied art in Brussels, and in 1926, he created his first surrealist work, *Le jockey perdu* [The lost jockey], a collage featuring a sepia-tone sketch of a jockey frozen mid-horsewhip, thundering through what appears to be a field of giant chess pawns. Plush red velvet theater curtains frame the scene.

In 1929, Magritte completed *La trahison des images* [The treachery of images], which features a briar pipe in profile, floating without context against a cream background. Whenever I look at it, I feel like I'm staring at a billboard-sized vocabulary flash cards, except underneath the image, where I'd expect *Une pipe* or *P est pour une pipe*, Magritte has printed, in perfect cursive, *Ceci n'est pas une pipe* [This is not a pipe]. The image is a visual joke on a schoolroom lesson: I anticipate *une pipe*, so much so that I can't help but see it already, even before I read what's written.

This is not a pipe is true. I can't smoke the painting, just as I'm not going to have a swig of soda from a magazine ad for Coca-Cola. (Huffing the paint, or rolling up the canvas into an enormous joint, is also unlikely.) *This is not a pipe* is also false. You know that the image represents a pipe, so to be told that it is not a pipe contradicts what you know it is intended to bring to mind.

La trahison des images is ironic process theory in action. If I tell you not to think of a pink alligator, the first image that's going to flash across your brain is. . . . Well, you've already seen it. By being told exactly what not to see, Magritte defines what you think.

The birthplace of the briar pipe is St. Claude, a small town nestled

in the Jura Mountains of eastern France. In the 1850s, craftsmen in St. Claude started manufacturing pipes out of briar, which proved more durable than cherry or clay. By the 1920s, 95 percent of pipes in France were made of briar, and most pipes today still use this wood. An enormous statue of a pipe stands outside the Musée de la Pipe et du Diamant, a museum dedicated to St. Claude's two historic industries. The statue of the pipe is a pipe, but it is no more a pipe than Magritte's pipe that is not a pipe.

Magritte's pipe recalls "Fumées," a calligram by Guillaume Apollinaire. Published in 1918 in *Calligrammes: poèmes de la paix et de la guerre (1913–1916)*, "Fumées" features a pipe made from words. In English translation:

SMOKE

And while war
Bloodies the earth
I hoist odors
Near the taste-colors

And I sm

      ok

        e

      tob

      ac

      co from

    the Zo.NE

Flowers barely touch the ground glimpse in whiffs
The ringlets of odors tousled by your hands
But I know too the perfumed grottoes

> Where smoke's unrivaled azure spirals
> Where softer than night and purer than day
> You sprawl like a god wearied by love
> > You bewitch the flames
> > They crawl at your feet
> > Those nonchalant women
> > Your leaves of paper

The word *pipe* never appears inside Apollinaire's calligram. The form describes the seduction of smoking, which makes the poem function as a pipe, not as a description of a pipe. As the smoke slides down the neck of the pipe to the bowl, I follow it to the tobacco from the zone. Initially, the gesture of describing smoking in the shape of a pipe seems over the top. But creating a pipe on the page is, in 1918, a poignant bit of magical thinking. In the war, normalcy turns upside down. What used to be the background of existence—daily routines like smoking whenever you want—have become rarities, and horrors of air raids and battlefields that are unthinkable in times of peace become bedrock in war.

Nearly forty years after *La trahison des images*, Magritte painted a sequel, *Les deux mystères*. This painting depicts an easel, propped on a stand, that displays a framed image of a pipe with *Ceci n'est pas une pipe* written underneath. Here, the pipe-not-a-pipe appears against a black background with the text in white cursive, as though on a chalkboard. Magritte's painting has gone from existential question to academic paradox. Above the painter's easel, a larger version of the pipe floats against the wall. *Les deux mystères* is a fun-house mirror. The first mystery begets the second mystery, which, it turns out, is exactly the same mystery. Is the second specter of a pipe a pipe, or is it another pipe dream? The bigger pipe floating on the wall has fewer details than either the original painting's pipe or the pipe in this representation of the original. The "original" in the new painting isn't only different in color; the period at the end of the phrase is gone, turning the definitive sentence into a slightly less definitive suggestion, and Magritte's signature at the bottom of the painting is gone. The image in this painting isn't meant to be the original, but a representation of the original. This is not "This is not a pipe."

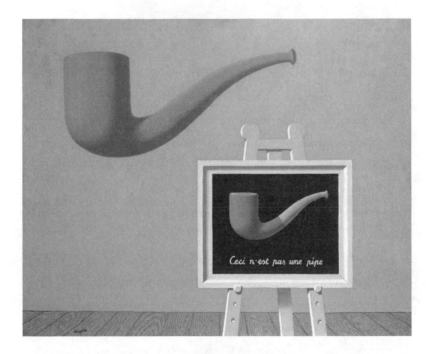

Yet the pipe on the wall is also not a shadow-pipe; since there's no visible light source, the pipe cast upward on the wall can't be the shadow of the pipe in the canvas. Nothing else in the painting has shading—the easel's legs rest on the ground without a shadow—and it would make no sense physically for a two-dimensional representation of an image within a painting to cast an enormous shadow on the wall behind it. Indeed, the pipe on the wall has more dimensionality than anything else in the painting, since it has a smooth texture and a body distinctly shaded so as to appear rounded. The pipe on the wall looks like a projection through a magic lantern, or as though the original painting were taking a photograph of a pipe, a meta-selfie. The first pipe has become so iconic that the image of the pipe has taken on pipe-like status of its own.

At the opening of an exhibit of Magritte's work at the Centre Pompidou in Paris, museum curator Didier Ottinger declared, "Magritte wanted to cross swords, meaning to engage in a theoretical combat with the philosophers, to prove to them that images can express thoughts in the same way that words can." Magritte does more than cross swords; his paintings do what crosswords do, which is to demand that you see both what is explicitly there and what is precisely *not* there.

In crosswords, you're not meant to hold the instability forever. For each clue, you're presented with a statement, and you're asked to come up with the word or phrase that that particular clue wants you to arrive at in that particular moment. You also get help from the visual logic of the crossword's grid. Once you know the size and shape of the thing that's not seen, and once other unseens come into vision, you can discover what is not there by virtue of inference from what is. Crosswords get you to *not* think of something so precisely that the answer is, ultimately, the only possibility.

"What are you going to do, then?" I asked.

"To smoke," he answered. "It is quite a three pipe problem, and I beg that you won't speak to me for fifty minutes." He curled himself up in his chair, with his thin knees drawn up to his hawk-like nose, and there he sat with his eyes closed and his black clay pipe thrusting out like the bill of some strange bird. I had come to the conclusion that he had dropped asleep, and indeed was nodding myself, when he suddenly sprang out of his chair with the gesture of a man who has made up his mind and put his pipe down upon the mantelpiece.

—Sir Arthur Conan Doyle, "The Red-Headed League"

For Sherlock Holmes, an x-pipe problem denotes the difficulty that a case presents to the detective, where x is the number of pipes—and therefore the amount of time and requisite brainpower—that Holmes must devote exclusively to deduction. A one-pipe problem is like a one-star Michelin restaurant, as being deemed worthy of Holmes's undevoted attention for any amount of time is no mean feat. A three-pipe problem is, therefore, a major conundrum.

The pipe is an active distancing mechanism between Holmes and the problem. As Maria Konnikova, author of *Mastermind: How to Think Like Sherlock Holmes*, points out, Holmes is not only thinking about the problem but also doing something else in the meantime. "A change in activity," Konnikova writes, "to something seemingly unrelated to the problem in question, is one of the elements that is most conducive to creating the requisite distance for imagination to take hold. Indeed, it is a tactic that Holmes employs often and to good effect. He smokes his pipe, but he also plays his violin, visits the opera, and listens to music; these are his preferred distancing mechanisms."

A crossword puzzle is a pipe. It's something you do to deliberately not think about something else. The crossword is just engaging enough that it demands all your attention, but it's not so taxing that it requires all your energy; on the contrary, the crossword pulls you outside your mind so that other processing can go on. Remember poet James Merrill doodling anagrams and word ladders on the sides of his manuscripts, churning through the letters of his name. Soldiers pick up puzzles while they're in barracks. I had a fight with a friend the night before being squashed together on a four-hour bus ride. Luckily, it was a Sunday. Once we'd worked our way through the large *Times* crossword, we had thawed enough to be able to talk.

A crossword is also not a pipe. Life is a distancing mechanism from the crossword puzzle. When you're stumped on a crossword, one of the best ways to solve it is to leave it. The crossword is a way to see your subconscious brain at work; you have to *not* think about the grid in order to let the mind stew and figure out what's going on. An "Easy Crosswords for Dummies Cheat Sheet," part of the "Dummies" how-to series, instructs stymied solvers to "walk away and come back to it a little later," as the answers will come when you "take a breather" and do something else. You can't get a clue, you get frustrated, you get away, get to bed, get up the next morning—and, suddenly, *aha!* The *aha* is addictive. Solvers remember where they were when they had their first one: when they slaved over the puzzle but couldn't work out the last bit, put it down, went to sleep, and the next morning, there it was—brain magic.

▢▢▢▢

Charles Layng, a Chicago-based reporter and editor, published *Layng's Cross-Word Puzzles: First Book* in 1924. "First" was an ambitious adjective: Layng hoped the description would bear fruit with as-yet-unwritten sequels. The publishers of Layng's book touted his collection as the public's much-needed "relief" from the "solid block idea" of crosswords, calling to mind an image of solvers trapped inside a grid, banging helplessly on the sides. The crossword's now-iconic square shape would eventually become part of the puzzle's lexicon: "This puzzle is one" is a clue for SQUARE from a 1979 *New York Times* crossword. But the first crossword puzzle, published in the *New York World* on December 21, 1913, is in the shape of a diamond, and soon, puzzles in the shape of the letters F, U, and N appeared in that paper. Layng leans into the idea of shaped crosswords, offering readers a smorgasbord: "The Liberty Bell," "The Elephant," "The Pin Wheel," "The Ice Cream Cone," "The Snow Man," "The House That Jack Built," and so on. Most clues don't relate too closely to the puzzle's shape, but some do: "Minor chess-men" is 2-Across in a puzzle called "The Pawn Shop."

One of Layng's puzzles is "The Pipe," a crossword grid in the shape of a briar pipe. "The Pipe" is not a pipe: the puzzle resembles its title in the loosest way possible, like a poorly pixelated doodle of a pipe in profile, and none of the clues are about pipes or piping hot pies or Pan or the Pied Piper or corncobs or Sherlock Holmes.

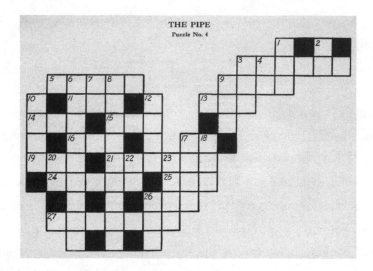

"The Pipe" begins by demanding that we see this crossword as a pipe. Then it asks us to ignore the fact that we're seeing a pipe and instead asks us to see the puzzle as a crossword to be solved. Once we've figured it out, we get to step back and again see the crossword as a pipe. There's no reveal that unveils a hidden joke about a pipe, or a pipeline of pipe-specific knowledge buried in the clues.

PIPE has appeared as an answer over 130 times in *New York Times* crosswords alone. When PIPE is the answer in a crossword, the clue doesn't want to make us think of "pipe" immediately. A crossword clue is the inverse of *Ceci n'est pas une pipe*; rather than tell us explicitly what not to think about, the clue's goal is to send us down a series of associations until we arrive at the pipe, that is, the place the clue has been leading us all along. Trying to get to "pipe" in a completely linear fashion dredges up too many other possibilities. Without eliminating the smoke surrounding the idea of "pipe," you move in a fog.

A pipe might be straightforward: "Appurtenance for Santa or Sherlock Holmes," "Corncob." Before Will Shortz took over as the *Times*'s crossword editor in 1993, "Meerschaum" had been used thirteen times as a clue for pipe; in the Shortz era, "Meerschaum" has yet to appear. Pipe means "speak" ("___ up (speak)") and "don't speak" ("___ down! ('Quiet!')"). Pipe can be an adjective, a "kind of organ or dream." Describing a pipe by its function gets trickier. "Water bearer" is ambiguous on first glance, as we might think initially of something we can see (a ewer, a vase). "It might need a fitting" might lead the solver into a different category at first, like SUIT. But why, on closer inspection, would a suit need a fitting? Though we think of clothes when we think of fitting, it's not the suit itself that needs to be fitted, but the person in the suit that needs the suit fitted to her. A suit goes instinctively into the context of things-in-the-world-that-need-fittings, but the suit, here, doesn't exactly fit. A pipe, on the other hand, often requires fittings to function—envision a pipe that's part of the plumbing, rather than one that Holmes might smoke. A pipe inspires William Blake's "Introduction to Songs of Innocence,": "piping down the valleys wild." There is no debate over the existence of the pipe; the poem only exists if the pipe exists. There's the Pied Piper of Hamelin, whose pipe lures the rats out of the city; when the mayor refuses to pay the piper, the piper comes again, this time leading the children away. No pipe, no piper; no piper, no rats gone; no rats gone, no children.

▪ ▪ ▪ ▪

A diagramless puzzle is a crossword in invisible ink. The puzzle gives a set of clues, like a crossword, but instead of a patterned grid, the diagramless presents an open field. There is a grid lurking underneath the white space—but you have to deduce where it is. As you fill in the answers, you also create the grid, building the black spaces like the cartoon gag of a train running on tracks that a wild-eyed conductor is freshly laying in front of it in a frenzy of crosshatches.*

The first diagramless crossword was an accident. The *New York World*'s original crossword triumvirate—Prosper Buranelli, F. Gregory Hartswick, and Margaret Farrar—went out to lunch to edit the next day's crossword, but they'd brought only the clues; the grid, they realized, was still at their desks. Rather than schlepp back to the office, Hartwick re-created the grid from scratch on the back of a napkin, filling in the answers and scratching off the inevitable blank spaces created. They'd hit on something. Diagramlesses never unseated the original crossword from the newspaper, but for papers that publish other complementary word games on a regular basis, they've remained in the stable of related variety puzzles on rotation, a moon orbiting its mother planet.

Most diagramless puzzles dilate to normal crossword-shaped grids, but some overachieve. When solvers completed an April 2018 diagramless by David Steinberg, the grid revealed a hole in the center, like a cookie cutter slicing out negative space, in the shape of a briar

---

*The climactic chase scene in *The Wrong Trousers*, a clay stop-motion animation film starring doddering Wallace and his whip-smart pet beagle, Gromit, features such an event. Through a complex chain of events, an evil penguin has attempted to pull off a diamond heist, and to escape the clutches of our heroes, he's hopped on a model train. Wallace and Gromit leap to a parallel train car to follow, but when the track runs out, Gromit grabs a sack of spare rails and furiously tosses them in front of the train, keeping just one track ahead of him at all times, so they'll be able to stay on the hunt.

pipe in profile. Above the pixelated pipe, a long horizontal clue read TREACHERY OF IMAGES; below, SURREALISM and THIS IS NOT A PIPE.

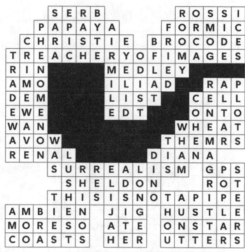

David Steinberg © 2018 *The New York Times*

Steinberg's pipe was not the only not-pipe to emerge in the crossword. Just a few months later, in September of the same year, a *Times* puzzle from Andrew Zhou featured the phrase CECI N'EST PAS UNE PIPE woven through the grid in circled letters; when solvers completed the puzzle and traced a line through each circle, a pipe emerged in the grid's center, mimicking Magritte's painting.

To create the crossword, Zhou "put an image of 'Treachery' into a vector graphics software, overlaid a twenty-one-by-twenty-one grid on it, and set out to find the key vertices of the pipe, seeing where they landed in the grid." He then arranged the letters of *Ceci n'est pas une pipe* in these vertices. "Hopefully," Zhou wrote in an explanatory note on XWord Info, the crossword omnibus website, "the surrealism of the original painting gains a new dimension here: a representation of a representation. The (benign) joke, which was the reason 'Treachery' was so enticing to invoke, is on detractors of this theme: if you finish the puzzle, play your bonus round of connect-the-dots, and declare 'that's not a pipe!' or 'that isn't anything like a pipe!,' you'd, of course, be fully correct."

Andrew Zhou © 2018 *The New York Times*

Crosswords are addictive because they tease out several kinds of desire at once: the yearning to solve a riddle, the desire to fill in a blank space, the obsession with perfection, yet also the ability to trust our guts and go with the thing that instinctively feels right. But crosswords are also repulsive. Smoking too many pipes in a row will make you sick, and crosswords without recourse to the natural world make your brain go loopy. They present the appearance of rigor without the depth of a true enigma. The crossword, on some level, has already been solved. Walled gardens can be Edens, but they can also be prisons: the mind can make a hell of heaven, a heaven of hell.

CROSSWORDS AND THE MEDIA:
THE CROSSWORD IN THE DIGITAL AGE

The *San Quentin News*, San Quentin State Prison's newspaper, is one of only a few American publications by and for incarcerated people. Inmates put together the entire monthly paper, from research to copyediting to graphics. Jonathan Chiu, who is serving a life sentence on charges of first-degree murder, is a *News* layout designer. He's passionate about sketch comedy, NPR, and running—he's done several of the prison's marathons, which consist of a hundred laps around the prison track. He's also a cruciverbalist.

After joining the *News* in 2015, Chiu started making crosswords for the paper. At first, the crosswords were simple, fact-based grids about prison life. But Chiu quickly got hooked on puzzle making, and he expanded his repertoire from San Quentin trivia to pop culture and wordplay. One of the guards complained, admiringly, that the puzzle had gotten too hard.

Cruciverbally speaking, the *San Quentin News* illustrates a law of crossword physics: if a newspaper—or any periodical—is in existence long enough, it will almost certainly acquire a crossword. Sometimes, that crossword languishes, but mostly, it gets a rabid enough following that the paper has to keep publishing it to maintain its readers. Crosswords are often cited as one of the few things that keep people buying hard copies of a paper.

Crosswords and journalism are genetically intertwined. Crosswords have evolved from a novelty to attract readers into an identifying factor; they're part of what makes a newspaper a newspaper. *BuzzFeed*, the online news and lifestyle site, started a crossword puzzle in the hopes that it would boost the site's prestige as a newspaper: "real" newspapers have good crosswords, so by adding a quality puzzle, *BuzzFeed* would lift its reputation from clickbait to news source. The BuzzPuzz, as no one called it, didn't last, but the perception of the puzzle as a necessity for newspapers persists. Readers of the *Minneapolis Star Tribune* complained when the paper switched its syndicated crossword from the *Los Angeles Times*'s puzzle to the *New York Times* crossword. "This puzzle makes me feel very, very stupid," wrote one reader. "I am not stupid. I am a physician. . . . You have ruined my morning. You have ruined my ritual."

But how would the crossword's relationship with newspapers translate into the digital age?

In 1994, the toy company Herbko International released the *New York Times* Crossword Companion Roll-a-Puzzle System, a piece of hardware technologically somewhere between a PalmPilot and a player piano. Solvers inserted a cartridge of puzzles into a slim black case and twiddled a wheel on the side to roll a new crossword into the frame.

The deluxe model, the Luminator, backlit the puzzle for use in low light and no light. Once the puzzle had been solved, you scrolled forward to the next one; once you'd gone through the lot, you replaced it with a fresh cartridge of puzzles. Like Plaza Publishing's original *Cross Word Puzzle Book*, the Crossword Companion came with an attached pencil.

The Companion did not catch on. The plastic black scrolls faded into eBay oblivion. Multimedia artist Camille Henrot's *Days Are Dogs*, an exhibit spanning the Palais de Tokyo museum in Paris, featured a cavernous room for each day of the week. Her "Sunday night," an archaeological-dig-cum-flea-market in insomniac blue walls, featured mementos of technology in carefully disheveled heaps. Inspirational posters such as an "Excellence" lion roared under visitors' feet; rotary phones with cords tangled in coital yet sterile intimacy. Next to the useless rotaries sat a heap of shrink-wrapped *New York Times* Crossword Companion Roll-a-Puzzle Systems.

Though the Companion itself was a flop, it was also the harbinger of the first seismic change in crossword-solving technology for a century. New technology meant new riffs on the crossword.

Michael Crick, son of Nobel laureate Francis Crick, the co-discoverer of DNA, believed that games represented the future of humanity. In an email to me, Crick wrote, paraphrasing Isaac Asimov: "Lions and tigers, when they are not searching for food, sharpen their claws but otherwise doze all day. By contrast, humans live by their wits, and need to keep continually sharpening their brains to stay in top form. The best adapted of us are genetically programmed to enjoy games and puzzles, sometimes to the point of addiction."

While studying neuroscience at Harvard Medical School in the

1960s, Crick got recruited by the team that was developing ARPANET, the military network that was the precursor to the internet. Crick later worked for Microsoft, where he developed a new spell checker. When Alexey Pajitnov, the inventor of *Tetris* and a fellow Microsoft programmer, asked Crick to make word games for Microsoft, Crick saw an opportunity to give crosswords a computer-age makeover, and so he created a type of puzzle he eponymously dubbed the Crickler. As Crick wrote to me, "Cricklers are really N-dimensional crossword puzzles projected onto one dimension—so they look like a quiz—where answers are conveniently next to questions—yet underneath they may be three-, four-, or even five dimensional." What this means is that Cricklers presented clues one line at a time, with each one corresponding to a location in a hidden grid. As solvers filled in the answers to each clue, corresponding letters would get pre-populated in later answers. Crick and his wife, Barbara, partnered with the *Seattle Post-Intelligencer* and the *Seattle Times*, and the first Crickler launched, in a freak of bad timing, on September 11, 2001. Though the Cricks pulled the puzzle down a few hours later out of respect, like lowering the flag to half-mast, they relaunched a few days later and soon expanded nationwide and worldwide. Crickler began as a news-based puzzle and required solvers to know something about the news, since grid patterns and guesswork were less helpful.

But Cricklers were no crosswords. Cricklers let crosswords masquerade as a quiz, but by taking away the grid—both the clues in the grid and the satisfaction of watching the solution bloom to life—Cricklers don't scratch the same itch.

Crosswords also got multimedia makeovers with new technology.

Puzzles could, theoretically at least, incorporate new types of clues—video clips, sound bites. "Homer and Lisa Exchange Cross Words," the sixth episode of the twentieth season of the television show *The Simpsons*, featured a puzzle that leapt from the page to the screen. In the episode, prodigious daughter Lisa turns into a crossword addict. She makes crosswords on the hopscotch court and enters the Citywide Crossword Tournament, run by a cartoon Shortz (and voiced by Shortz himself). Eminent crossword constructor Merl Reagle, who wrote the puzzles for the episode, also made a coordinating Sunday *New York Times* crossword that contained corresponding messages from the show. Rather than simply creating a Simpsons-flavored puzzle, Reagle used the crossword as connective tissue between the experiences of watching the episode and solving the puzzle. There are two meta-puzzles in this crossword. Lisa finds one of them in the episode: a diagonal along the solved grid reads DUMB DAD SORRY FOR HIS BET. But Homer tells Lisa she's missed the extra puzzle. All the initial letters to the 144 clues form an acrostic, which is a message from Homer to Lisa: DEAR LISA, YOU MAKE ME SO HAPPY. REALLY, REALLY, REALLY HAPPY. SORRY, HE TOLD ME I NEEDED A HUNDRED FORTY-FOUR LETTERS. WHAT WAS MY POINT AGAIN? OH, RIGHT. BOUVIER OR SIMPSON, I CHERISH YOU.

For a special sound-focused edition of the *New York Times* magazine, Joel Fagliano constructed a crossword in which fifty-one of the seventy-eight clues appeared to be blank. Readers were directed to a link where Will Shortz read the empty clues aloud. "1 Across. [Pause.] What are the first two words of this song?" The beginning of an orchestral arrangement of "The Star-Spangled Banner" played, then cut out after the first phrase. Pause. Then Shortz proceeded to the next blank. Most of the sound-based clues relied on definitions—"What word represents this sound?" Shortz asked, and a tinned sneeze erupted, cuing ACHOO—but some required more intricate logical leaps. "9 Down. What state capital is suggested by this band?" Kansas sang the first few bars of "Carry On Wayward Son," for the answer TOPEKA.

The audio crossword turned the puzzle into a guided meditation, gently but firmly moving the solver at a steady pace through each suggestion, neither faster nor slower than a moving walkway at an airport. You couldn't speed-solve the audio crossword; you had to wait until Shortz took you to the next blank spot. If you listened to the clues like an audiobook, without filling in the grid, the effect felt like the fulcrum between a John Ashbery poem and BBC Radio's Shipping Forecast: deeply allusive, yet all its meanings were far away.

The version that's thrived in the digital landscape is the original crossword. Computers have hardly made the crossword obsolete. In the digital age, the puzzle has only continued to prove its cockroachlike ability to adapt while remaining exactly the same.

The *New York Times* launched its digital crossword in 1997, fifty-five years after the puzzle's print debut in that paper. The digital *Times* puzzle was developed to be the equivalent of carrying around a folded-over Arts section in your pocket, something that follows you on all your screens. You can begin the puzzle on your phone in the subway, plug away on your desktop at work, and finish it on your tablet at night.

Originally, the online version, like its print counterpart, got bundled with the paper; a subscription to the digital *Times* also gave you access to that day's crossword puzzle online. But in 2012, for the first time in the then-seventy-year history of the *Times*'s crossword, the puzzle—at least, the digital version—got monetized. If you subscribed to the *Times* digitally, you would no longer automatically get the crossword; now, you had to pay a separate fee and download separate software to play the puzzle on your devices. You also didn't automatically get a subscription to the *Times* if you bought a *Times* crossword subscription. Until this point, a newspaper's crossword solvers also had to be its readers, even if they did nothing with the rest of the paper except flip through it to get to the puzzle. But now, the *New York Times* and the *New York Times* crossword became distinct entities.

The *Times*'s crossword app has been housed in-house since 2014. Before then, the *Times* had outsourced the game to another company's platform, but since the app was doing so well, corporate decided to expand the operation. In 2019, the *Times* crossword app had over half a million subscribers, double what they'd had the previous year. At $39.99 a subscription, that's over $20 million in crossword bucks per year. And the *Times*'s app is hardly the only game in town. Crossword apps are legion—Redstone Games's Crossword Puzzle, Penny Dell Crossword Daily, Crossword Quiz+, Clean Crosswords, Little Crosswords—and when you include word game apps in general, the list explodes.

The digital crossword soon launched an entire Games department at the *Times*. Although the flagship of Games is the crossword, the department's programmers, marketers, designers, and editors have developed a flotilla of ancillary puzzles, some retooled old favorites, some new for the site: Letterbox, Set, KenKen, Sudoku, Spelling Bee, and more.

The print crossword, technologically speaking, has changed only in that Shortz emails completed files to Manhattan rather than using fax or snail mail. By contrast, over a dozen full-time *Times* employees are dedicated to running the Games department smoothly: back-end programmers making sure that the puzzle works; front-end program-mers who translate games to all platforms; API and iOS specialists who fix compatibility issues; development managers; a designated games marketing team; designers who build new games; and designers who foresee and precorrect problems, like making the Mini crossword more prominent on the site to addict new users.

In 2014, the *Times* introduced a bite-sized version of a crossword, only on its digital app. The *Times* wanted to be able to offer something for free to hook solvers into paying for a crossword subscription, so Joel Fagliano created a miniature amuse-bouche. The Mini is usually a five-by-five grid, in comparison to the daily fifteen-by-fifteen, and the clues are, on average, much more straightforward. A difficult daily might take half an hour, minimum; the toughest Mini might take two minutes, max.

Crossworders initially greeted the Mini with mixed reviews. In a *Slate* article with the demure title "The *New York Times* 'Mini Cross-word' Is an Utter Disgrace to the *NYT* Crossword Brand," contributor Ruth Graham lambastes the Mini in maximal bombast; like the *Tamworth Herald* writer who dreamed up the hyperbolically hysterical hya-cinths in "AN ENSLAVED AMERICA," Graham is at once serious in the substance of her gripe and giddy with the vitriol of her style. The Mini, she argues, devalues the *Times*'s brand, dubbing it "the *People* magazine crossword puzzle of the *New York Times*." Mini, she writes, "is a four-letter word for 'Are you kidding me?'" (There are other four-letter words unsaid.) "It doesn't tickle your mind," she continues, "so much as punch you in the brain with its blatancy. It's so clearly designed as a mere loss leader for the actual crossword that finishing it has the exact opposite effect that a good puzzle should have—it's less a tiny surge of accomplishment than the sense that you've wasted an entire minute of your time." The Mini's sins are threefold: First, it's too easy; it's too obviously mere marketing bait for the paid puzzle; and, most importantly, it's a waste of time.

Graham's complaints about the Mini echo the moralistic finger-wagging of cross Brits in the twenties. The crossword still taps directly into our horror of wasted time, or that we haven't maximized every minute if it's possible to do so. If we're not working, we should be working on something else: relaxation, exercise, an artistic project, after-school activities, cooking, meditation, a second job, a third. We should be constantly grooming to become the smarter, faster, better versions of ourselves.

The crossword proper is now culturally accepted as better than doing nothing: done day after day, the crossword might even actively strengthen your brain, a mental equivalent of holding a plank pose. Yet the puzzle is still deeply tethered to our abhorrence of wasting time. We use techniques such as memory studies to help ourselves rationalize this addiction to the crossword, or to the routine of opening up the puzzle, but however we react—pride, rationalization, acceptance, rejection—the crossword is an activity that forces us to confront why we waste time, or, rather, why we keep ourselves occupied all the time, even when production produces nothing. But the Mini, Graham argues, is not just a nuisance and a disgrace; it's a menace. Unlike the crossword proper, it's a time-suck that's a waste of time.

The day after *Slate* published Graham's piece, the Mini took its revenge. Though the clues themselves were banal enough, the completed grid spelled out as close to a fuck-you as the family-friendly puzzle would allow:

Joel Fagliano © 2015 *The New York Times*

(Fagliano claims it was a coincidence, but that K, U, F, C cluster in the northeast corner cuts it a bit close for Sunday breakfast.)

The Mini began life marketed as a gateway drug to the regular crossword, but it's now become a distinct form in its own right. Although the Mini might be regarded as a waste of time by self-identifying cruciverbalists, who have justified their regular puzzle to themselves, non–regular solvers see the Mini in the opposite light; while the crossword itself might be too big and too time-consuming for every day, the Mini is not a time-suck but a whetstone, sharpening the mind for the day to come. A few years after beta-testing in the app, the Mini found a home in the print paper: not in the hinterlands of Arts & Leisure with the regular puzzle, but in prime real estate on A3, right under the space Tiffany & Co. has advertised in since 1896. To mimic the print experience, the analogous right-hand corner of the website featured a link to the crossword, inviting readers to "play today's puzzle." The hand extended in greeting is also a hand extended for cash: to play today's puzzle, you have to pay.

On the other hand, the Mini also extends a hand to people who might not have otherwise found a place in the puzzle proper. Fagliano told me that his favorite moments of the job are when college students and recent graduates approach him, excited about the little puzzle. The Mini is porous and immediate. Because Fagliano can make them so quickly and the turnaround time is so short, Minis can absorb a lot of the of-the-moment pop culture that regular puzzles, with their long lag between acceptance and publication and with their need to maintain shelf life, can't always accommodate. The Mini also gives an entry point into this world of crosswords.

Where technological advances have changed the crossword most dramatically is in construction.

The overlap between crossword wonks and computer programming types is vast. Many crossword constructors were early adopters of Excel; they'd trace puzzles by hand using graph paper, then translate the grids into spreadsheets. During the 1990s, crossword constructors began creating programs dedicated to construction, and by all accounts, they really did build a better mousetrap. In the Ernie Bushmiller days, newspapers needed an experienced cartoonist to draw proper crossword grids. Now, for about fifty dollars, anyone can buy a program that will automatically give you a beautifully symmetrical, technically perfect crossword grid. The hard part is no longer making sure the grid itself has perfect symmetry—the hard part is finding clues that will work in that symmetrical surface. The computer helps with this too. Nearly all constructors use a program such as CrossFire or Crossword Constructor, which creates a grid that automatically corrects for rotational symmetry and suggests answers. Construction software can warn you when you're going down a treacherous route, and it can suggest word combinations that will work in any given area. The default auto-fill, though, gets pretty random and bland, sort of the *Lorem ipsum* of crosswords.

That's where a new major part of crossword construction comes in: the word list. Crossworders have compiled enormous databases of words and phrases that will fit into a grid, and each word gets a ranking based on its inventiveness as well as its commonness. Words that are technically in the dictionary but are too crosswordy—plural versions of anagrams like NNES (north-northeasts), for example—get low marks, whereas phrases of common words might get higher ones.

There's a tech-bro machismo among many constructors today, because part of being an expert constructor is having a really robust list of words and phrases that the computer can use to create its fill. Length comparisons abound. (Though, many constructors have assured me, size doesn't matter; it's about quality.)

Computers, on the whole, are much better at playing games than we are. Humans began submitting to computers at games in 1979, when

Luigi Villa, the reigning world backgammon champion, lost a $5,000 winner-take-all match in Monte Carlo against BKG 9.8, a computer program developed at Carnegie Mellon. But humans still have the edge in crosswords. Though Matt Ginsberg tries to best humans each year at the ACPT with Dr.Fill, his solving program, constructors have yet to create a crossword that can't stump the machine. Computers can spit out functional crosswords, and they can fill in the grids, but whether they're any good, or if they're right, is another story.

And, it turns out, computers can help humans sniff out a cruci-verbal scandal.

The crossword-puzzle world of the early twenty-first century was a Venn diagram, with the crossover section in the middle nonexistent. "I don't ever do the *USA Today* puzzle," said Michael Sharp, author of the *Rex Parker Does the New York Times Crossword* blog. "I don't even know people who do the *USA Today* puzzle." Crossword devotees of one set of puzzles typically didn't venture into the Universal Press Syndicate and *USA Today* puzzles, and vice versa.

Nevertheless, in February 2016, crossword editor Ben Tausig smelled a rat. A crossword database had recently been created by software engineer and recreational solver Saul Pwanson, which gave people the ability to cross-check puzzles across many outlets. Tausig learned that a puzzle he'd written in 2004 had been changed very slightly by puzzle editor Timothy Parker in 2008 and run as a Universal Press Syndicate puzzle with the byline Bruce Manders; then, in 2015, the puzzle had appeared again, this time under Tausig's name. Tausig did some digging and discovered that the story went much deeper: Parker had liberally borrowed, to say the least, from over sixty crosswords.

Timothy Parker began his career as the crossword writer for Universal Press Syndicate, eventually serving as founding editor for the Universal Uclick line of syndicated crosswords. (Universal Uclick is the renamed synthesis of Universal Press Syndicate's print and online offerings.) In 2000, Parker earned the Guinness World Record for world's most syndicated puzzle compiler. Continuing to serve as Universal's editor, in 2003, Parker also became the crossword editor at *USA Today*. Like Fernando Pessoa, the Portuguese writer who published work under more than seventy-five different names, at *USA Today*, Timothy Parker released puzzles with the bylines of more than sixty constructors, all of whom were Parker. Parker is a Baptist pastor, dedicated to both crosswords and the cross; in addition to his mainstream media work, he's also published *King James Games*, a collection of Bible-themed word puzzles.

Merv Griffin, television producer of *Jeopardy!* and *Wheel of Fortune* fame, hired Parker to write puzzles for the last game show that Griffin conceived. On *Merv Griffin's Crosswords*, contestants competed to fill in answers one by one to that day's crossword puzzle, earning and losing money based on whether their responses were correct. As the show progressed, contestants called "spoilers" took the stage, lurking behind the two main solvers; if one of our heroes got a clue wrong and a spoiler got it right, the spoiler could jump in to take over in the front row.

According to a Universal Press Syndicate profile of Parker, Griffin hand-selected Parker to write for the show. "Merv called me on my phone in my home office in Baltimore and invited me out to Beverly Hills to help with his new show," Parker gushed. "I'll never forget getting off the elevator in his building and looking up to see Merv sitting behind his enormous desk. I was even more thrilled when he told me he solves four crosswords a day but the *USA Today* puzzle is his favorite." Griffin died shortly after production began. The show aired in September 2007 to disappointing ratings and was canceled by May 2008.

Journalist Oliver Roeder, writing for the statistical website *FiveThirtyEight*, helped prove Parker's plagiarism beyond a shadow of a doubt. (One of Parker's less convincing moments: "I'll be quite honest with you," Parker told Roeder. "I'm not a fan of the *New York Times* crossword. I never have been a fan of the *New York Times* crossword. I don't even know how I would access old *New York Times* crosswords, unless they're in some older books. I wouldn't even have access to older *New York Times* crosswords." The entire archive of *Times* crosswords, Roeder pointed out, is available online, both at the *Times* website and at XWord Info.) In May 2016, after a two-month investigation into the allegations, *USA Today* dissolved all ties with Parker.

Writing for *Slate*, constructor Matt Gaffney broke down the difference between a theme that might get reused without suspicion and a deliberately plagiarized puzzle. For example, a *New York Times* crossword from 1994 created a theme entry out of an Oscar Wilde quotation broken into three fifteen-letter segments: TO LOVE ONESELF IS | THE BEGINNING OF | A LIFELONG ROMANCE. A quotation by a famous author that breaks into even segments spanning the width of a crossword grid doesn't immediately smack of direct plagiarism; indeed, the quotation had already run in two *Times* crossword puzzles (in 1987 and 1992). But other copycat grids were much more suspicious. A 1997 *Times* puzzle featured four theme clues in a pinwheel pattern: TABLE HOPPER, SHOW STOPPER, NAME DROPPER,

TEENY-BOPPER. Timothy Parker published a puzzle in 2006 that not only featured these four clues in the same pattern, but three theme clues that were identical to those in the *Times*. The combination of clever-but-unusual theme answers combined with identical cluing structures reeks not of mere coincidence but of something much more deliberate.

As Shortz explained to me, there was no question that the puzzles Parker edited were of inferior quality to the puzzles that solvers talk about online; the clues were simple without being elegant or imaginative, and the grids were indifferent. Puzzles don't need to be hard to be respected, Shortz stressed, but they do need to be constructed with care to be taken seriously.

THE HARDEST CROSSWORD

1-Across: Marie had fun with them on April Fool's

19-Across: Dinner would often be served ＿＿ because Marie didn't know what time it was

21-Across: Marie wanted to go to the Cloverleaf Tavern on this night: Abbr.

2-Down: Marie confused this with her toothbrush

27-Down: "＿＿ Geometries": geology book Marie kept since HS

In December 2016, many crossword solvers found a baffling puzzle in their newspaper. Every clue in the puzzle was about someone named "Marie," and every clue referenced something that only "Marie" would know. The puzzle seemed simple—if you were Marie.

The crossword looked like a neck riddle: a one-sided riddle to which the solver can't possibly ever figure out the answer. In *The Hobbit*, J. R. R. Tolkien pits our hero, Bilbo Baggins, against the seething cave creature Gollum in a riddle contest. Bilbo and Gollum exchange riddles back and forth. If Gollum gets stumped, he has to show Bilbo the way out of the caves; if Bilbo loses, Gollum gets to eat him. They trade riddles until Bilbo, desperate, asks Gollum: What do I have in my pocket? Of course Gollum doesn't know the answer; furious, he concedes the victory, and Bilbo's neck riddle has saved his neck. In fairy tales, such a maneuver is "outriddling the judge": if an accused figure can stump her judge with a riddle, she'll be set free.

Marie's crossword was, indeed, a neck riddle—but also for Marie. "Marie's Crossword" was part of a public awareness campaign by the Alzheimer's Foundation of America. The foundation brought in Will Shortz and Fred Piscop, a prolific constructor and editor who specializes in custom crosswords, to develop three puzzles—"Marie's Crossword," "Pat's Crossword," and "Katherine's Crossword"—each based on a real-life person with Alzheimer's. Family members who'd witnessed their relatives go through the disease provided testimonials, and Shortz and Piscop translated this information into crossword format. Every clue and answer came from some aspect of the person's life that she couldn't remember anymore.

The crosswords ran in several major publications—the *New York Times*, the *Wall Street Journal*, the *Daily News*—camouflaged to look exactly like that paper's normal crossword and placed where the puzzle typically appeared. They were titled "The Hardest Crossword," and solvers were finally tipped off by a revealing ad at the bottom of each puzzle. *Can't find the answers?* the banner read. *Neither can Marie.*

The idea behind the campaign was to create as close an analog as possible to the experience of actually having Alzheimer's. "Crossword puzzles make it hard to find simple answers," a promotional video for the campaign declared. "So does Alzheimer's disease." Would-be solvers were stumped by seemingly simple but unsolvable clues, like a person with Alzheimer's who finds herself facing a world she can no longer figure out.

Each crossword was also a tribute to that patient, a cryogenic scrapbook of lost memories. The PSA gave the family members a personal keepsake. When my grandfather entered the memory-care floor of an assisted living center, the caregivers asked us for information about his past—memorable moments from his career, things he'd been proud to achieve, places he'd gone, signature phrases and stories. One of them made a memory box to go outside his door, a little diorama découpaged with a bow tie for the department store he'd owned, pens for the books he'd written, a microphone and lectern for the speeches he'd given.

There was also a whiff of magical thinking in the campaign. Like a paralytic woman rising and walking at a revival after twenty years using a wheelchair, if Marie or Katherine or Pat could just solve her puzzle, she'd be cured.

The limbic system is a set of brain structures underneath the cerebral cortex and above the brain stem that governs emotion, behavior, motivation, and memory. On each side of the brain, a ridge runs around the floor of the temporal horn of the lateral ventricle, cradling the other structures in the limbic system. In 1564, the Venetian anatomist Julius Caesar Aranzi named this ridge the hippocampus, after the Greek for "seahorse," because the structure looks like a seahorse's tail and head curling around a little sticky-outy belly. (For a few decades in the early nineteenth century, the "hippocampus" was a "hippopotamus."* In 1779, German anatomist Johann Christoph Andreas Mayer mistook the terms, and several other authors followed the bestial mix-up until physiologist Karl Friedrich Burdach figured out the error in 1829.) That little belly, the fornix, is a C-shaped bundle of nerve cells connecting the hippocampus's output with the rest of the brain; if it gets damaged, memory loss ensues.

One of the buzziest memory-loss cases in the twentieth century is that of Henry Molaison. Born February 26, 1926, Molaison had intractable epilepsy, possibly brought on by a childhood bicycling accident. By age twenty-seven, Molaison's seizures had worsened to the point where he couldn't work anymore. He approached prominent neurosurgeon William Beecher Scoville for a cure. Scoville determined that the epilepsy was caused by Molaison's medial temporal lobes and proposed their surgical excision. On September 1, 1953, Scoville removed these areas of the brain, effectively lobotomizing Molaison's hippocampus. The medical zeugma[†] took away Henry's seizures and his

---

*Writers of natural history in antiquity and the Middle Ages held the theory that specific marine parallels existed for all land creatures. "It used to be a common belief that everything on the earth had its counterpart in the sea," British author T. H. White (of *The Once and Future King* fame) explained in his translation of a medieval bestiary. "The horse and the sea-horse, the dog and the dog-fish, the snake and the eel, the spider and the spider-crab. . . . What was more, if there were whales on sea and land, why should there not be men in both? Mermen? And if men, why not kinds of men? Why not bishops, for instance?" White continues: "The creation was a mathematical diagram drawn in parallel lines. . . . Things did not only have a moral: they often had physical counterparts in other strata. There was a horse in the land and a sea-horse in the sea. For that matter there was probably a Pegasus in heaven." T. H. White, Appendix, *The Book of Beasts* (New York: Putnam, 1960), 250ff.

†A zeugma is a figure of speech in which one word is used to apply in two different senses: "He took my cloak and my honor"; "Eggs and oaths are soon broken"; "[The

short-term memory, turning Molaison into a mirror-image Dorian Gray; Molaison remained suspended at twenty-seven in his mind, yet he continued to develop and age in the physical world.

Patient H.M., as Molaison is known in medical literature, became the most famous amnesiac in history. His anterograde amnesia was perfect. He retained fully functioning language, long-term memory, cognitive skills, and physical and emotional capabilities, but no ability to lay down short-term memory tracks. Scoville had managed to sever the precise portion of the hippocampus that made H.M. the exact figure memory studies didn't know it needed until it had been ghoulishly created for them. H.M. inspired Christopher Nolan's 2000 thriller *Memento*, starring Guy Pearce as a short-term anterograde amnesiac who is solving a crime. Pearce has to rely on an elaborate system of notes, because he loses his memory every few minutes; gradually, he begins to question whether he can trust his own notes, or trust himself.

Long-term memory can be divided into two parts: explicit, or declarative, memory; and implicit, or procedural, memory. Declarative memory, or "knowing what," involves consciously recalling facts and past events and using them to perform tasks. Procedural memory, or "knowing how," engages the unconscious memory of skills and experience to perform tasks.

H.M.'s lobotomized brain did hang on to many parts of his personality, and one of the most important ones was that he remembered he liked the crossword. H.M. did puzzles regularly and frequently.

---

boys] covered themselves with dust and glory" (this last from Mark Twain, *The Adventures of Tom Sawyer*).

Suzanne Corkin, an MIT professor with a dubiously firm grip over H.M.'s care,* supplied him with crossword books, as did his friends and family and other researchers.

In 2004, Brian Skotko, then an undergraduate at Duke, read about H.M. and wanted to see what the crosswords could reveal about H.M.'s memory, and what crosswords might show us about the intersection of short- and long-term memory formation. Skotko worked with Corkin to investigate how memory tracks might be laid down, even for a brain that supposedly couldn't create new recollections.

Skotko, Corkin, and the rest of her team created five different puzzles for the crossword experiments. The pre-1953 puzzle consisted of clues and answers that referred only to figures and events that took place before 1953. The post-1953 puzzle consisted of fifteen clues that had historical figures and events popularized after 1953, which H.M. was not expected to solve, and five clues with the same constraints as the pre-1953 puzzle. The researchers then created three pre-post puzzles, with slight variations. The first used post-1953 clues for pre-1953 answers; the second was identical but with clues randomly rescrambled; and the third had a new set of clues with the same constraints as the original pre-post puzzle.

The experiments gave the same grid but with different clues; how well could H.M. solve a puzzle with only the preoperative facts? Was he using postoperative clues subconsciously? For example, for the clue

---

*The ethics of Corkin's control over H.M. have been much disputed. Some, including Luke Dittrich, Scoville's grandson who has written extensively about H.M.'s case, consider her care not dissimilar to the particular admixture of kindness and iron that the clones' caretakers have in Ishiguro's *Never Let Me Go*. Others, including Brian Skotko, see Corkin as eminently professional.

"The National Academy of Recording Arts and Sciences recognized this male American dancer with a Lifetime Achievement Award in 1989," was H.M. using only "male American dancer" to solve the puzzle, or had he somehow also absorbed the award, even though it hadn't occured until after his memory loss? If H.M. could form no postoperative memories, he should do well with a grid that used only the preoperative fragments of the clues—only, for example, "male dancer." But if he didn't do well, the result would suggest that H.M. was using postoperative facts to solve the puzzle. As a control, ten participants from the Harvard Cooperative Program on Aging in Cambridge, Massachusetts, were also asked to solve the puzzles. The healthy volunteers were matched to H.M. by age (seventy-four, on average) and education level (twelve years); only two of the volunteers solved crosswords habitually, giving H.M. a slight upper hand in that regard.

H.M. performed as expected on the pre-1953 puzzle: he answered well and exactly the same time after time. He consistently omitted CHAPLIN and GERSHWIN, but the other puzzlers in the group also agreed that those were among the most difficult clues, and maybe H.M. hadn't ever been familiar enough with those performers, pre- or postoperation, to call them readily to mind. H.M. was as consistently bad at the post-1953 puzzle and didn't improve after repeated tests. (He also failed to get any faster at filling in the grid, suggesting that he also wasn't developing any muscle memory of repeating the same physical action over and over.)

But on the pre-post puzzle—the one with post-1953 clues for pre-1953 answers—H.M. got significantly better over time. Although he demonstrated no learning on the post-1953 puzzle, he did show learning when he could link information from after 1953 to things he'd absorbed before the operation. When he was given only the clue "Male American dancer," he never got ASTAIRE. On the fifth consecutive day of solving, though, he was able to answer ASTAIRE from "The National Academy of Recording Arts and Sciences recognized this male dancer with a Lifetime Achievement Award in 1989." So H.M. could have been learning from the postoperative material. Or the pre-operative information could have been too general to ever support his learning (after all, if he didn't know CHAPLIN from "Famous entertainer in silent movies of the 1920s," arts and leisure might not have been his strong suit to begin with, and "Male American dancer" is hardly the most specific cue). H.M. might also have had such inflexible learning that he required the same clue in the same precise order to learn anything, so the partial clue wouldn't work.

Amazingly, it turned out, H.M. *did* learn. From the crossword experiments, Skotko and the other researchers figured out that H.M. could learn post-1953 information when he could anchor it to something that had been meaningful to him before the operation. Over the course of the experiment, H.M. successfully associated postoperative knowledge with six preoperative answers: POLIO, HISS, GONE WITH THE WIND, IKE, ST. LOUIS, and WARSAW. The clue for POLIO, for example—"Childhood disease successfully treated by the Salk vaccine"—contained the pre-1953 fragment "Childhood disease" but the post-1953 information about the vaccine. (Although Salk did technically announce successful tests of his vaccine in March 1953, it didn't become widely available until 1955, and at the time of H.M.'s surgery, the vaccine wasn't common knowledge.) Even though H.M. almost certainly didn't know about Salk, he did know about polio, so he could link the post-1953 information to the pre-1953 knowledge through the emotional anchor.

Before the crossword experiments, H.M. had shown that he could connect pre- and post-1953 knowledge, particularly of people. When asked whether President John F. Kennedy was alive or dead, he immediately answered that he had been assassinated; though he could have known who JFK was before 1953, JFK was inaugurated in 1961 and killed in 1963. The crossword experiments, though, corroborated that through repetition, nondeclarative memory—knowing "how" to do something—could be strengthened without conscious awareness and could create declarative memories—the conscious recall of facts.

␣␣␣␣␣

Crosswords are more famously touted in the memory-loss world not as reconstructive tools but as preventive medicine. "Do Crossword Puzzles Really Help Prevent Alzheimer's?" one *Huffington Post* headline asked in 2015. (*HuffPo* affirmed.) Writer John McPhee told me that he does the Mini *New York Times* crossword every day, first thing in the morning, as a vitamin. ("I'm addicted," he confessed.) A federal judge does the Mini puzzle every morning as a diagnostic tool—if he can solve, this morning, the morning's Mini, he's sharp enough to stay on the bench. In 2011, five years before "Marie's Crossword," puzzle expert Merl Reagle developed a crossword for the Alzheimer's Foundation as part of its National Brain Games Challenge. Reagle's crossword wasn't meant to simulate Alzheimer's but to promote prevention and brain health; as he told the trade publication *Aging Today*, "This is a thinking person's contest to help the thinking impaired."

Crosswords are less a silver bullet to combat memory loss and more Centrum Silver for the mind. They help the brain cross-train so that it might take longer to notice that your marbles are disappearing. In an experiment with participants in the Bronx Aging Study, researchers found that doing crossword puzzles delayed the onset of accelerated memory loss by 2.54 years. But the team also found that once memory loss did finally kick in for the crossworders, the rate of decline was faster than for the non-crossworders. The human brain is great at compensating. Even though neurons in certain areas may be decaying, the brain deploys its cognitive reserves to cover for the losses. Doing crosswords is like the boy with his finger in the dike; they won't stop dementia, but they can build a stronger cognitive dam in the meantime.

Part of the connection between crosswords and memory may be that people who are attracted to puzzles, or people who choose to do puzzles as their mental Pilates regimen, are less likely anyway to develop memory loss. Another longitudinal study, this one in Britain, analyzed data from over sixty-five thousand adults to examine the connection between cognitive functioning and "cognitively stimulating leisure activities" like Sudoku and crossword puzzles. Participants self-reported how frequently they did four types of games—crosswords, Sudoku and Sudoku-type puzzles, brain-training computer games, and non-brain-training computer games—as "more than once a day," "once a day," "once a week," "once a month," "occasionally," or "never." The results showed that the frequency with which people reported playing these games was positively associated with high performance in grammatical reasoning and episodic memory, areas particularly vulnerable to age-related cognitive decline.

If you're the kind of person who's doing the crossword—especially if you think it's going to stave off dementia—you're also probably the kind of person who's taking lots of other steps to prevent memory loss. You might also be the kind of person who's not predisposed to memory loss at all. I have one grandfather who did word puzzles called "crypto-quips" well into his nineties, and his memory remained intact until the last few weeks of his life. My other grandfather, never a puzzler, was the one who developed dementia. Brian Skotko, the researcher who studied H.M. and crosswords, wasn't really interested in puzzles at the time; however, as he aged, he found himself, almost subconsciously, turning to the crossword as his own form of preventive medicine. Crosswords may not help, but they can't hurt.

A CROSSWORD CROSSING

A CELEBRATION OF THE *TIMES* CROSSWORD,
DAILY PROGRAMME

DECEMBER 08—DECEMBER 15

In 1942, The New York Times *printed its first crossword puzzle; it
became a daily occurrence in 1950 and one of the paper's most
popular features. To celebrate the Crossword's 75th anniversary,
join* Times *puzzle editors on a seven-night transatlantic sailing
aboard the luxurious* Queen Mary 2®. *With daily game sessions,
private lectures and exclusive access to the* Times *experts, solve
your way across the Atlantic.*

—*New York Times* Journeys catalog

Day One, Port Day: The Journey Begins

One summer, my friend casually forwarded me an email that would change my life. *Look what my mother found—the* New York Times *is offering a crossword-puzzle-themed cruise this winter! YOU HAVE TO GO*, she wrote.

She was joking. I was serious. During graduate school, I'd worked as a tutor on the side, and I drained every cent of my squirreled-away tutoring savings to put down the money for the deposit. If a ship was sailing filled with crossword fiends, I was going to be on it.

That was how, a few months later, in the middle of a hotel in Midtown Manhattan, I found myself within a high-speed elevator, too wired to sleep. After scrutinizing several wall signs, I took the express elevator down to the second floor, then the local back up to the eighth, where I finally alighted upon the windowless, empty gym and ran on a treadmill to nowhere.

In a few hours' time, I would embark on the *Queen Mary 2*, sailing from New York to London.

▭ ▮ ▮ ▭

The *New York Times*'s Journeys division curates travel experiences tailored to particular readership niches. *Times*-selected experts give lectures and run events based around a particular topic. Journeys range from the far-flung ("Antarctica and Climate Change") to the stone's-throw ("Dumbo, the New Brooklyn"). In 2017, in honor of the seventy-fifth anniversary of the crossword puzzle in the *New York Times*, there was a weeklong crossword-themed Journey aboard the *Queen Mary 2*, a luxury ocean liner. About sixty-five puzzle enthusiasts signed up for the trip, joining the two-thousand-plus at-large guests for the at-capacity voyage. Technically, this was not a cruise but a crossing, a one-way trip with a destination, not a round-trip ticket to nowhere. (Note: some names have been changed, here and throughout the epilogue.)

The *Times* selected four expert cruciverbalists to lead our Journey.

Joel Fagliano, the digital games editor at the *New York Times*, would be our crossword master of ceremonies on board. Natan Last, one of the prodigious cruciverbalists of his generation, served as Joel's comrade-in-arms and co-chief of crossword construction. A graduate of Brown University, Natan had been constructing since he was a teenager, and in addition to freelancing puzzles, he led construction classes at the Jewish Association Serving the Aging (JASA) in New York. Some of JASA's puzzles had even made it into the *Times*.

Deb Amlen, the *Times*'s crossword blogger, was the solving guide, both omniscient and empathetic. Deb had begun as a hunt-and-peck solver. She was a humor writer with a passing interest in crosswords when she began to write *Wordplay*, the *Times*'s crossword blog. *Wordplay* became a place on the internet for word nerds who weren't necessarily crossword fiends. Deb made sure the *Times* crossword was intimate, not intimidating. She spearheaded helpful features on the site like beginner's guides to crosswordese.

Ben Zimmer, a lexicographer who wrote regular columns about all things word-related, was our resident linguist. Zimmer wasn't really a crossword-specific expert; he was more there as the eyes and ears of words.

Most notable was the absent expert: Will Shortz. When the whole group gathered for our first muster-en-masse in the *New York Times* building in midtown Manhattan, the morning before we set sail, Shortz met us for a special champagne brunch, sporting a boat-ready anorak over his uniform of polo and khakis, and played a couple of word games to jolly up the crowd. But as Journeyers chatted after the game, waiting for the bus to take us to port to set sail, Shortz slipped away to stay on dry land.

▭ ▮ ▮ ▭

The *Queen Mary 2* is the only ocean liner—that is, a passenger ship primarily used for transportation across seas or oceans—currently in service. She is the flagship vessel of the Cunard Line, a fleet of luxury ships that include the *Queen Victoria* and the now-retired *Queen Elizabeth 2*, and is the most posh* way to cross the Atlantic.

When she sails at capacity, the *Queen Mary 2* carries 2,620 guests and 1,253 crew. If she were vertical, she'd be 86 feet taller than the *New York Times* building at the top of its tower and 123 feet shorter than the Empire State Building. The chefs serve seven thousand boxes of strawberries and approximately ninety metric tons of pineapples per year. Amenities on board include five swimming pools, a two-story spa, a library, a casino, a shopping promenade, a planetarium, and kennels that have British-style and American-style facsimile lampposts to make canine guests from both sides of the pond feel at home.

---

*POSH: Port out, starboard home. There are berths on both sides of the ship, but being posh means knowing on which side of the ship you should book your berth so that you'll be on the left side leaving, right side returning. This, as John McPhee has pointed out to me, was because in the days when there was no air conditioning, passengers wanted to be on the side away from the sun: port sailing east, starboard sailing west.

The *Times*'s Journey is the first crossword-themed ocean crossing, but not the first crossword cruise. For eleven years, *Newsday* crossword editor Stanley Newman organized an annual Crossword University Cruise through the Holland America line. Newman's cruises included group sessions on puzzles, such as "Puzzling 101" and "Tackling the Toughies"; crossword construction lessons; one-on-one personalized solving tutorials; and a cruiverbal scavenger hunt. Passengers like Maurine from Florida loved it: *My favorite memory was the way our reputation spread at the ship's daily Trivia Contests. (I believe that each and every time we entered a team, we won!)*

The *Queen Mary 2*'s Daily Programme, which appears every night under our doors, is our only news source all week. It lists every event on the ship, from Sea Shanties with Tommi-with-an-i to the Christmas Marketplace to Shuffleboard on Deck Twelve. Below the weather forecast, the Daily Programme notes the next evening's dress code: Casual, Cocktail, or Formal. In addition to the Programme, crossworders get the following day's *New York Times* crossword, which is how I can keep track of the days of the week.

Day Two, Sea Day: Black-and-White Ball

At first, it's weird that Will Shortz isn't here. There are hundreds of gents in polo shirts, khakis, and I scour them, Where's Waldo–style, expecting to see him hiding in plain sight.

But soon, I forget to keep looking for him. Shortz helms such a strong ship that the *Times* crossword sails on, with or without him.

▱▰▰▱

Every day begins with Deb's coffee klatch in the sky-blue-and-cream Carinthia Lounge on Deck Seven, where a dozen or so of the crossworders gather to talk through the puzzle that'd been delivered the previous night. Monday's solve is more gossip circle than troubleshoot. But as the week progresses, the circle on Deck Seven gets a little bigger, and a little more befuddled.

Though it may not seem kosher, Deb's all in favor of looking up the answers. "I don't believe it's cheating," Deb tells us. "It's your puzzle. You bought it, you own it." On the crossing, though, since the internet comes in dribs and drabs at about two dollars a minute, it takes more effort to "cheat" than not.

▱▰▰▱

After Deb's klatch, Ben the linguist gives a lecture on some aspect of wordplay. These talks are held in the planetarium, where Ben stands against a plush galactic backdrop, as though constellated in crosswords. Anyone on board can come, even the noncruciverbalists, and he draws a packed crowd, especially for the one on Briticisms and Americanisms. Ben leans into his audience rivalry: *got* (British) versus *gotten* (American); *film* (British) versus *movie* (American). To great waves of chuckling, Ben shows anachronistic *Downton Abbey* clips: for instance, head of the manor Lord Grantham, new to automobiles, would never have said, "Step on it."

I explore the *Queen Mary 2*'s library, the largest library on the high seas. The books are backlit behind glass cabinets, glittering like jewels. There are crossword-puzzle dictionaries and various reference books, which make "cheating" easier. The library also offers a daily cryptic crossword, independent of the *Times*'s journey.

Every day we're on board, time accelerates in small increments. When the clock rings for high noon, noon disappears, and turns into one o'clock. We are gradually shifting into Greenwich Mean Time, and instead of transferring all at once at the beginning or the end of the journey, we tilt more swiftly every day toward dinner.

Tonight is the Black-and-White Ball. The Black-and-White Ball is a tradition that has nothing to do with crosswords, but I can't help ascribing some significance. Dinner's dress code is Formal, and at the stroke of five, the ship changes over from activewear to formal attire. The dance floor clears off after every song, as though every song is the last: self-contained units, little puzzles that you enter, complete, leave.

Day Three, Sea Day: Crossword Construction on the High Seas: Act One

Several members of the crossword crew gather in Cunard ConneX-ions, a windowless, thickly carpeted conference room on Deck Two, flanked by the two Games Corridors, which run the length of the ship. Joel and Natan lead us in the first of several crossword

237

construction sessions. By the end of the crossing, we'll have com-
pleted a puzzle. About half the crossword crossers attend the ses-
sion, and half of those are extremely vocal: Who is the pun-master
of the sea?

DRAMATIS PERSONAE:

* Joel and Natan, Masters of Ceremonies

* The Disaster Twins (*two sisters who called themselves "The*
Disaster Twins" because of their uncanny ability to sail dramatic
ocean voyages together, yet escape unharmed)

* Terry (*the best Scrabble player on board*)

* Bunny (*in a different jewel-toned tracksuit every day*)

* Phil (*a retired radiologist*)

* Fanny (*a retired secretary with an excellent memory for place*
names)

* Claire (*furtively playing Solitaire on her phone*)

* Sylvie (*with lots of handmade jewelry*)

* Eileen (*a romance novelist*)

* Gary (*who's brought his guitar to play the songs he makes up*
about puzzles)

* Norm (*from Atlanta; wears natty glasses*)

* Chorus (*less individually vocal but equally invested crossword*
crossers)

Natan's computer screen has been projected so that everyone can
watch him fill and refill the grid in real time.

Joel: Today, we've got to do the all-important work of brainstorming the theme for our puzzle. I like to start by thinking about what's around us. So—boats, seas, ships, crossings.

Phil: Ooh! SHIPSHAPE.

Natan types SHIPSHAPE into the grid, slightly off-center.

Joel: How about black squares moving across the board like a boat?

Fanny: WET 'N' WILD. DECK. ROLLING.

Bunny: We should have all the crew members! PURSER. YEOMAN. CAPTAIN.

Terry: How about the oceans looping around the grid like circumference lines of a globe! ATL—ANTIC. IAN—IND. IFIC—PAC. Phrases that begin with IFIC: If I Cared, If I Could.

Fanny: SEA CHANGE. BERING SEA. SOUTH CHINA SEA.

Claire: We've got to work NAUSEA in there—get it, nau-sea.

Natan: What about anagrams?

Joel: ARAL anagrams to LARA—that could have a Dr. Zhivago clue. RED—DRE. Let's go in another direction—what about ships?

Chorus: JUNK, LINER, SLOOP, CLIPPER, CUTTER, OILER, TANKER, CARGO, WHALER.

Bunny: I like WHALER!

Natan: Does anyone remember that *Times* puzzle with NINAS in it—the one where "nina" got put in the middle of other words?* NINA and PINTA might work—SPINTABLE—but probably not SANTAMARIA. Okay, scratch that.

Joel: What are words and phrases that include a kind of ship hidden in them?

Terry: CARGO—ESCARGOT. KETCH—KETCHUP.

Claire: JUNK EMAIL.

Joel: ENDLESS LOOP for SLOOP.

Natan: KRAFT MAC 'N' CHEESE.

Terry: KRAFTDINNER. It's a Canadianism. That's what they call Kraft Mac 'n' Cheese.

The Disaster Twins: What about BOATNECKSWEATER?

Fanny [*aside*]: Boatneck sweater—that's such girl knowledge.

Phil: Ships crossing bodies of water, ships crossing the ocean. What if the embedded ships are the Across clues, and then the oceans are the Downs?

Norm: NAIL CLIPPER.

Joel: Okay, that's eleven letters—what can match that?

Claire: JUNKYARD DOG.

Phil: LINER—LINER NOTES, but that's ten.

---

*Al Hirschfeld, the caricaturist, hid *NINA* in nearly all the sketches he drew after his daughter, Nina, was born.

Joel: Is LINE READING a thing?

Natan: If we do LINER NOTE, we can do LA CLIPPER for symmetry.

Joel: SPOILER in the center spot works nicely.

Natan [*surveying grid*]: Okay. Bodies of water have to cross the parts of words that are actually the ships. So the N of ENDLESSLOOP can't cross with the N of ATLANTIC, because the ship wouldn't be crossing the ocean.

Eileen: Aren't there a specific Seven Seas? [*She pulls out an iPad.*]

Terry: No, that's what's great about the seas—there are so many of them, you can pick any seven.

Natan: We have to decide: Do we want to use any three bodies of water for our crossings? Are we only using oceans, or ocean/sea/lake?

Gary: Ocean, sea, lake.

Norm: Only oceans.

Eileen [*emerging from iPad*]: There's a specific set of seas that are the Seven Seas.

Sylvie [*aside*]: How did you get on the internet?

Natan: So if we do oceans, we'll have to use only three oceans—Atlantic, Indian, Pacific. If we include Arctic, then the only one we've left out is the Southern Ocean. Missing two is fine, because it's a sample, but missing only one makes the grid feel lopsided and random.

Fanny: We should put all of them in!

Natan: It'll be very tough to cram all five oceans into a fifteen-by-fifteen. But we can easily do three.

Joel: Okay. Back to LINER. LINERNOTE is nice, and it lets ATLANTIC be 1-Down, which looks nice. [*Joel watches as Natan tests fill.*] No, we're locked into some massive white space chunks in the corners. ONLINE RADIO. Is that a thing? Clued "Pandora, for example"?

The Disaster Twins: Line dancing! Inline skating!

Gary: No, it has to include that R of LINER.

A bell rings. Session is over for the day.

Sylvie: I just never would have thought to think about words this way before this trip! Marvelous.

Bunny: What happened to WHALER?

Day Four, Sea Day: A Very Cunard Christmas

It's "Christmas" on board, which means that there's a two-story Christmas tree spanning Decks Two and Three. When noon flips to one o'clock, hundreds of guests gather around the tree to sing Christmas carols, led by Sea Shanty Tommi.

In the real world, it's the first night of Hanukkah. At dinner, you can choose latkes. We discuss the *aha*: that click when a puzzle snaps into place. Both Joel and Natan described having the feeling of falling asleep with a puzzle and waking up knowing the answer. You see your mind at work; you can actively feel that your subconscious is real, because you know something now that you didn't know before simply by deep-diving into the brain's benthic zone. Crosswords become a tool the mind can use to let you see the subconscious, usually invisible, visibly at work.

"Do you remember the last time you got the *aha*?" I ask the table. "Sure!" says Fanny, one of the most enthusiastic constructors. "I got it this crossing, on the Sunday puzzle. I had figured it all out—it was a rebus—and then I was looking for the last theme answer, I knew it was an actor's name that was going to have a body part as a rebus in it somewhere, but I thought it would come later in the name. I figured out (EAR)THA KITT, DENZEL WA(SHIN)GTON, and I was looking for the rebus later in the name. But then I had my *aha* moment—LIVER—OLIVER PRATT."

Day Five, Sea Day: Crossword Construction on the High Seas: Act Two

Everyone is shouting ideas for clues at a rapid-fire pace.

PEGLEG: "A pirate has one." "Flamingo's support."

GRASS: "Kind of skirt." "Weed." "Writer Gunter."

AIR: "Folk tune." "Fresh ____." "Light as ____." "Scuba diver's need."

SKIPOLE: "Mogul's personal assistant." (Unfortunately, it doesn't quite work: the mogul isn't the one using the pole.) "Winter plant?"

LAUREN: "Humphrey's bride." "She taught Humphrey how to whistle."

PEC: "Short kiss." ("That's 'PECK' with a K!"; "That's the point—it's a *short* kiss.")

OOPS: "Two alleys?"

IT WORKS: Can't be "It might be broken but," because there's an "it" in the answer. "Triumphant shout." "Reason to keep an old appliance."

Day Six, Sea Day: Insomnia

By the final night, I can't sleep. Crosswords are no help. I'm trying Thursday's crossword, and I think I know the theme, but I'm not quite sure. Something with AX-ing letters, because this is how the theme answers are filling in; there aren't enough squares for the answers I think are correct, so I assume there's some sort of rebus going on. SIT BACK AND (RE)LAX. NONE OF YOUR (BE)ESWAX.

I'm halfway through an Agatha Christie mystery from the ship's library, but I can't focus to read. Hercule Poirot is grilling the characters: Where were you when Arlena Marshall (*née* Stuart) was murdered this morning? My heart creeps into my throat. Where was I? What square was I in?

I give up trying to sleep and wander to the Commodore Club on Deck Nine, not to be confused with the similarly alliterative Churchill's Cigar Room across the hallway. None of the crossworders are here, yet I can't escape words. "I've found a typo in the menu," a rosy bald man confides to me. For spirits, they give two columns, one with prices for a one-ounce pour, the other with prices for a two-ounce pour, but on the cognac page, they've printed "$/2oz" on both columns.

"I was a proofreader," the rosy man says. "I'm retired, but when I see a mistake, now, I can't not see it."

Day Seven, Port Day

Though the *Times* assistants promised they'd send it to all of us, I never did see the end of that SHIPSHAPE crossword. I don't know if we kept KRAFT MAC 'N' CHEESE, or Bunny's beloved WHALER. Finishing it wasn't the point.

Doing a crossword might feel like you're running to nowhere, but it's a crossing, not a cruise. I wake up before sunrise, when we're officially set to disembark, but we've already arrived: I'd stopped noticing the thrum of the ocean until now, when it was gone. I walk out to the deck on legs surprised by steadiness. It's not the thrill of an *aha*, but the relief of a journey fulfilled.

finished writing this book at the 2019 42nd Annual American Crossword Puzzle Tournament. The mayor of Stamford read a proclamation declaring that the ACPT's final day would thenceforth be Stamford Crossword Tournament Day. Some things have stayed the same. Miriam Raphael—we may be distant relatives, since our last names are both versions of the same Polish name that got truncated at Ellis Island—has won the over-ninety division again. (She missed the first-ever ACPT, but otherwise, as of 2019, she's had perfect attendance.) Dr. Fill, the computer solver, did the puzzles in lightning speed but missed a few squares, so humans are still superior to machines, cruciverbally speaking.

But some things change. This year, the tournament had its largest turnout ever: nearly seven hundred fifty participants, over two hundred of them rookies. The competitors filled two hotel ballrooms. For the first time, the final ACPT puzzle's constructor was female.

And change is spreading across the crossword world. The *New*

York Times is hiring more editors, partly to deal with its backlog, but mostly to bring more voices into the room. Cruciverbalists Will Nediger and Erik Agard created a Puzzle Collaboration Directory to match mentors with new talent. High school chemistry teacher and crossword constructor Nate Cardin organized Queer Qrosswords, a pack of puzzles to benefit LGBTQ+ charities. Crossword editors Laura Braunstein and Tracy Bennett founded the Inkubator, a subscription service that publishes crosswords by cis women, trans women, and women-aligned constructors.

The crossword puzzle was once a sleepy corner of the newspaper, but now, it's increasingly woke. The current generation of solvers and constructors has a far different relationship with the puzzle than their parents and grandparents did. The crossword's always going to have an aspirational aspect—what would be the fun if it didn't feel like at least a smidgen of a challenge? But the crossword also represents a far wider cross section of society than it ever has.

And the crossword continues to thrive. The resilient little puzzle can be whatever you need it to be. Combatant, interlocutor, punching bag, security blanket: the crossword is there for you.

The crossword isn't a state of mind—it's a way of life.

A C K N O W L E D G M E N T S

First and foremost, I would like to thank my wonderful editor, Will Heyward, for hearing "crossword" and seeing a book. Will has been an unflagging shepherd throughout this process, and this book would not exist without him. Thank you to the entire team at Penguin Press, including Ann Godoff; Scott Moyers; my production editor, Alicia Cooper; and my copy editor, Amy Schneider. Thank you to Ilya Milstein for the delightful cover illustration.

Thank you to my incredible agent, Melanie Jackson, who saw this book before I could see it, and without whom none of this would have been possible.

My dissertation advisers believed in me when I did not, and trusted me with astonishing faith. Thank you for your unflinching support. To Elaine Scarry and Stephanie Burt, for shepherding the project through all its forms; and to Peter Sacks and Louis Menand, for understanding and encouraging me faithfully. Thanks, also, to David

Alworth, Daniel Donoghue, Philip Fisher, and Helen Vendler. Special remembrance for Daniel Albright. My profound thanks to Jorie Graham.

I am humbled by the generosity and warmth the crossword community has shown to this project, and I have been honored to enter this world. All the brilliant crossword constructors, editors, and solvers have been so kind with their time, information, humor, intelligence, wit, spirit, patience, and encouragement.

Will Shortz has been an extraordinary benefactor. I could not have written this book without his amazing generosity and openhearted spirit. Joel Fagliano and Sam Ezersky have been terrific sports. Ben Tausig introduced me to many aspects of the crossword-puzzle world at crucial early stages of the process. Ben Zimmer and Natan Last have also been generous sounding boards throughout. To the crossword crew aboard the *Queen Mary 2* in December 2017: that was a week to remember.

Special thanks to the following: Erik Agard, Deb Amlen, Howard Barkin, Jeff Chen, Alan Connor, Michael Crick, Kevin Der, Dan Feyer, Matt Ginsberg, Elizabeth Gorski, David Haglund, David Hague, Jim Horne, Wyna Liu, Caleb Madison, Ruth Margolin, Liz Maynes-Aminzade, Myles Mellor, Mike Nothnagel, Brendan Emmett Quigley, Michael Sharp ("Rex Parker"), Anna Shechtman, Mike Shenk, Brian Skotko, Michael Smith, David Steinberg, Jacob Stulberg, Ross Trudeau, and Finn Vigeland. Thank you to Geoff Chalkley for help with cryptics. I had the privilege of speaking with Merl Reagle a few months before he passed away, and I hope that something of his spirit radiates through the book.

Thanks to David Remnick and Leo Carey for valuable feedback

on a very early version of this story. Thanks to Fatimah Asghar, Ian Bogost, Alice Notley, Michael Silverblatt, and Stephen Sondheim.

During my first semester of college, one of the first poems I wrote for James Richardson's poetry workshop was a crossword-inspired bit of word golf that turned the "black" into "white" and "white" into "black": thank you, Jim, for supporting me ever since. As a sophomore in college, I took John McPhee's creative nonfiction seminar, which changed my life. An assignment for that course was to write a "set piece," that is, a self-contained but tangential narrative within a larger story about something else entirely. I imagined a long-form essay about code breaking, and my set piece was about the crossword puzzle in World War II—essentially, what's now chapter six. (I never did get around to writing the "actual" story.) Thank you, as well, to Sarah Anderson, Jeff Dolven, Diana Fuss, Joshua Katz, Brenda Shaughnessy, and Susan Wheeler.

Thank you to the Princeton Writing Program and the Works-in-Progress Colloquium at Princeton, especially Amanda Irwin-Wilkins, Christopher Kurpiewski, Srishti Nayak, Brian Pietras for the subtitle inspiration, and Jennifer Schnepf.

Thank you to Mark Levine for egging on my puns. Thanks to Jim Galvin, Rick Kenney, Robyn Schiff, and Cole Swensen. To the incredible editors I've worked with, in particular Vauhini Vara; I will never forget the night I found the subject line "write for newyorker.com?" in my inbox. To Jessica Laser and Alex Walton for teaching me about form, and for my paint-chip crown. Thank you: Bianca Bosker, Ashley Colley, Jen Finkle, Jessie Gaynor, Suleika Jaouad, Thessaly La Force, Jessica Lander, Anthony Madrid, Tara Manon, Chris Martin, Ted Mathys, Ben Mauk, Mark Mayer, Jeff Nagy, Margaret Ross, Chris

Schlegel, Sara Shaw, Rachel Greenwald Smith, Tony Tulathimutte, Caitlin Tully, Lindsay Turner, and Josephine Wolff.

Many thanks, as well, to Amanda Auerbach, Taylor Cowdery, Helen Cushman, Thomas Dolinger, Laura Forsberg, Eliza Holmes, Elizabeth Phillips, Hannah Rosefield, Teresa Trout, Emmy Waldman, Erica Weaver, and Michael Weinstein. Thank you to everyone in all the workshops.

Writing group has been my home: Sara Deniz Akant, Rawaan Alkhatib, Katie Fowley, Callie Garnett, Dan Poppick, Colby Somerville, and Bridget Talone, thank you.

Thanks to Nicholas Nardini for the Saturday crosswords, and to Mariam Rahmani for the Sunday (and everyday) Styles. To Jenny Mackenzie: Who knew that my senior year capstone project on crosswords would persist? Special thanks to Christopher Spaide for wordplay at every opportunity, and to Emily Silk for her endless support.

Thanks to the fellowships that have provided generous support for this dissertation: the Dexter Summer Research Travel Fellowship, the Helen Choate Bell Term-Time Fellowship, and the Dissertation Completion Fellowship from the Harvard University English Department. Thanks to the Jerry Slocum Collection of the Lilly Library at Indiana University for allowing me access to their treasure trove of puzzle materials. Thanks also to the New York Historical Society and to the Dorothy and Lewis B. Cullman Center for Scholars and Writers at the New York Public Library.

Thanks to the Mastheads team for providing a beautiful black box, a month to write, and so much encouragement (Tessa Kelly, Jeff Lawrence, Chris Parkinson, Aaron Thier, Sarah Trudgeon); thanks to my fellow residents in 2018 (Jean Chen Ho, Matthew Kramer, Jenna Lyles, Lincoln Michel); thanks to Alex Reczkowski.

Finally, thank you to my family. To my aunts, uncles, and cousins, for their kindness and enthusiasm. To my grandparents, Billie and Irv Raye, and Ruth and Murray Raphel: I'm honored to follow in your footsteps. To Ben Raphel, for being a champion. And, with infinite gratitude and love, to my parents, Neil Raphel and Janis Raye, for always being there for me, inside and outside the box.

NOTES

1. FUN: Arthur Wynne, Margaret Petherbridge Farrar, and the Origins of the Puzzle

1 **shut down for several days:** "Manton Marble, Publicist, Dead. Editor and Owner of the *New York World* from 1862 to 1876 Dies in England at 82. Noted Political Writer. His Famous 'Letter to Abraham Lincoln' Followed President's Suspension of His Newspaper. His Letter to President Lincoln." *The New York Times*, July 25, 1917.

2 **over one million subscribers daily:** Paul Karasik and Mark Newgarden, *How to Read Nancy: The Elements of Comics in Three Easy Panels* (New York: Fantagraphics Books, 2017), 31.

5 **(to-day, ice-cream, bumble-bee):** David Crystal, *Making a Point: The Persnickety Story of English Punctuation* (New York: St. Martin's Press, 2015), 264.

6 **a typical patent lawyer's fee:** "First Deficiency Appropriation Bill, Fiscal Year 1920," Hearings before Subcommittee of House Committee Appropriations, 66th Cong., 1st Sess. (Washington, DC: U.S. Government Printing Office, 1919), 431.

6 **difficult to create a crossword:** Ian Bogost, Simon Ferrari, and Bobby Schweizer, *Newsgames: Journalism at Play* (Cambridge, MA: MIT Press, 2010), 85.

7 **"second week in December, 2100":** Helene Horovec, "A Crossword Hall-of-Famer: Margaret Farrar," *CROSSW_RD Magazine*, November/December 1992, 5.

8 **"The only thing I give a hang about":** Horovec, "A Crossword Hall-of-Famer," 5.

8 *cruci-,* **"cross,"** plus *verbum,* **"word":** "cruciverbalist, n.," *Merriam-Webster.com*, 2019.

12 **"a cross word puzzle card":** Arthur Wynne, "Puzzle or Game," US 1558071, U.S. Patent and Trademark Office, October 20, 1925.

12 **(Teen Bushmiller's other career option):** Karasik and Newgarden, *How to Read Nancy*, 31.

13 **The thickness of his lines:** Karasik and Newgarden, *How to Read Nancy*, 35.

14 **a frustrated squiggle:** Clare Briggs, "Movie of a Man Doing the Cross-Word Puzzle," *Morning Oregonian*, October 3, 1922.

2. The *Cross Word Puzzle Book* and the Crossword Craze

15 **their telephone exchange:** Alan Connor, *Two Girls, One on Each Knee: The Puzzling, Playful World of the Crossword* (London: Penguin Books, 2013), 143.

16 **"The Cross-Word Puzzle Book is out today":** Connor, *Two Girls, One on Each Knee*, 144.

17 **"My, / What pronoun":** "The Cross Word Puzzle," Newman Levy, from F.P.A.'s "Conning Tower" in *The New York World*, reprinted in *Simon & Schuster 75th Anniversary Vintage Crossword Treasury: A Collection of 75 Classics from 1924 to 1950, From the Original Crossword Publisher*, ed. Prosper Buranelli, F. Gregory Hartswick, and Margaret Petherbridge Farrar (New York: Fireside, 1999).

17 **"that magical definition":** Horovec, "A Crossword Hall-of-Famer," 5.

18 **Cal dives into a stack:** Karasik and Newgarden, *How to Read Nancy*, 42.

18 **physically blocked with mailed-in orders:** Herbert Mitgang, "Margaret Farrar, 87, Editor of Crossword Puzzles, Dies," *The New York Times*, June 12, 1984.

18 **largest book order to date:** Connor, *Two Girls, One on Each Knee*, 144.

19 **Gelett Burgess, a humor editor:** A. N. Wilson, *After the Victorians: The Decline of Britain in the World* (New York: Farrar, Straus and Giroux, 2015), 290.

19 **"The fans they chew their pencils":** David Crystal, *Language Play* (Chicago: University of Chicago Press, 2001), 88.

20 **"you're certain to fall victim":** Stephan Benzkofer, "How Crosswords Got in Tribune's Cross Hairs," *Chicago Tribune*, December 29, 2013.

20 **for the next forty years:** Benzkofer, "How Crosswords Got in Tribune's Cross Hairs."

20 **"a fad with New Yorkers":** Busybody, "Jottings about Town," *The New Yorker*, February 21, 1925, 30.

21 **to promote a missionary campaign:** Roger Millington, *The Strange World of the Crossword* (London: Hobbs, 1974), 20.

22 **a one-thousand-dollar prize:** Blake Eskin, "They Shoot Adverbs, Don't They?," *The New York Times*, December 25, 2005.

23 **"the Ottawa Public Library":** Quoted in Alan Connor, "Crosswords: The Meow Meow of the 1920s," *Crossword* blog, *The Guardian*, December 15, 2011.

23 **"to protect its legitimate readers":** *Report of the New York Library for 1924*, (New York Public Library, 1925), 24.

25 **told the *New Yorker*:** E.J. Kahn, "Renewed Acquaintance," *The New Yorker*, November 26, 1979: 38.

26 **a fashionable hat:** "The Hour Glass," *The New Yorker*, April 4, 1925, 7.

29 **"the *pus* of *flan breton*":** Quoted in Ruth von Phul, "Not a Leetle Beetle" (FW 417.3–4), *James Joyce Quarterly* 6, no. 7 (Spring 1969): 265–66.

29 **"dead with existential or neurotic angst":** von Phul, "Not a Leetle Beetle," 265.

30 **"What a paradox":** Quoted in W. D. Lewis, "Game: Curious Criticism," *Harper's* February 1974, 94.

31 **"something to sit on":** "Nomenclature," *The New York Times*, January 26, 1978, 20.

31 **"a ludicrous women's lib neologism":** Ruth von Phul, "Letters: On Nomenclature: When a Chair Is Not a Chair," *The New York Times*, February 1, 1978.

31 **"crossword puzzle composer and champion":** "Ruth Franc von Phul," *New York Times*, April 1, 1986.

3. How to Construct a Crossword

33 **"Mycroft's specialism is omniscience":** Sir Arthur Conan Doyle, "The Adventure of the Bruce-Partington Plans," *Sherlock Holmes: The Complete Novels and Stories, Volume II* (New York: Bantam Classics, 1986), 360.

34 **"everything is pigeon-holed":** Doyle, "Adventure of the Bruce-Partington Plans," 360.

37 **both technical and aesthetic specifications:** "Submit Your Crossword Puzzles to the *New York Times*," nytimes.com/puzzles/submissions /crossword, 2019.

40 **judgment, revision, and publication:** "How to Make a Crossword Puzzle: The Series," nytimes.com/puzzles/submissions/crossword, 2019.

42 **"fool's gold":** Eugene Maleska, *A Pleasure in Words* (New York: Simon and Schuster, 1987), 397.

42 **"early 1950s custom":** Michelle Arnot, *What's Gnu?: A History of the Crossword Puzzle* (New York: Vintage, 1981), 124.

42 **FIRST AID STATION, SECONDHAND SMOKE, THIRD BASE UMPIRE, FOURTH CLASS MAIL:** Kevin McCann, "Theme Types," 2011, http://cruciverb.com.

43 **GREER GROANS (Garson):** Maura Jacobson, "The Lady Changes Her Name," ed. Will Shortz, *The New York Times*, November 24, 1996.

43 **America's version of BBC English:** Louis Menand made this observation to me in conversation, and it's proven enormously useful as cultural shorthand for the vast majority of crossword consumers in midcentury America.

44 **"The fashion wears out more apparel than the man":** E. T. M., "Stepquote," ed. Eugene T. Maleska, *New York Times*, June 7, 1981. See William Shakespeare, *Much Ado about Nothing*, act 3, scene 3.

44 **dead white men:** Eugene Maleska, "Stepquotes: Puzzles with a Philosophical Point of View," XWord Info, accessed May 3, 2019, http://www.xwordinfo.com/Stepquotes.

44 **TIME FLIES OVER US | BUT LEAVES ITS | SHADOW BEHIND:** Nathaniel Hawthorne, *The Marble Faun* (Boston: Ticknor and Fields, 1860).

45 **"if there's any 'aha' moment":** Brendan Emmett Quigley, "Puzzle 29 & More Rambling about Quote Puzzles," *Brendan Emmett Quigley* blog, February 11, 2009, http://brendanemmettquigley.com/2009/02/puzzle-29-more-rambling-about-quote-puzzles.html.

45 **"There's the quote. It's a quote, alright. The End":** Rex Parker, "Thursday, November 20, 2008," November 19, 2008, http://rexwordpuzzle.blogspot.com/2008/11/thursday-nov-20-2008-pete-muller.html.

45 **a cornucopia of objects:** Charles Layng, *Layng's Cross-Word Puzzle: First Book* (Chicago: Stanley, 1924).

46 **words pertaining to Coca-Cola:** Jamal Booker, "Coca-Cola Crossword Puzzle," *Coca-Cola Journey: History*, November 17, 2011.

46 **"refreshing thirst quencher":** Booker, "Coke Crossword Puzzle Answers," *Coca-Cola Journey: History*, November 22, 2011.

52 **scores of swastikas:** XWord Info, accessed May 12, 2019 http://www.xwordinfo.com/Grids.

4. Pleasantville, New York: Will Shortz

61 **"Quint Mint," a gum brand:** Christopher Short, "From Point A to Point B: Crawfordsville's Cleverest Son Holds Forth on His Hoosier Half," *Paper of Montgomery County Online*, May 17, 2010, https://thepaper24-7.com/Content/Social/Social/Article/From-Point-A-to-Point-B/-2/-2/26132, accessed May 12, 2019.

62 **The essay received a B-plus:** Stephen Hiltner, "Will Shortz: Profile of a Lifelong Puzzle Master," *The New York Times Insider*, August 1, 2017.

63 **"Think of the gotcha gang":** David Steinberg, "Interview with Mel
   Taub," *The Pre-Shortzian Puzzle Project*, January 5, 2013, http://www
   .preshortzianpuzzleproject.com/p/pre-shortzian-constructor-interviews
   .html.

63 **the Gray Lady:** Meyer Berger, "The Gray Lady Reaches 100," *Life,* September 17, 1951, 153.

65 **a computer programmer in the Netherlands:** Clive Thompson, "The
   Puzzlemaster's Dilemma," *New York* magazine, June 7, 2006, http://nymag
   .com/arts/all/features/17244/.

65 **The Ping-Pong prodigy:** Charles Bethea, "Will Shortz and the Ping-
   Pong Prodigy," *The New Yorker,* November 2, 2015, https://www.newyorker
   .com/sports/sporting-scene/will-shortz-and-the-ping-pong-prodigy.

70 **With traditional two-dimensional construction tools:** Kelsey
   Campbell-Donaghan, "Frank Gehry at 83: Still Obsessed with Fish," *Fast
   Company,* January 14, 2013, https://www.fastcompany.com/1671622/frank
   -gehry-at-83-still-obsessed-with-fish.

71 **previously the stuff of fantasy:** Lian Chang, "The Software behind
   Frank Gehry's Geometrically Complex Architecture," *Priceonomics*, May
   12, 2015, https://priceonomics.com/the-software-behind-frank-gehrys
   -geometrically/.

71 **an extra bingo:** Kevin G. Der, Crossword, *The New York Times,* February
   12, 2010.

5. The Crossword Hyacinth: England and the Cryptic Crossword

77 **"Here all is joyous":** William Hogarth, "Remarks on Various Prints," in
   *Anecdotes of William Hogarth, Written by Himself: With Essays on His Life
   and Genius* (London: Nichols, 1833), 64.

78 **"wild hyacinth of American industry":** "Cross-Word Puzzles: An
   Enslaved America," *Tamworth Herald*, December 27, 1924.

79 **"unprofitable trifling":** "Cross-Word Puzzles: An Enslaved America."

81 **"THIS IS NOT A TOY!":** Tony Augarde, *The Oxford Guide to Word
   Games* (Oxford, UK: Oxford University Press, 2003), 60.

81 The *Western Times* of England: Quoted in Connor, "Crosswords: The Meow Meow of the 1920s."

82 "a fragile creature in six letters": Quoted in Connor, *Two Girls, One on Each Knee*, 110.

83 Early British crosswords frequently featured Latin: Alan Connor, "The Return of Latin," *Crossword* blog, *The Guardian*, October 19, 2015.

83 detective stories for the *Guardian*: Emily Cleaver, "Torquemada and the Torturous Literary Puzzle," *Litro*, June 26, 2010.

84 until Mathers's death in 1939: John Halpern, *The Centenary of the Crossword: The Story of the World's Favourite Puzzle* (London: Andre Deutsch, 2013), 30.

84 "I see him sitting cross-legged": Quoted in T. Campbell, *On Crosswords: Thoughts, Studies, Facts, and Snark about a 100-Year-Old Pastime* (New York: Köhlerbooks, 2013), 153.

84 in person or over the telephone: Campbell, *On Crosswords*, 153.

85 "I wouldn't have chosen the timing": Quoted in Connor, *Two Girls, One on Each Knee*, 37.

86 "'Bantu hartebeest'": Stephen Sondheim, "How to Do a *Real* Crossword Puzzle, or, What's a Four-Letter Word for 'East Indian Bezel Nut' and Who Cares?," *New York* magazine, April 8, 1968.

6. World War II and the Gray Lady

90 "Eccentric Club Minesweepers' Fund": Connor, *Two Girls, One on Each Knee*, 100.

91 "'a matter of national importance'": Michael Smith, *The Secrets of Station X: How the Bletchley Park Codebreakers Helped Win the War* (London: Biteback, 2011), Kindle edition, Chapter 7.

91 "contribution to the war effort": Smith, *The Secrets of Station X*, Chapter 7.

93 nearly five thousand puzzles: Alan Connor, "Leonard Dawe: The Man behind the Infamous D-Day Crosswords," *Crossword* blog, *The Guardian*, May 26, 2014.

93 **no two-word answers:** Connor, "Leonard Dawe."

94 **"I have kept that oath until now":** Tom Rowley, "Who Put Secret 'D-Day Clues' in the 'Telegraph' Crossword?," *The Telegraph*, April 27, 2014.

95 **"it will be forgotten":** "Topics of the Times: Sees Harm, Not Education," Editorial, *The New York Times*, March 10, 1925.

95 **"the Insidious Game of Anagrams":** "All About the Insidious Game of Anagrams," *The New York Times*, December 29, 1929.

96 **"should the supply be cut off":** Richard H. Tingley, "Cross-Word 'Brain Teasers' Still Hold Their Popularity," Letter, *The New York Times*, February 1, 1930.

96 **"relaxation of some kind or other":** "75 Years of Crosswords," *The New York Times*, February 14, 2017.

97 **"You can't think of your troubles":** "75 Years of Crosswords," *The New York Times*.

97 **"diagramless puzzles of a general nature":** Horovec, "A Crossword Hall-of-Famer," 6.

98 **the average word length was 5.36:** Charles Erlenkotter, "Headlines and Footnotes," ed. Margaret Farrar, XWord Info, February 15, 1942, http://www.xwordinfo.com/PS?date=2/15/1942.

7. The Oreo War: Race, Gender, and the Puzzle

102 **EYELOVEU:** Campbell, *On Crosswords*, 18.

102 **DELIVERED:** Beverly Seward, "*The New York Times* Crossword, Tuesday, April 1, 1975," ed. Will Weng, XWord Info, http://www.xwordinfo.com/PS?date=4/1/1975.

102 **"his children are constructing puzzles":** Alex Haley, "Crossword Puzzles," *Boys' Life*, October 1966, 48.

103 **"Most beautiful girl on campus":** James T. Barron, "Eugene T. Maleska, Crossword Editor, Dies at 77," *The New York Times*, August 5, 1993.

103 **When Jean showed her roommate:** Eugene Maleska, *A Pleasure in Words* (New York: Simon and Schuster, 1981), 10.

103 **Many of the puzzles:** Maleska, *A Pleasure in Words*, 384.

104 **"[Maleska] was your hero":** Marc Romano, *Crossworld: One Man's Journey into America's Crossword Obsession* (New York: Broadway Books, 2005), 6–7.

104 **"DIPLOMATIC IMMUNITY":** Randall Rothenberg, "Puzzle Makers Exchange Cross Words," *The New York Times*, August 10, 1988.

104 **"NOSE XRAY":** Rothenberg, "Puzzle Makers Exchange Cross Words."

105 **jiggling "jigsaws":** Campbell, *On Crosswords*, 21.

105 **five and a half hours on every issue:** Campbell, *On Crosswords*, 21.

105 **Emily Cox and Henry Rathvon:** Campbell, *On Crosswords*, 22.

105 **bread and butter of crossword grids:** Michelle Arnot, *Four-Letter Words: And Other Secrets of a Crossword Insider* (New York: Perigee Books, 2008), 14.

106 **"there's not much unanimity there":** Rothenberg, "Puzzle Makers Exchange Cross Words."

107 **"HALL OF FAME":** "Mark Diehl's American Crossword Puzzle Academy Treasures," David Steinberg, The Pre-Shortzian Puzzle Project, February 15, 2014.

107 **"Mountainous cookie?":** Clue results for OREO, "Find Clues or Match Patterns," XWord Info, accessed May 3, 2019, http://www.xwordinfo.com/finder.

107 **status symbol for serious cruciverbalists:** Fred Piscop, "The *New York Times* Crossword," ed. Will Shortz, March 2, 2016, XWord Info, http://www.xwordinfo.com/Crossword?date=3/2/2016.

108 **"too black to be white":** Danzy Senna, "An Overlooked Classic about the Comedy of Race," *The New Yorker*, May 7, 2015.

109 **refusing to update its vocabulary:** Adrianne Jeffries, "The NYT Crossword Is Old and Kind of Racist," *The Outline*, June 6, 2017.

109 **"the bioscope of the American crossword":** Mangesh Ghogre, "Letter from Mangesh Ghogre," *American Crossword Puzzle Tournament*, 2012.

109 **comment on Rex Parker's blog:** Jeffries, "The NYT Crossword Is Old and Kind of Racist."

111 **"the fix is super easy"**: Jeff Chen, *"New York Times*, Tuesday, January 1, 2019," XWord Info, https://www.xwordinfo.com/Crossword?date=1/1/2019.

115 **the need for "transparency"**: "A Note on Crosswords and Bylines," *WSJ Puzzles*, January 17, 2019, https://blogs.wsj.com/puzzle/2019/01/17/a-note-on-crosswords-and-bylines/.

115 **"Masks the problem"**: Rex Parker (@rexparker), Twitter January 18, 2019, 7:43 a.m., https://twitter.com/rexparker/status/1086290700508020736.

116 **"boysplained"**: Anna Shechtman, "Puzzle Trouble: Women and Crosswords in the Age of Autofill," *American Reader*, August 2014.

116 **"free-floating virginity"**: Shechtman, "Puzzle Trouble."

117 **$1,500 for a Sunday puzzle:** Will Shortz, *"New York Times* Crossword Contributors to See Pay Raise after Jan. 1," *The New York Times*, December 18, 2018.

117 **juggling career and family:** Shechtman, "Puzzle Trouble."

8. Krossvords and *Mots Croisés*

121 **"I fill in the gaps"**: Vladimir Nabokov, interview with Herbert Gold, *Paris Review* 41 (Summer/Fall 1967), 102.

121 **"the hardly pronounceable: *kzspygv*"**: Vladimir Nabokov, *Speak, Memory: An Autobiography Revisited* (New York: Vintage, 1989), 34–35.

122 **"none of these callings has been mine"**: Nabokov, *Speak, Memory*, 273.

122 **the first crossword puzzle in Russian:** Nabokov, *Speak, Memory*, 273.

123 **etymological whiffs of a Christian cross:** Joseph Clayton Mills, ed. and trans., *Nabokrossvords: Selected Puzzles from the Russian Émigré Newspaper* Rul', *1924–1926* (Chicago: Sibilance Press, 2012), iii.

123 **Knut Hamsun character to Ibsen:** Mills, *Nabokrossvords*, iv.

123 **"unmistakable political overtones throughout"**: Mills, *Nabokrossvords*, iv–v.

124 **Nabokov and Véra were married:** Vladimir Nabokov, *Letters to Véra*, trans. and ed. Olga Voronina and Brian Boyde (London: Penguin Classics, 2014).

127 **"the butterflies it would engender"**: Nabokov, *Speak, Memory*, 119–20.

130 **"a tedious, meticulous, maniacal task":** Georges Perec, "Thoughts on the Art and Technique of Crossing Words," trans. Henri Picciotto with Arthur Schulman, *The Believer* 4, no. 7 (September 2006): 33–34.

130 **"imprecise neighborhood" of a word's definition:** Perec, "Thoughts on the Art and Technique of Crossing Words," 34.

131 **"though progress has been made":** Georges Perec, *Life: A User's Manual*, trans. David Bellos (Boston: Godine, 1987), 106.

9. Tournament of Champions

134 **"history of literary and intellectual thought":** Will Shortz, *"The History of American Word Puzzles to 1860,"* undergraduate thesis, Indiana University, 1974: 2.

135 **"the last couplet":** Shortz, *"The History of American Word Puzzles to 1860,"* 55.

135 **declared Yale victorious:** The *Harvard Crimson*'s baleful reporting notes that Yale easily beat Harvard, but that the wife of a Harvard man, who was on the Bryn Mawr team, "distinguished herself especially, even in defeat." "Yale Adds Another Sprig to Its Athletic Laurels by Taking Intercollegiate Crossword Puzzle Championship," *Harvard Crimson*, January 6, 1925.

144 **French women declared it "hideous":** "Cross-Word Stockings Is Fad of American Women in Paris," *The New York Times*, January 2, 1925.

146 **"it does fit awfully well":** Alan Connor, "Would You Solve Your Workmate's Puzzle?," *Crossword* blog, *The Guardian*, January 18, 2016.

147 **"glitterati of the crossword world":** Deb Amlen, "Puzzle Lovers Find Their Tribe at a Crossword Tournament," *The New York Times*, March 26, 2018.

10. Decoding the Crossword

169 **made of cloth:** Kate Summerscale, *The Suspicions of Mr. Whicher: The Shocking Murder and the Undoing of a Great Victorian Detective* (New York: Bloomsbury, 2008), 68.

170 **the pieces of the puzzle:** Franco Moretti, "The Slaughterhouse of Literature," *Modern Language Quarterly* 61, no. 1 (March 2000): 207–27.

171 **"By 'discovering' the grid":** Rosalind Krauss, *Grids: Format and Image in 20th Century Art* (New York: Pace Gallery, 1980), 2. The ellipsis is Krauss's.

172 **SATOR AREPO TENET OPERA ROTAS:** Marcel Danesi, *The Puzzle Instinct: The Meaning of Puzzles in Human Life* (Bloomington: Indiana University Press, 2002), 51.

172 *Abracadabra*: Hugh Chisolm, ed., "Abracadabra," *Encyclopedia Britannica*, 11th ed. (Cambridge, UK: Cambridge University Press, 1910).

173 **Queen Victoria:** Gregg Hecimovich, *Puzzling the Reader: Riddles in Nineteenth-Century British Literature* (New York: Peter Lang, 2008), 17.

174 **"a couple of bogus letters":** Colin Dexter, *The Wench Is Dead* (London: Macmillan, 1989), 234–35.

175 **impatient with games:** Colin Dexter, *Last Bus to Woodstock* (London: Pan Books, 2017), 17.

177 **"'South African quadruped in six letters'":** Dorothy Sayers, "The Fascinating Problem of Uncle Meleager's Will," *The Complete Stories* (New York: Bourbon Street Books, 2013), 56.

178 **"Pagliacci":** P. G. Wodehouse, *Summer Moonshine* (London: Penguin Books, 1996), 236.

178 **"Sun God Ra":** P. G. Wodehouse, *Something Fishy* (New York: Abrams, 2008), 56.

181 **"should be a fortress":** W. H. Auden, *Collected Poems*, ed. Edward H. Mendelsohn (New York: Modern Library, 2007), 714.

181 **"if the pagans were anything":** Alan Levy, "On Audenstrasse—In the Autumn of the Age of Anxiety," *The New York Times*, August 8, 1971.

11. This Is Not a Crossword

189 **Magritte's pipe recalls "Fumées,":** See Michel Foucault, *This Is Not a Pipe* (Berkeley: University of California Press, 2008), 60.

189 **"Fumeés":** Guillaume Apollinaire, *Calligrammes: Poems of Peace and War (1913–1916)*, trans. Anne Hyde Greet (Berkeley: University of California Press, 1980), 114–16.

192 **"Magritte wanted to cross swords":** "'This is not a pipe': Magritte's 'Treachery of Images' Beguiles Paris," Reuters, September 22, 2016, http://www.reuters.com/article/us-france-art-magritte-idUSKCN11R308.

194 **"preferred distancing mechanisms":** Maria Konnikova, *Master-mind: How to Think Like Sherlock Holmes* (New York: Penguin Books, 2013), 132.

195 **"The Pipe" is not a pipe:** Charles Layng, *Layng's Cross-Word Puzzles: First Book* (Chicago: Stanley, 1924).

196 **over 130 times:** "Pipe," XWord Info, https://www.xwordinfo.com/Finder?word=PIPE, accessed May 15, 2019.

197 **"piping down the valleys wild":** William Blake, "Introduction to Songs of Innocence," *Songs of Innocence and of Experience*, Poetry Foundation, https://www.poetryfoundation.org/poems/43667/introduction-to-the-songs-of-innocence.

199 **"where they landed in the grid":** Andrew Zhou, "Notes," "The Art of Puzzle-Making," XWord Info, September 23, 2018, https://www.xwordinfo.com/Crossword?date=9/23/2018.

200 **"you'd, of course, be fully correct":** Zhou, "Notes."

12. Crosswords and the Media: The Crossword in the Digital Age

203 **the puzzle had gotten too hard:** Dan Kopf, "The Quirky San Quentin Crossword Puzzle Features Prison Slang and Solange," *Quartz*, October 21, 2017.

204 **"You have ruined my ritual":** Quoted in Ian Bogost, Simon Ferrari, and Bobby Schweizer, *Newsgames: Journalism at Play* (Cambridge, MA: MIT Press, 2010), 98.

207 **I CHERISH YOU:** Campbell, *On Crosswords*, 130–31.

215 **under Tausig's name:** Oliver Roeder, "A Plagiarism Scandal Is Unfolding in the Crossword World," *FiveThirtyEight*, March 4, 2016, http://

fivethirtyeight.com/features/a-plagiarism-scandal-is-unfolding-in
-the-crossword-world/.

217 **"the *USA Today* puzzle is his favorite":** Kathie Kerr, "Black History
Month Profile: The Puzzle Brain behind Merv Griffin's *Crosswords*," Universal Press Syndicate, February 10, 2008, https://www.prweb.com/releases
/2008/02/prweb687744.htm.

217 **The entire archive of *Times* crosswords:** Roeder, "A Plagiarism Scandal Is Unfolding in the Crossword World."

218 **something much more deliberate:** Matt Gaffney, "How to Spot a Pla-
giarized Crossword," *Slate*, March 10, 2016.

13. The Hardest Crossword

220 **Bilbo's neck riddle has saved his neck:** J. R. R. Tolkien, *The Hobbit: 75th
Anniversary Edition* (Boston: Houghton Mifflin Harcourt, 2012).

220 **couldn't remember anymore:** "The Hardest Crossword," Alzheimer's
Foundation of America, http://www.thehardestcrossword.com.

225 **same physical action over and over:** Brian G. Skotko et al., "Puzzling
Thoughts for H.M.: Can New Semantic Information Be Anchored to Old
Semantic Memories?," *Neuropsychology* 18, no. 4 (2004): 756–69.

226 **the partial clue wouldn't work:** Skotko et al., "Puzzling Thoughts
for H.M."

227 **the emotional anchor:** Skotko et al., "Puzzling Thoughts for H.M."

227 **"This is a thinking person's contest":** Alison Biggar, "Word Wizard
Designs a National Brain Game Challenge to Fight Alzheimer's," *Aging
Today*, https://www.asaging.org/blog/word-wizard-designs-national-brain
-game-challenge-fight-alzheimer's.

228 **the Bronx Aging Study:** Jagan A. Pillai et al., "Association of Crossword
Puzzle Participation with Memory Decline in Persons Who Develop
Dementia," *Journal of the International Neuropsychological Society* 17, no. 6
(November 2011): 1006–13.

228 **faster than for the non-crossworders:** Pillai et al., "Association of
Crossword Puzzle Participation with Memory Decline," 1006.

228 **"cognitively stimulating leisure activities":** Nicola Ferreira et al., "Associations between Cognitively Stimulating Leisure Activities, Cognitive Function and Age-Related Decline," *International Journal of Geriatric Psychiatry* 30 (2015): 422–30.

228 **age-related cognitive decline:** Ferreira et al., "Associations between Cognitively Stimulating Leisure Activities," 422.

IMAGE CREDITS

INDEX

Note: Page numbers in *italics* refer to illustrations.